A TRUE STORY

SURVIVOR

From childhood abuse to a life of crime and prostitution

TARA O'SHAUGHNESSEY

WITH JOHN F. MCDONALD

EBURY
PRESS

1 3 5 7 9 10 8 6 4 2

Ebury Press, an imprint of Ebury Publishing
20 Vauxhall Bridge Road
London SW1V 2SA

Ebury Press is part of the Penguin Random House group of
companies whose addresses can be found at
global.penguinrandomhouse.com

 Penguin
Random House
UK

First published by Ebury Press in 2019

www.penguin.co.uk

A CIP catalogue record for this book is available from the
British Library

ISBN 9781785039263

Typeset in 11/14 pt ITC Galliard Std
by Integra Software Services Pvt. Ltd, Pondicherry

Printed and bound in Great Britain by Clays Ltd, Elcograf S.p.A.

MIX
Paper from
responsible sources
FSC
www.fsc.org   FSC® C018179

Penguin Random House is committed to a
sustainable future for our business, our readers
and our planet. This book is made from Forest
Stewardship Council® certified paper.

To my mother, who brought me into the world
and who I love, despite everything.

To my children, Daniella and Christopher,
who I love very much – thank you for
putting up with me.

To my grandchildren, who I love more than
life and who are the future.

To my aunt Christine, who was always
there for me, even through the darkest times.

To my friend Francis, who had faith in me,
even when I had none myself.

To all the children who feel written off or
different – you're beautiful.

Contents

Chapter 1

The Black Lamb

When I was young, I used to care what people thought of me, what they saw me as, what I appeared to be to them. Now I regret worrying about the vinegar in their hearts, about the venom in their eyes and the jaggedness of their words. When I was younger, lying on the floor in my mother's bedroom, like a dog – and even afterwards, when I was a prostitute – they said I was pretty, even though I wasn't. Not when I was young. At least I don't think I was. Maybe if they'd said I was ugly it would have been different and I wouldn't have been molested so much. But it doesn't really matter now, because I've discovered that external beauty can't bring happiness. I know that's a cliché, but it's true: only internal beauty can truly satisfy – the light that falls on you from the hope you feel, from the belief that there is something good, even if everything around you is bad. The other things can bring a false kind of happiness: fame, or fortune, perhaps. But it's imitation, an imposter – not real. It belongs to other people and they loan it to you because they like the way you look or the way you fuck. But they always want it back in the end; one way or another. And it turns sour and leaves the bad taste of regret in your mouth – like a lie.

I was born on 4 January 1972 on Alderney, one of the Channel Islands. My father was Patrick and he left when I was two years old. I raised myself from then on, because my mother was no good at it. She was no good at anything or to anyone, including herself. She had lots of men friends who abused us both, shouted at us with hard voices, threw stones at us like they did at sinners long ago, sneered at us and spat on the ground, shook their furious fists at us and called us names. My mother was Angela and I was an only child. Angela became the black sheep of the family after Patrick ran away from her. She was bad and, by definition of being her daughter, so was I. She said I was just like my father – she told me I had his eyes and teeth and temper – and she hated me for it and gave me his religion, even though it wasn't hers. My father was Catholic and there weren't many Catholics on Alderney. There was one less when he left, so I took his place.

One of my earliest memories is of my mother having sex with my stepfather, who wasn't really my stepfather because he never actually married her. I saw this because I slept in the same room. You see, we only had a one-bedroom flat after my father left and that's because my mother's rich family controlled her budget when she decided to become the black sheep and go drinking and writhing on top of men.

My uncle was the richest man on the island and he bought her the flat, which cost a lot of money, I'm sure, as property wasn't cheap on Alderney. They, the family, told me that I should be proud of my birthplace, the rich islands with so many prosperous people and such a well-balanced way of life. But they didn't live in the one-bedroom flat with my mother. My father ran back to Ireland, where he came from, and I knew nothing of his family over there. All he left me was his name – and his eyes and teeth and temper. No, the only family I knew was my mother's – local people of French ancestry, who made their money from land and fishing and building and carpets and furniture. That kind of thing. Their rule of measurement was money and status and image and nothing bad ever happened to them – until my mother decided to go off the rails.

My uncle, Auguste, was the richest of all and he was the patriarch, after my grandfather – whose name was also Auguste – retired. The island was very beautiful, very picturesque, and surrounded by beaches like Corblets, where people went wind-surfing; and Maggie's Bay, named after my grandmother, where I used to collect coloured stones; and Arch Beach, full of little nooks and crannies and tide-pools; and Platte Saline, where the undercurrent would take you if you weren't careful; and Saye Beach, where the water was so blue you'd swear you were abroad. Palm trees swayed in the wind and, inland, wooded glades were full of magic and mystery. Alderney was an idyll – an Elysium, a mythical place. But it had a dark heart at the centre of its labyrinth: the flat where I lived with my mother, and the Minotaur she slept with.

They didn't allow just any old person to come and live on the island. You had to be rich, you had to have the sickly sweet stink of money on you, you had to occupy a large space in your own ego. People had beautiful houses and domestic staff and wonderful cars; money was a vulgar subject that was never spoken about, but always understood: always an enveloping force, like the air they

3

breathed, or the champagne they drank. And you had to have a certain status and not have any black sheep in your cupboards with the skeletons – at least, none that anyone knew about. My mother was the youngest of four siblings and was always accompanied by the shrill sound of wolf-whistles and the click-clack of seven-inch heels.

I was an only child and I knew I was different from the very moment I plunged into the world. I had a number of cousins, but they weren't like me and I wasn't particularly close to any of them – except Adele. Adele was my childhood hero. She was around the same age as me, but she looked like something out of *Vanity Fair*, with curly blonde hair and big blue eyes. Everybody wanted to be her friend. She liked me too, for some reason, even though I lived with the black sheep in the one-bedroom flat that cost the family a lot of money. Or perhaps it didn't cost them a lot of money – perhaps they owned it, just like they owned the rest of the island, and they allowed my mother and me to live in it like a glasshouse, or a folly.

Where the family could keep an eye fixed on us.

I was allowed to visit Adele's luxury house and jump on her luxury bed and touch her luxury posters of Boy George and Bananarama and pretend to be her luxury self – just for a while. Everything smelled of lilies and lavender and they served scrumptious food and I didn't know if this was normality or if 'normal' was my life, in the flat full of antiques and dust and men's shoes and empty cognac bottles … I'd run to the off-licence for Angela when I was four, for her next bottle of sherry. She'd call and order and say the 'girl' would be around to collect, as if I were her little maid and she was some aristocrat from the seventeenth century and could they put the Domecq Amontillado on her account.

Thank you so very much.

I don't know why my father didn't take me with him. I mean, it wasn't as if my mother desperately wanted me or that it would have broken her heart into a thousand pieces if I had gone. I was a convenience and an inconvenience to her – convenient for running errands and for extracting money from the family; inconvenient for having to sleep in the same room as her and the men who owned the shoes. She never spoke of my father and I wondered who he was. I imagined him as a dark gypsy: a Heathcliff, or a Roibin from *Sky West and Crooked*. I believed he'd come back for me some day – just turn up out of the blue on a silver horse or in a golden carriage and whisk me away before my mother could stop him. But he didn't. And I was disappointed.

My mother was exotic, to say the least. She had green eyes and full lips and long wavy hair and eyelashes like spiderlegs. She wore the tightest jeans and the highest heels and the lowest tops and she turned heads wherever she went. She didn't believe in routine, so there were never set mealtimes or bathtimes or schooltimes, and I was more or less left to my own devices when I was young. My 'stepfather' was called Bruno and he came into my life when I was about three. He was never a permanent fixture, like a real father would have been – or maybe not. He drifted in and out and came and went; he wasn't from the island and that annoyed the rest of the family a great deal. They considered him to be an opportunist adventurer and that's why they kept a careful eye on the money allocated to my mother.

Bruno looked the part: a sailor with a mop of hair like a thunderclap, tanned and fit, and there was that aura around him – that ambient sense of hazard that some men have, men that a woman knows she should stay away from but is drawn to like a moth to a flame. He had a loud walk and he lived his life spirally, not sequentially, always returning to the past before moving forward to the future, and rarely visiting the reality of the present. In that sense they were a perfect couple, Angela and Bruno, being equals in extroversion and ostentation, in disgust and despondence. He subsidised her allowance from the family and she climbed naked on top of him at every opportunity.

Despite her dual sources of income, my mother spent most of her money on having a good time, which usually meant expensive cocktails or other forms of alcoholic liquor. One of her favourites was a mixture of brandy and sherry which she called a 'shandy', for obvious reasons.

'Mix me a shandy, Tara, there's a good girl.'

I could perform that task to perfection long before I even started school. Because of my mother's penchant for the more expensive escapism, the interior decor of the flat suffered. Cuttings of carpet that didn't match were scattered on the floor like stepping stones across a fetid pool, and we had two old faded sofas and a record player that only worked when it wanted to. We didn't have a cooker or a washing machine – my mother took the washing around to one of her sisters' for the domestics to do, and I lived on junk food and crisps. The bathroom had a bath, of course, and a toilet, but dampness came through the ceiling and the walls were mould-coloured. The bedroom contained my mother's big, king-sized bed while on the floor, in one of the corners, I had a mattress that smelled, as I shared it with the dog. There was a cupboard that all the clothes were flung into and a chest of drawers with Angela's make-up on and a mirror for her to make sure she looked tragically glamorous, like a modern-day Medea.

Because I slept in the same room as her and Bruno – on the smelly old mattress with the pile of unruly dog blankets – I was too ashamed to ever have any of my friends over. This is what my so-called mother had reduced us to and I resented her for it, because I could have been a little princess like my cousins if she'd stayed within the fold and behaved herself. But that was never in my mother's nature and perhaps that's why my father left and ran away – with the gypsies, into the sky west and crooked.

My first day at school came when I was five. I was really excited. I crept out of bed as quietly as I could, so I wouldn't wake my mother, who might start playing horsies with my stepfather if I did. I went to the living room and dressed in my new uniform and thought how smart I looked on this special day. I checked my schoolbag to make sure I hadn't forgotten anything, then I noiselessly opened the front door and slipped out. In my excitement, I tripped and fell over: blood stained my new white socks and stones embedded themselves in my grazed knees. I wanted to cry and call for my mother, but there was no time for that and, anyway, she would just have sighed and shrugged her shoulders and poured herself a drink. So I picked myself up and made my way to school.

It was something I'd got used to from as far back as I could remember – looking after myself.

My school was St Anne's, which was a very aloof establishment and looked as if it was far too good for the young people going there to get an education. It was like an old aristocrat, watching the children with half-closed eyes and a kind of disdain for the transience of their young time

I didn't like school to begin with, mainly because school didn't like me. It mocked me for being the brat of a black sheep – a black lamb that was wild and feral and bad. The teachers always asked the girls what their fathers did, probably because their fathers were donating money to the school and they liked their daughters to be able to get up and brag about their wonderful philanthropic ways. When they asked me, I said my father was a gigolo, even though I didn't know what the word meant and had only heard my mother use it on some occasion or other, but it sounded impressive, exotic. The teacher smiled embarrassedly and passed along to the next girl, and I was never asked about my father again.

St Anne's was a Protestant school and I was the only Catholic girl going there. I was segregated from the others at assembly time and taken away to a separate room by Sister Francis, who taught me the catechism and confession and benediction and about the Crusaders of the Blessed Sacrament. She also taught me the words that John the Baptist said when he saw Jesus: 'Behold the Lamb of God, who taketh away the sins of the world.' It stuck in my mind. It was repeated every time I took communion: 'Lamb of God, who taketh away the sins of the world, have mercy on us,' and I formed a picture of that lamb in my little mind. It was a white lamb and I was a black lamb and there was a rueful kind of affinity between the two of us: white and black, good and bad, forgiving and forlorn. And I knew it would have mercy on me for all the sins I was about to commit in my sordid life.

There were many different groups in school: groups of country-club children and groups of golf-club children, groups of pony-club children and groups of stinkless-shit-club children. I didn't fit into any of those groups, and there were no clubs for children-with-black-sheep-mothers. They weren't allowed to play with me, the others, as I was considered to be a bad influence. So, I kept to myself, and was given the silent treatment by some of the girls, and the not-letting-me-pass-in-the-corridor treatment, and other ridiculous rituals like that. My mother was a figure of fun to them; they had a name for her – 'Raquel Munch', which was meant to be some kind of juvenile parody of the film star with the enormous boobs. They had obviously heard their own mothers talking about Angela and knew of her wild behaviour and her many men.

They also cast aspersions on the fact that my father had run off, and I was constantly reminded that I was dadless. Apparently, my many stepfathers didn't count in their estimation of paternity. I remember once, on a school trip to Dorset, they were all whispering and giggling behind their hands and speaking in some kind of code which they'd devised, and I couldn't take any more of it. I exploded and started fighting and punching. I was sent to the head when we returned and was made to feel so ashamed, even though I had really nothing to be ashamed of. Because she was my mother after all, and it wasn't for them to denigrate her, down into the dirt.

That was my prerogative.

They left me alone after the attack.

It's not that the rest of the family didn't worry about me every now and then, left alone with the black sheep – they did, in their own, self-contained way. But I was never sure if they worried about me or about what the other rich families on the island thought about them for deserting us the way they did. I mean, the name Cloutier was well respected, or so they liked to think, and it was a constant embarrassment to have Angela misbehaving and me living the life of a feral child – and being beaten for it by Bruno, with a dog lead – on such a happy hideaway as Alderney. Sometimes they came to the flat to see how I was, but my mother screamed at them so much they soon left again, glancing ruefully in my direction on the way out. It was never good to cause too much of a scene. I mean, what would the other yacht owners say?

As I got older, I became feisty and argumentative, and people kept away from me even more than before. I said I didn't care about any of them, even though I was crumbling inside from the lack of love and no sense of belonging in life. I became disruptive and used to set off fire extinguishers and shoplift and go into the woods and eat magic mushrooms. The family even threatened to have me put into the militia cadets.

'She's out of control and she needs discipline!'

But my mother wouldn't let them.

I hung around with the bad boys, because the good girls were scared of me. I became an urchin, with dirt under my fingernails and unruly hair, and trousers rolled up to my knees. My mother locked the flat whenever she went anywhere, whether I was there or not; if I wasn't and I returned before her, I'd be locked out. So I went roaming here, there and everywhere and lived in my own wild little world. I had a tape recorder and I used to listen to Nena singing '99 Red Balloons' and dance around the flat with no curtains and rewind it and play it again and again and sing the words to the people passing by outside. Sometimes they smiled back, but mostly they scowled.

My mother and Bruno were always fighting and the flat was always getting smashed up. She had other boyfriends when he wasn't about. Many boyfriends. And I had many stepfathers, so to speak. They ignored me for the most part, and some would give me money for sweets to get me out of the way, but on bad days they'd be drunk and abusive and I'd have to huddle in a corner. Bruno also had other women besides my mother.

I could never understand why Angela wanted to be with someone who beat her and beat me, and why she kept on taking him back. I was outside playing one day when I heard terrible screaming and the fire brigade and ambulance turned up. I was ushered away by Mrs Moore, who lived upstairs, and to this day I don't know the full truth of what happened. But it was said he threw boiling water over her and she had burn marks down her arms and on her stomach. Another time he pushed her into the grate. I used to sit there and put gauze dressings on her back until she healed.

Let me be quite clear: my mother wasn't a monster who beat me every day. It was only Bruno who hit me with the dog lead, and that was because of his sadistic nature. Some members of the family knew I was being beaten, but they tended to turn a blind eye: it was bad enough I was from a broken home, without me being taken away from my mother.

And so I believed I wasn't important to anyone or anything and my life was totally meaningless. I thought this was normal for children like me, and that all worthless people went through this kind of life.

Angela's problem was her lack of self-worth, which manifested itself in a self-absorption that left little room for anything else. The men were her way of proving she was alive and also a way to spit in the eye of the family who contributed to that darkness inside her soul.

I lost myself in books for a while, from the age of six onwards. I'd sit on the library steps, swinging my legs and reading *The Famous Five* or *The Secret Seven*. I liked Enid Blyton a lot. I absorbed myself in their imaginings and lived their adventures in my head. Reading took me to other places, away from Alderney and Alderney people – to Neverland and Wonderland and Camelot and wild heathland where dark princes roamed magical woodlands and princesses were held captive by wicked witches wearing high heels and too much mascara. I'd take six books at a time from the library and could finish three in one night. Elisabeth Beresford lived on the island and I used to visit her in her house and talk about comets and violins and clouds and sea-birds and life and loneliness. It was another world for me, where I could be someone else – not Tara O'Shaughnessey, the wild waif of Alderney.

Despite this, I still wanted to be liked at school – who didn't? To be good at sports was to be popular at school, so I decided to be good at netball. But, like everything in my life, I tried to make it overcompensate for my isolation: I would practise in the pouring rain in my lunchbreak and for hours after school, until it got too dark to see. I'd practise with them all watching me through the windows.

After two years, however, I got so good they had to take me into the team. Once I got on court, I was aggressive. I played goal attack and everyone knew that when Tara had hold of the ball, she was going to score. It was one of the brighter times of my schooldays – a time that swelled my heart like a singing bird and the small world I knew blew kisses back and the loneliness left me for a while and went to live with someone else. I always loved sport and I played lacrosse and hockey when they let me. I went swimming in the sea regularly and I was as fit as any of the boys. But netball was my favourite and getting on the team was like all my dreams coming true – finally, I was part of something. I ended up being team captain and representing the school all over the Channel Islands.

But that was later, after the blow-jobs.

I was always scared of Bruno, from the moment he came into my life. He was probably the only thing I was really afraid of. Not because he hit me with the dog lead, but because of the way he looked at me sometimes. It was a narrow look, the sort of stare that said: 'I know you know I'm looking at you' – that kind of look. He was always doing it, ever since he came through the door of the flat when I was just a baby. It was a leer rather than a look, a glower rather than a glare. It crept out of his eyes and slithered across the floor and assaulted me.

Every Saturday, my mother would go shopping and leave me alone with Bruno, whenever he was around, and I couldn't really get away from him when I was very small. Sometimes he'd be around when she wasn't there and he'd give me that look.

'Where's your mother?'

'I don't know.'

Then he'd pour himself a drink and just sit there, staring at me, leering at me, until I left the flat and went outside.

As my cousin Adele was my idol, I always wanted to impress her. One day after school I asked her to come to the flat, as I had something to show her. She didn't want to at first, but I said it was something really cool that I'd found in the bedroom and she eventually agreed. I had been bored one day and started rummaging around in the drawers under my mother's bed. I know now they were pornographic magazines, but I didn't know then, as I was only about seven. But I knew there was something wrong about looking at them, because there were men's willies and women's titties and all sorts of other stuff. Adele and I spread the magazines out all over the floor and giggled and touched the pictures with our fingers, until we heard the front door open.

Bruno's footsteps came closer and closer as I tried to gather up the magazines and stuff them back into the drawers, but he came into the bedroom and caught me before I could. He looked at Adele and she looked back at him and then he looked at me. I turned away and he left the room.

I didn't think any more about it until the following Saturday when my mother had gone shopping. Bruno was in the bedroom supposed to be getting dressed and I was in the living room playing my tape recorder. He called me to come in and, when I did, I saw he was lying on the bed with a towel over his midriff. His eyes looked glazed, like marbles, and there was a kind of sneer on his mouth.

'You've been a naughty girl, haven't you?'

I didn't answer. I just stood there, looking away from him, towards the window.

'You've been looking through your mum's magazines.'

I swallowed hard, but still didn't answer.

'You're a little whore, just like your mother.'

Then he grabbed my arm and pulled me onto the bed beside him. One of his hands snaked around the back of my head and his other hand removed the towel from his erect penis. He told me to open my mouth and pushed me down over the penis. It almost went through my throat and I couldn't speak and I was gagging and trying not to throw up on top of him. Tears were stinging my eyes and he was making noises as if he was in pain, as he pulled and pushed at the back of my head. Then this white, messy stuff squirted out into my mouth and onto my face and down my shirt. He pushed me away and I retched violently as he wiped himself with the towel.

'Good girl, Tara. Now I won't tell your mother about you looking at her magazines.'

I went to the bathroom and washed my face and rinsed my mouth. My legs were shaking, but I was relieved that he wasn't going to tell my mother.

Then something happened – some memory freed itself from the back of my mind, from the dark place where it had hidden itself. I remembered the smell of him – that stench of him. It had been lurking in the house, stalking me. It was everywhere, in the walls and the floors and the doors and the windows and inside my senses. It had been there for a long time – at the back of my consciousness somewhere, buried, lying dormant. This wasn't the first time I'd had to suck Bruno's penis; I realised I'd been doing it since I was four years old.

And I said my prayer – the one I would always say now, after he'd do this to me.

The one that would stop me going to hell.

'Lamb of God, who taketh away ...'

Chapter 2

Skin Deep

Bruno got bored with blow-jobs and with me masturbating him at the edge of the bed, coming all over my face and throwing his boxers at me to clean myself.

One day, he decided to 'break me in' and forced his fingers up into me. Blood spilled through my underwear like a secret, and my mother thought I'd started my period. Later, he sat watching me with the smile of a spider and I ran from the flat.

He stopped short of having full intercourse with me but, until I was nine years old, he did everything else to me. I sometimes ran down to my grandparents and I'd lock myself in the toilets to get away from him. But I was always brought back – always had to go back. There was nowhere else, nobody else who wanted me.

I'd beg my mother not to leave me alone with him on Saturdays, but she never listened and I'll never know if she realised what was going on. If she did, she didn't say anything. Bruno was a sadistic and violent man, and perhaps she was afraid of what he might do to her, if she tried to stop what he was doing to me.

The abuse from Bruno wasn't just physical, it was psychological as well. If he couldn't get me on my own to sexually abuse me, he'd tell my mother that I'd lied or misbehaved in some way and then he'd get to punish me by hitting me with the dog lead. He was a sadistic bully and he'd leave welts on my body. He'd throw me outside in the cold with no clothes on for hours at a time; he'd pinch the backs of my legs when no one was looking, and dig me in the ribs.

Mrs Moore, who lived in the flat upstairs, had five sons. She was often able to hear me screaming and she took me up there whenever she could to have supper with her boys. I loved going up to Mrs Moore's because she gave me beans on toast, and I wasn't used to cooked food. She tried to keep me with her one night when Bruno was around, but my mother came up to get me: I could hear shouting at the door, then my mother dragged me out. A few days later social workers called, but Angela told them I was a little liar and always looking for attention. We never heard from them again, and I was banned from playing with the Moore boys.

When I was about nine, I knew their relationship was coming to an end because Bruno wasn't around as much as he used to be. Angela was out partying a lot with her best friend, Jane, who had one blue eye and one green eye. I liked Jane, as she reminded me of a mermaid. She had long blonde hair and she managed an upmarket clothes shop and rode a motorbike. One night I was woken by the sound of loud music and laughter. I walked into the lounge rubbing my eyes. Angela had invited a group of squaddies back and she was perched on one of their knees while Jane was dancing with another. I wouldn't go back to bed and the men were getting a little agitated because I was in the way of whatever they had planned. Jane promised she'd let me ride on the back of her bike if I was good and went back to bed. She kept her promise the next day and took me for a spin around the island. I loved the free feeling of the wind on my face, holding on tightly to this woman who I knew so well and didn't know at all.

As Bruno wasn't around much any more, my mother was meeting different men all the time. One night she dragged me with her to meet this German who'd come over to the island. I don't know how she met him, and he lived miles away. His house was like a hospital, clean and clinical and painted all white. I was shoved into a bedroom with crayons and paper to draw on, while my mother stayed in the living room with the German. I could hear strange noises and went to investigate. When I poked my head around the door, all I could see was Angela in between his legs and him pushing her head down.

It reminded me of what Bruno did to me.

There were naked men and women on the television and I gasped – could they be the same ones from the magazine? My word!

Angela must have heard me, but she and the German just ignored me and pretended I wasn't there.

I went to the German's house with my mother many times. I was always given something to occupy my attention and sent to the bedroom, and I'd always sneak into the lounge when they were at it. They always knew I was there and watching, but they didn't seem to care. I think they believed I didn't understand what was going on and, as Angela used to do it with Bruno when I was in the same room, this was no different. I don't know what the German thought about it – perhaps he was too enthralled by what my mother was doing to him? Some time later I heard he was on the run and the local police came round to ask Angela some questions. I thought we both might have to go to prison, but she denied knowing him and they seemed to take her word for that. He was eventually arrested and deported.

Bruno wasn't gone completely, however, and one night he came round when my mother was out. My papa – that's what I called my grandfather Auguste– was in the flat with me. Bruno had some things he said were valuable antiques and he wanted to take them away with him. When my papa said he couldn't do that without Angela's consent, Bruno headbutted him and knocked him out. I was in the bedroom sleeping, but the commotion woke me and I saw what happened. I saw my grandfather fall to the floor, clutching his side and I screamed. Bruno grabbed some stuff from the flat and left. The door was wide open and my papa was unconscious and I was screaming, not knowing what to do.

Someone called for an ambulance.

One good thing came from it: the end of Bruno. He was prosecuted for assault and taken to court. He pleaded guilty and was fined and given a restraining order. I was standing with my aunt Christine when he came out and she went up to him and slapped him across the face. I've always had a close relationship with Christine – I know she would have helped me more if she could. But my nightmare with Bruno was over because he wasn't allowed to come near any of the family ever again.

That didn't stop Angela having other boyfriends and I was always in the firing line. I was subjected to mental and emotional abuse by them. They'd shout at me and watch porn and have sex with my mother in the bed, while I was lying on the floor.

One morning, I was woken by a lot of shouting and banging at the window. Angela was standing in the room, wearing only a top; her bottom half was bare. Some men were outside the window looking in, and she grabbed me and held me in front of her like a shield, just as a brick came flying through, sending glass everywhere.

I was so frightened I peed myself.

This kind of treatment drove me to self-harm when I got older. Once, I slashed my wrists, my arms and my face with broken glass that was on the ground outside a local pub. When they found me I was ashamed of what I'd done, so I said I'd walked out into the road and was hit by a car, which drove off. I was taken to hospital and the police were called. They asked me questions, but I just said I couldn't remember anything. I still have some of the scars. Another time I took an overdose of paracetamol and was hospitalised again. My mother came and took me home but it was never spoken about, just brushed under the carpet.

Apart from hand-me-downs that were donated from my cousins, I got all my clothes from jumble sales and I wore what I liked, whether it was in fashion or not. Paisley shirts and long black skirts and duffle coats. Hi-Tec trainers were all the rage when I was growing up, but I knew full well I'd never have those because they were far too expensive, so I wore winklepicker shoes and old Doc Martens instead. One of my rich uncles gave me a £5 note once, which was like a million to me. I bought myself a pair of bright blue jelly shoes and thought

I was the chicest girl in town for a while. I used to plait my hair at night so next morning it would fall about my face in ringlets. I was the only girl in the school to have such long hair – it was right down my back. I had huge blue eyes and straight white teeth that I'd inherited from my father.

One Christmas, Papa bought me a boombox and a *Now* CD that had all the chart music I liked: Sister Sledge and George Michael and stuff. I'd go to the school yard on Sunday afternoons and skate around in circles and pretend I was Jayne Torvill, the famous ice skater. I'd gate-crash dances I wasn't invited to and whirl like a dervish; I lived this fanciful life that belonged only to me and no one else.

My mother's string of boyfriends continued and it was a mystery to me what she was looking for. None of them lasted long and none added any value to her life or mine. She came from such a good family and I could never understand why she kept choosing bad men. But I was growing up and trying to loosen the grip she had on me. I became defiant, coming home late and hanging with a gang and smoking and sneaking into the pubs the fishermen frequented – the Chez Andre was a regular haunt.

I was starting to feel different – adolescence was creating a hormone storm inside my body and it was as if something inside me was trying to break free and run naked along the beaches and into the sea.

I was made netball captain when I was fifteen, and the headmaster at St Anne's made me deputy head girl as well. I was confused and a little bit bemused and slightly scared by this – I mean, I wasn't exactly the most popular girl in school and I didn't know why I was chosen for such a responsible role. I suppose it might have been because I was tough and didn't take any nonsense from anybody – if there was a problem with bullying or misbehaviour in the playground or in the corridors, I was the one to sort it. I think my mother was proud of me for that – she never said anything, but I got the feeling she secretly admired my achievement.

I felt proud, too, with my little hexagon badge on my jumper.

I was something.

The summer of 1988 came and Whitney Houston and Madonna and Gloria Estefan were in the charts – all irrepressible idols of mine.

Alderney Week was held every year in August. It was a week full of carnival and sports days and boat races; Miss Alderney would be chosen a few weeks earlier so she'd be ready to prepare for her duties during the week.

They held the Miss Alderney competition in the Belle Vue Hotel. Ball gowns were worn and the only rule was that you had to be a local girl. My cousin Adele had been maid of honour in the past and had also taken the title once. It was a tradition in our family to enter Miss Alderney, but it held no interest for me because I knew I'd never be chosen.

I was hanging around outside the Belle Vue with my gang of uncouth companions when Adele arrived with some of her fashionable friends and insisted that I enter the competition.

'Are you kidding?'

'No, Tara, please! Please enter.'

'No way!'

It was about three hours before the competition was due to begin and I had no dress and no one to do my make-up. But Adele kept on insisting because none of the other girls in the family had entered that year.

'Oh, go on, Tara!'

'I haven't got a dress!'

'You can wear mine.'

'What about make-up?'

'I'll do it.'

'No!'

'There's free champagne.'

That swung it.

So, against my better judgement, I allowed myself to be persuaded, 'for the sake of the family'. I went ahead and got made up like a Barbie doll – they had to squeeze me into the bodice of the big pink dress with a coat-hanger.

All the families on Alderney were packed into the ballroom, hoping their daughters would be chosen – except for my mother, she didn't know I'd entered. The organisers came backstage to talk to us, asking what our hobbies were and what we planned to do with our lives after school. I was swigging the free champagne and I told them I liked sports and my ambition was to be a vagabond like my father. I didn't really know what a vagabond was, but it sounded romantic.

There were three judges on stage and I waited in line for my name to be called. Finally, my turn came.

'And now we have Tara O'Shaughnessey, aged sixteen, who's cousin Adele Boucher took the crown three years ago.'

I stumbled onto the stage in the high heels I wasn't used to wearing, like a tipsy pink blancmange, and tried to hear the questions they were asking, but the noise from the crowd was deafening.

I didn't know whether people were laughing or cheering, or both.

'So, Tara, I see you want to be a correspondent?'

'What's a correspondent?'

'A journalist ... a writer.'

'Do I? Yes, I do!'

'Very good. Very original.'

All the other girls had said they wanted to be fashion models or film stars or pop stars or something equally vainglorious. Of course, I never said I wanted to be a correspondent – I said I wanted to be a vagabond, but they probably thought the organisers misheard backstage and that I must have said I wanted to correspond. I don't remember answering the rest of their silly questions and I was relieved when I could stagger off to what was left of the champagne.

The waiting was finally over and the drums began to roll – there was no way I'd be picked, I just knew it, standing backstage with all the other contestants. The prizes were awarded in reverse order, with the two maids of honour being called first and Miss Alderney last. I felt a bit of a fraud to be there at all, and I was halfway out of the pink monstrosity when the announcement was made.

'And in third place, Miss Tara O'Shaughnessey!'

It didn't really register that I'd won a place. It must have been some kind of joke and they'd all be laughing and pointing mocking fingers at me when I went back out on stage. I tried to get the rest of the pink dress off so I could make a run for it, but I was stuck in the tight bodice. The other girls pushed me out onto the stage and I stood there like a rabbit caught in headlights. Then the cheering started, and whistling, and clapping, and I could see my aunt Christine smiling in the crowd. They placed a royal blue sash over my shoulder and a tiara on my head. My arms were full of flowers and chocolates and a voucher to be cashed or spent in Guernsey. Everyone was on their feet, cheering.

It was half dream and half nightmare, and I'd wake up soon, on the bedroom floor with the dog.

The other maid of honour and Miss Alderney were crowned, and us three winners were ushered out to a float and paraded around the island. Music played and all the pub-goers came out onto the streets, cheering. My mother was outside a pub – she knew nothing about me entering the contest and I'm sure I detected a rare expression of surprise and pride on her face. Later we attended discos at the Belle Vue and the Old Barn, where lots of people came up and congratulated me – except my mother. I was still wearing the monstrosity and some of the girls from school came up, sniggered and ran away, because it was impossible to dance to AC/DC in that fussy frock.

Alderney week itself went by in a hazy daze. We had lots of things to do, like a cavalcade and interviews and photo shoots and judging a baby competition and a strongest man competition. We sat on three thrones, like a queen and her princesses either side, and I waved like royalty from the horse and carriage we travelled in. Once I got used to the fact that I wasn't hallucinating after eating magic mushrooms, I loved every minute of it and didn't want the week to be over. On the last night, there was a torchlit procession down to Butes and everybody followed our carriage. There was a huge bonfire and live bands and beer tents and food stalls and marquees and parties in the underground bunkers – and then it was over. That was the end of Alderney Week for another year. I felt like Cinderella when she lost her glass slipper.

I'd already done my mocks and I was due to be taking my GCSEs when I went back to St Anne's in September. In truth, I didn't even know what they were or why I was taking them. My priorities were surviving with my mother and having enough to eat. I'd done no studying and I was sure I'd fail everything, so what was the point? At home, my mother had an alcoholic living with us who she believed was madly in love with her. But it was just another man using her. I wanted out – away from her and away from the claustrophobia of the island, but I didn't know how to achieve that.

The post-Alderney Week comedown was depressing and I went out to a pub with some friends to try and prolong the party. There was a group of older girls there, from another island, when we arrived. One of them took a shine to a boy in our group and his girlfriend took objection to her advances. One thing led to another and it ended up in a brawl that spilled out onto the street. I got punched in the face and lost a shoe in the melee. When it was over I thought, 'I can't go home to my mother like this, she'll go insane.' So I slept at a friend's house that night and woke with a black eye and a swollen lip and one foot covered in mud. That was bad enough, but then the police came and we were arrested and brought to the station. We were cautioned and the sergeant told us there was a chance it would go to court, if the other group decided to press changes – even though they'd started it and were a lot older than us.

I had to tell my mother, what else could I do?

Just as I thought, she flew off her broomstick and I was grounded for being the worst daughter of all time. But I was becoming more rebellious as I got older and something snapped in me and I stormed out of the flat. I had the money I'd won at the Miss Alderney contest and I decided it was time to go.

Later, I sneaked back home and threw some stuff into a bag.

Angela arrived home while I was packing.

'What are you doing?'

'I'm leaving this island and I'm leaving you.'

'You can't do that, Tara.'

'I can and I am.'

I was still only sixteen and legally under age so she could probably have stopped me. But I think she knew I'd do it anyway, when she wasn't looking. I hugged her and told her I'd be in touch. Then, like Huckleberry Finn, I made my escape.

I walked to Alderney Airport, which was about a mile away. I only had £100 and the fare to Heathrow would take twenty of that. I bought my ticket at the departure counter. Because I was under age, I was afraid they wouldn't let me on the plane, which was a little yellow G-Joey Trislander, with a propeller on each wing and another on the tail.

As I sat there huddled inside my donkey jacket, I thought that, any minute, the family would march through the door and drag me back from my dream. Unable to sit still, I paced up and down, watching the unmoving hands of the clock above the booking desk, until at last they announced that my flight was ready to leave. I picked up my rucksack and headed out across the tarmac.

Every step brought me closer to my new dimension and became its own self-contained little lifetime. Birth and life and death. And again. And again. And again.

And then I was on the plane and the propellers were turning. I hunched right down in the seat so no one would see me through the window, until we were in the sky, soaring.

Looking down at the clouds from heaven.

Chapter 3

Pole Dancing

The flight from Alderney to Heathrow was short: it only seemed to take five minutes and I didn't have time to worry about having never been in an aeroplane before. I arrived in the early evening. Everyone was gathering their big suitcases and I had nothing but a small bag of second-hand clothes. They all looked so sure of themselves, like they knew where they were going, had somewhere to go.

I didn't.

Heathrow was huge: I was in awe at the size of it. I had all the time in the world, so I just waltzed around the place, looking at the shops and going up and down the escalators. I knew I couldn't stay there indefinitely, so I went outside and found a coach station. I wanted to get to the centre of London, so I asked people which bus would take me to Piccadilly Circus. I knew Piccadilly Circus was in the middle of London – it was probably one of the few places I'd heard of.

'That one goes into central London.'

'Thank you.'

The driver said he could drop me at Victoria and that wasn't far from Piccadilly Circus. Good enough. I bought a ticket and hopped on the coach.

Travelling into London in the twilight was a wonderment. I'd never seen a place that big – street after street after street – the shops, the houses, the traffic, the people all jumbled together like liquorice allsorts and rushing and pushing. We came in past Kew Gardens, through Chiswick and Hammersmith, past the Victoria and Albert Museum and Buckingham Palace, and down to Victoria Coach Station, where I got off.

It was starting to get dark when I emerged onto the street and followed the crowd north, along a road called Eccleston Place. I didn't have a clue where I was or what I was going to do. I knew nobody in London and I had to find somewhere to stay before nightfall.

I decided the best place to go would be a pub – people were always friendlier when they had a drink in their hands.

The first establishment I came across was called the Phoenix and I went inside. What if they wouldn't serve me because I was under age? But I mustered enough courage to go to the bar and order a half of lager and a packet of crisps. The barman was a big fellow with a balding head and very hairy arms; he placed the drink on the bar with the expression of a silverback gorilla that had just had its belly scratched.

'One an' 'alf sovs to you, me darlin'.'

I hadn't a clue what that meant: the London slang was a foreign language to me. Someone close by saw my perplexed expression.

'He means one pound fifty.'

'Oh … right. Thank you.'

I took a sip and looked at the gorilla.

'Where's the ladies'?'

'Up the apples and pears.' Now the guy was using cockney on me!

The interpreter pointed to the stairs.

After a few lagers I was getting a bit merry and I decided to play the jukebox. It was five plays for 50p and I found Nena and played '99 Red Balloons'. It made the place seem friendlier. I started to dance to the music, on my own, singing along.

The pub had filled up by now, with quite a few young people, and some of them danced alongside me. It wasn't long until I was sitting at a table with a mixed group, who thought my accent was cool. I made up a story about how I had escaped from an evil stepmother on a little island in the middle of the sea, and now I wanted to make a new life in London. They were fascinated and thought I was some kind of changeling girl, like Odette or Cinderella or Bridget Cleary. They said I could stay with them for the night and, when the pub closed, we went back to a house in Chester Square.

It was shared accommodation, which was new to me, even though I'd been sharing the flat on Alderney with my mother's lovers for my whole life. This was different. They were all young and, in my parochial opinion, so sophisticated and chic. Everything was new, everything was cool, everything was exciting. Punk music was blaring out and it seemed like there were no rules in this house, which suited me. Some of them looked like zombies, with jet-black hair and black make-up and black clothes. Those people were called goths and they were mostly middle-class kids whose parents had lots of money. They were smoking cannabis and they passed me a joint which made my head spin, so I found a space on the floor and lay down. The loud music and people moving around me and banging doors kept me awake for most of the night, but I finally fell into a fitful sleep and dreamed about being chased into the sea at Corblets Beach by drunken sailors and swimming out towards the bright lights of London, away in the distance.

When I woke the next morning, I could see a blinding sun was shining through the window – after I'd separated my eyelashes from my cheekbones, that is. I stepped over comatose bodies to get to the cluttered kitchen and make a cup of strong coffee. It took me a while to realise where I was because I was disorientated and confused, but then it struck me like a slap in the face: I was free. I was finally free. I'd made it.

One of the guys from the pub the day before came in and I asked him if I could stay at the house for a while, until I could find a place of my own.

'No can do.'

'Why not?'

He explained that the night before was a one-off. A party. Once everyone woke up, they'd leave and only the people paying rent would be left.

'I can pay rent.'

'It's not as simple as that.'

'Why not?

'This is Belgravia.'

'So what?'

He explained that Belgravia was an exclusive part of London and I'd have to have a three-month down payment, which would come to nearly £1,000. It looked like I'd have to go walking the streets.

As I was leaving, I bumped into another girl, who was also leaving.

'Who're you?'

'Who're you?'

'I'm Tracey.'

'I'm Tara.'

We got talking as we walked down the street together. I was starving, and as I couldn't remember the last time I ate – apart from the crisps in the pub – we went into a café for some breakfast. It turned out that Tracey had left home, too, because she'd fallen out with her parents, and had come down to London to escape. She was working in a bar and I asked her if she could get me a job there.

I meant pulling pints of beer, but that's not what Tracey was doing. She gave me a funny look and said it was dancing. I was really naive, replying that I loved dancing and that I had a natural rhythm – everyone back home said so. I could whirl like a dervish when I wanted to.

After a breakfast of sausage and beans, Tracey took me to Victoria tube station. I'd never been in the Underground before and I didn't know whether to be fearful or fascinated. I followed her down a steep escalator, holding on for dear life, to the claustrophobic corridors below, which Tracey navigated with easy familiarity. The platform was crowded and I couldn't understand how nobody ended up under the train that came in, asthmatically pushing air before it. We jumped into a carriage before the closing doors could trap an arm or a leg – to be mutilated along the flying tunnel walls. I could imagine all kinds of craziness being carried out down here in this eerie place – with pimps and procurers and perverts and the Pilgrims of Arès.

We sped northwards five stops to King's Cross, then back up another huge escalator where I almost had my bum pulped by the automatic ticket gates. I was glad to get back out into the sane, bright sunlight, away from the dryness and the dust.

The bar where Tracey worked was called Lucy Lightfoot's and it was a bit of a dive. It was rickety and rough with dirty floors and sodden beer mats and the smell of something nasty and unidentifiable. There were four different rooms, with music playing in each and large poles erected in the middle of the floor. It still hadn't dawned on me what I'd be expected to do. It wasn't open at that time of the day, but the manager let us in. His name was Mervin and he was the ugliest man I'd ever seen. He had a massive belly and a big afro and a gap between his two front teeth. When he spoke, his eyes roamed all over me, abusing me, looking me up and down and inside out, like he was assessing my potential.

'Can you pole dance?'

'Sure she can.' Tracey answered for me – I didn't know whether I could or not.

My mouth was dry and my heart was racing. Tracey kept nudging me so I just nodded my head.

'OK, I'll give you a try.'

'I'll go first, show her what's expected.'

Well, Tracey got on this pole and she was wrapped around it like a serpent, sliding up and down, holding on with one hand and making suggestive gestures with her body. I needed this job, so I grabbed the pole after her and thrust myself up along it. I was strong from doing lots of sports at school and I had to make Mervin like me. I looked straight at him, puckering my lips and gyrating my hips and flinging my head up and down so my hair went whirling everywhere, just like I'd seen on *Dirty Dancing*. Then suddenly I slipped, and banged my elbow on the floor. But Mervin was impressed and I got the job.

Now I just needed somewhere to sleep. Tracy had a room in a shared house and she said I could stay with her.

'What about the three months' rent?'

'It's not like that Belgravia place. They're all rich kids. You'll be OK with me.'

In actual fact, the house belonged to Mervin, but I paid rent to Tracey. A couple lived in the next room and a single guy next to them. They kept to themselves and I didn't see any other people there. The couple looked like something from *The Texas Chainsaw Massacre*: the guy was a bodybuilder type with long hair at the back in a mullet. He was a bully and used to shout at his partner a lot and I could hear them through the wall. It reminded me of Bruno and my mother. He worked at the club as a barman but I never had a lot of contact with him because we worked different shifts. The single man was a musician and he used to play the guitar and smoke marijuana. The house itself was basic. Everything in our room was basic: cord carpets, nicotine-stained net curtains, a small portable television and two single beds, which Tracy and I pushed together to make more room. It became like a double bed and we slept together in it. The house was terraced, with no garden – just a slab of concrete out the back. The paint was peeling off the walls but, for now, it was home.

So I went to work as a pole dancer at Lucy Lightfoot's and Tracey and I lived and hung out together. She let me wear her clothes until I was able to afford some of my own, then we'd swap so it looked like we both had a larger wardrobe than we actually did.

I got to know the lie of the land around King's Cross but, even though I was settling into life as a pole dancer, I wasn't earning very much money and there were no tips. Mervin expected blood for the wages he paid and I had to work long hours for him, sometimes 6 p.m. to 6 a.m., without much of a break. There were no proper facilities and we had to get changed into our dancing costumes in the ladies' toilet.

But, when I was on the pole, I felt liberated. My body shape was changing and I was getting leaner. I started smoking, which suppressed my appetite, and taking speed helped keep me awake. I'd dab it on my gums or wrap it in a Rizla paper and bomb it, which meant getting it onto the back of your tongue and swigging it down with a drink. It was all new to me, but I was learning fast.

Mervin gave me a maid's outfit to wear on stage, which consisted of a flimsy black mini-dress with a white frilly apron across the middle. It had buttons up to a collar with a white string to tie it up at the back, and I was given a feather duster to tease the clients with. But I had to supply my own underwear and shoes, which I got from a sex shop on Pentonville Road. They were specifically for pole dancing, with huge platforms and black PVC crossovers studded with imitation diamonds. I loved them – they gave me so much confidence. Tracey wore a red see-through catsuit and she looked stunning when her hair was down, with bright red lipstick and black mascara.

The club was like a cattle market. The clientele at Lucy Lightfoot's was rough, like the bar itself – builders and drunks and old men in dirty raincoats, and unruly stag parties. Mervin didn't care much who came through the doors, as long as drinks were being bought at inflated prices. There weren't a huge number of girls and I think Mervin just had us there so he could charge the drinkers extra for his booze. I can see them still, munching on pork pies and slurping down pints of Stella while watching us girls perform. I was never asked to do private dancing for the men, but I did go topless – you made more money the better your performance. I wasn't too keen on going topless, as I have a birthmark next to the nipple on my left breast and I was self-conscious about it. I just used to imagine myself at the beach back in Alderney sunbathing – I told myself it was the same thing, only I was dancing instead of lying on a towel. I never engaged much with the clientele and always avoided eye contact.

Lucy Lightfoot's was a free-for-all. There was no stage, just very dim lighting and the drinkers could get right up close if they wanted to. They loved to drink and, the more they drank, the more they leered. I was always worried about the lack of security and protection for the girls. The men could grope us and the barmen would be expected to come and sit them back down, but wouldn't throw them out, so they'd just do it again. The stag parties were the worst – all these boys drunk out of their brains, spilling beer and shouting.

'Get yer tits out, ya slag!'

The only time they got evicted from the club was if there was a fight, and there were plenty of those. Us girls would just duck for cover when the glasses and bottles started flying. I got really hard-nosed after a while and

I'd watch where they hung their jackets. When they got drunk I'd go and steal money from their wallets. I know it was wrong, but back then I reckoned they deserved anything they got for being so perverted. I got so cocky I'd just walk behind the bar and help myself to vodka and cigarettes. Mervin wouldn't say anything, just rub himself up against me when I walked past him. I started to hate him.

One night this guy came in and sat in the front row while I was on. He kept staring at me, but not in a perverted way – more like he was interested in me for some reason, if you can describe a guy looking at a pole dancer like that. He was wearing an expensive suit and his hair was immaculate, and he had a big gold watch on his wrist. He wasn't like the other regular denizens of Lucy Lightfoot's and he came over to me and Tracey at the bar after we had finished our shift.

'Can I buy you ladies a drink?'

'No, thanks.'

Tracey answered before I could accept. This annoyed me, as it was clear the man had money; maybe he had connections, too, and maybe he could get us out of this place. She seemed to shiver and pulled me away from him.

'Why did you do that, Tracey?'

'For your own good.'

'Who is that guy?'

She didn't answer.

Taking speed made me feel like I was plugged into a generator – I felt so energised. I had boundless energy and could go for long periods without sleep. Tracey supplied me and when she couldn't get any, the comedown was bad. My legs would ache and I'd get griping pains in my stomach. I'd be boiling hot on the outside, but cold on the inside. I didn't know it, but I was beginning to have a habit. To ease the pain of the comedowns, I started smoking weed, so my body and mind began to be all over the place: I was wired on the speed and woozy on the weed. These habits cost money and I wasn't earning enough to afford them, so I decided to try to find a better job.

After about six months with Mervin, I started putting out feelers amongst the punters at the bar, asking them where else they went and what the other pole-dancing clubs were like. They told me about this place called SINatra's, down in Fulham.

By now I'd turned seventeen and I was used to the Underground. When I had some time off, I took a ride over to Fulham Broadway. SINatra's was down a side street, next to a chip shop, and looked very nondescript from the outside. I had to go down a steep stairwell, and it felt like I was walking into a dungeon. It was dark and dingy but it had lots of room inside, much more than I expected from the outside. It was like a maze, with big concrete posts and, just when you thought there was no more room, another door opened, like *Alice in Wonderland*. It was decorated nicely, not like Lucy Lightfoot's – glitz and silver and big mirrors and drop-down chandeliers and disco balls. The music was techno and upbeat and the bar staff were all dressed in black. It had an eerie feel to it, but in a sophisticated way. There was only one dance area, where smoke billowed out every twenty minutes or so, which I found fascinating. There were sofas for the clients to sit on and the girls had their own dressing rooms. Very impressive.

I was a lot more confident now than when I first came to town, so I went to the bar, ordered myself a drink, and asked to see the manager. I was told it was a manageress and there were vacancies, so I found myself a corner to sit in and waited. It wasn't long until I saw this woman coming towards me. I'd never seen anything like her before: she was like a swan, elegant and beautiful, and dressed to kill. She seemed to float across the floor, rather than walk, and her voice was educated when she spoke.

She introduced herself as Madame Jane. I guessed she was about forty or so, but could have been older. She asked if I had experience and I said no. Tracey warned me not to say I worked for Mervin: he was known to be rough and the girls who worked for him got the reputation of being rough, too. Madame Jane would never employ me if she knew I was coming from Lucy Lightfoot's.

Having no experience, as she thought, wasn't a mark in my favour. But I got to my feet and performed a few moves in front of her. I think she liked my youthful enthusiasm and the fact that I loved to dance, so she agreed to give me a try. She said she ran a tight ship: her girls were expected to fall into line and do as they were told. There was a strict dress code and no fraternising with the clientele. On stage there would be no bare legs: it was stockings and suspenders and always high heels, which I'd have to supply myself – oh, and it was topless. Unlike Mervin's there was no fixed wage: all earnings were tips and I'd be expected to hand over 30 per cent of what I took from the clients.

I was excited and disappointed at the same time. Where would I get the money to buy stockings and suspenders and high heels? But I still said yes.

'When can I start?'

Madame Jane gave me a week to get myself sorted out, which I reckoned would be enough time to square things with Mervin. The only thing I was worried about was the room I shared with Tracey. If I left Mervin, would I have to leave his house as well? I'd see what Tracey had to say about that.

I hadn't thought about my family since I'd left Alderney and now I wondered what they'd think if they knew what I was doing. The apprehension didn't stay in my mind for long, however; I dismissed it and it fell by the wayside of my insouciance. I suppose it was like a big adventure to me, and I wasn't really aware of any danger. In any case, I believed Alderney was closed to me now and I couldn't go back. I also believed nobody would miss me or want me back. I wasn't really that important to anyone at home and they were probably relieved I was gone.

I was nervous about going to work for Madame Jane: I didn't know if I could do what would be expected of me. I always had a rebellious streak against authority and never liked to be given orders. Lucy Lightfoot's might be a dump, but it was easy-going and there weren't many rules.

I had a week, so I could still do a few more shifts for Merv the Perv, as the girls called him – he was always spying on us and giving us the leer. To make things even more difficult, Tracey decided to go back to her family and that left me to pay full rent on the room, which I couldn't afford, plus find the money to buy the gear I needed to work at SINatra's.

I told Mervin I was worried about the rent and he invited me upstairs to his flat above the bar so we could 'talk about it'. The flat was really nice compared to the bar below: white leather couches, a huge television screen, dimmed lights, blue satin on the bed – this guy was making a lot of money off us dancers, and he wasn't sharing it. He poured me a drink and leaned over me to put it on the elaborate coffee table.

'You want to stay the night, Tara?'

'Not really.'

'There's no electricity in your room.'

'How come?'

'Tracey didn't top up the key before she left.'

I didn't know anything about pay-as-you-go electricity keys – I just gave her the money and left all that up to Tracey. Maybe he was telling the truth, maybe he wasn't. Then I realised this might be an opportunity to solve all my problems, so I agreed to stay.

There was only one bed and it meant Mervin and I sleeping together, so I kept topping up his glass and he got very drunk. I kept my clothes on when we eventually got into bed and he was too inebriated to do anything naughty. He tried to touch me a few times but I pushed him away and he eventually gave up and started snoring.

After cat-napping through the night, I was up and gone before Mervin woke in the morning. I took his cigarettes and a £20 note from his wallet and left a message saying I'd see him at work that evening. Then I went to the room with no electricity and packed up all my things. Later, I ordered a taxi to pick up me and my gear.

I told the taxi driver to wait while I went back to the bar to see Mervin. I told him we could be together, but Tracey had left a pile of debts that needed to be sorted out, otherwise people would come after me. He fell for it and gave me an envelope with £250 in it, which was a fortune to me. Perhaps I should have felt guilty about this, but I didn't. I felt it was what he deserved for exploiting me and the other girls in his seedy club. My lack of remorse also reflected my hardening attitude to life, which would increase with experience. I left my cigarettes and the room key on the bar and told him I'd return in half an hour to start my shift.

I never looked back.

Chapter 4

Essex Gangsters

SINatra's was in a different league to Lucy Lightfoot's, even though it didn't seem like that from the outside. The girls were prettier and classier – at least, that's the way they seemed to a seventeen-year-old like me. They had bleached-white hair, wore basques and fishnet stockings, and bright red lipstick. It was über-clean and we had proper dressing rooms. I felt a bit out of my league at first, but Madame Jane must have seen something in me – probably that I was young and naive ... 'fresh meat' as they used to say.

They didn't just let anyone in: you had to be a member and it was mostly business people who were well dressed and well heeled. I heard one the girls calling them 'yuppies' and I guessed that meant they were the opposite to 'hippies' – clean and well off, instead of scruffy and broke.

I managed to get into a little bed and breakfast in Prothero Road, which I found advertised in a local newspaper. It was just a bus ride away from SINatra's and I felt really at home there. It was a private house with a picturesque garden with hanging baskets and a manicured lawn. The old lady who owned it was called Marjorie and she let out a room to me. There was a big coal fire in the lounge and I had a really comfortable double bed, with an old-fashioned bedspread, all flowers and swirls. For the first time in my life, I felt safe and happy. But I knew somehow that it wasn't going to be permanent, so I never hung my clothes up in the wardrobe, just keeping them in a bag next to my bed.

I think Marjorie liked having me there, because she always had a cooked breakfast waiting for me when I came in from my shift, and we talked about Elisabeth Beresford, who she loved, and who I'd known when I was being blown about by the winds of neglect around Alderney.

I told her my job was working nights as a pole dancer. She asked what a pole dancer was and I told her. She found it fascinating.

I had used speed and weed while I was at Mervin's club, but here the drug of choice was cocaine. It was everywhere – the clientele snorted it by the bucketful, as did all the girls. The first time I took it was off the cistern in the toilets. I sniffed it through a rolled-up £10 note and I could feel it hitting my throat – chalky, like a bad medicine taste. Within seconds, though, I had a massive rush, my eyes began to bulge and my heart felt like it was exploding in my chest. It seemed as if I was outside myself, outside the room – outside the club. Nothing or nobody could touch me. I was invincible. Indestructible. It gave me so much confidence and I danced like I'd never done before. I was famous, I was a movie star – and everybody loved me.

The cocaine was £25 a gram, so it wasn't cheap, and you couldn't let Madame Jane catch you, or you'd be out the door, but she knew what was going on and, as long as you didn't get caught, you were OK. I knew I had to be careful about who I bought from: I didn't have Tracey to keep me supplied any more and the dealers would try to pimp you out with the promise of coke and fabulous amounts of money, most of which they'd keep for themselves. Some girls were gullible enough to fall for their lies, but I was becoming more streetwise by the day.

Our bags were checked for drugs on the way in and out, and we all had our own methods of concealment. Most of the girls hid the coke in their knickers, which was an obvious place, but I always preferred to keep mine in my hair, which was long enough to conceal a housebrick.

Unlike at Lucy Lightfoot's, I was expected to perform privately at SINatra's, and I'd get a lot of money slipped into my bra or thong. I had learned how to cover up my birthmark with concealer, so I didn't mind going topless any more. My figure was in amazing shape, my legs were toned and I could hold on to the pole more rigidly than before. I had real definition on my body, with a six-pack of abdominals and I was more confident than ever – especially when I was on the coke. I became very popular with the regulars.

It was like this: we were on shift work – at least six girls to a shift, because some of the clients liked blondes and some liked brunettes, some liked big breasts and some liked dark skin, and so on – Madame Jane catered for all tastes. The end of the month was the best time, when most of the clients got paid – weekends, bank holidays, even Christmas, that's when we made the most money – and there was a lot of competition to work those busy times. It was dog eat dog to get those shifts, and the girls were choosy about who they worked with, because a popular girl like me would take a lot of the work from them. That's why I didn't make many friends at SINatra's – they resented me because I was younger and fresher.

Friday nights were the busiest. I'd start at 4 p.m. and work right through till 4 a.m. I was making at least £100 a night from tips or money that would be thrown at me, along with bits of paper with men's names and phone numbers on. Madame Jane was always on our case, checking that everything was pristine with our appearance, otherwise we wouldn't be allowed out to dance. At the end of each shift we had to give her a third of everything we made. Madame Jane was ruthless – she monitored how many private dances we did and how much the clients paid us. It was basically working freelance and paying to use the club. If a girl didn't make money, she was out. I was lucky, as I was popular and did a lot of private dancing and group dancing.

A new girl called Mandy came to work at SINatra's – she was blonde and very pretty and came from Liverpool. She didn't have a place of her own, so I asked Marjorie if she could stay with me until she found somewhere. We got on well and shared a bed, just like Tracey and I used to. One morning after we finished work, we sat drinking vodka and she asked me if I was bisexual. I was offended – did I look like a butch lesbian?

'Of course I'm not!'

'How do you know?'

I didn't.

'Don't knock it till you try it.'

One drink led to another and then we danced together and she kissed me. I expected it to be gross, but it wasn't – much the same as being kissed by a boy. We went back to the room and ended up in bed together, but this time not to sleep. It was a strange experience for me. I'd never been with a girl before and, although it wasn't totally abhorrent, it just didn't seem right.

Despite my misgivings, I liked Mandy and we got on well together. So we embarked on a relationship of sorts and, even though I didn't enjoy it as much as her, it somehow made me feel more confident than ever. I had a true friend who was like me and drank vodka and snorted cocaine and danced semi-naked for men. It was the first time I'd experienced this sense of camaraderie. But Mandy wanted to have sex all the time – in the toilets and the dressing rooms. Mostly it was all right, but I didn't like performing cunnilingus on her. I could do it only when I was intoxicated, if my mind was blank and what we were doing was distorted. When I was sober, I didn't want to have sex and that upset her.

Mandy and I didn't last. It was more of a fling than anything else, and just something different. We grew apart but stayed friends for a while. I never saw myself as a full-blown lesbian – I suppose it was exciting to have someone give me some attention, but I didn't have any feelings of love for her, not in the way I imagined I would have if the right person came along.

Over time, I had several sexual encounters with women. A number of my friends were bisexual and we'd experiment with mutual masturbation or coy cunnilingus if we were high or under the influence of alcohol. But it was all very immature and it would be a number of years before I experienced what a true and deep relationship with another woman was like.

As time went by, I could feel myself slipping deeper into this life of an erotic dancer, and it started to become part of me, to define me. It was who I was – Tara the pole dancer. I loved the music they played at SINatra's and I loved the dancing. I loved getting on the pole, the smoke swirling as I performed. I felt in control: of myself, and of the men who were watching me. It was a feeling of freedom and power. I was still one of the busiest girls there, sometimes working back-to-back shifts. I was also changing – you could say growing up. But it was more than that: I was becoming insensitive, colder, more mercenary. I didn't really make any friends, as it was a very competitive place and everyone was out for themselves, and when I wasn't working, I'd sit at the bar and have a drink and wonder if this was my life from now on. The place was becoming like home to me – I had money, I had nice clothes, I had a nice place to live and life was good. But what about when I got older? I'd have fleeting images of my mother, but I dismissed them as soon as they entered my head. I didn't want to think about becoming like her – if that was what was ahead of me.

This one particular mid-week night, when it wasn't too busy, about a year after I first came to London, I was sitting at the bar and a woman came in. She was in her late thirties and had an amazing figure, really thin, with big breasts and long, dark, wavy hair and smooth olive skin. She sat beside me at the bar and I thought she was stunning, so I was happy for her to strike up a conversation with me.

I thought I was really streetwise at that time but now, looking back, I was still incredibly naive.

'Hello, I'm Mary.'

'Hi, I'm Tara.'

'Nice name, is it real?'

'Of course, my father gave it to me—'

'That was generous of him.'

'—before he went away.'

Mary told me she lived in Essex, in East Barking to be precise, and she was waiting for a male friend. She waited and waited, but he didn't turn up. She said she was a saleswoman for ladies make-up, all the top ranges, and she made a lot of money. She had her own house and her own car and she asked if I'd be interested in a career in sales – a good-looking girl like me could do well.

I thought about her proposition for a while. Did I really want to get out of the pole-dancing game that I'd become so familiar with? Again I thought of what might happen in a few years' time – there would always be young girls coming into the business and the clients always wanted 'fresh meat'. A saleswoman in cosmetics would be a respectable job that paid well and had unlimited prospects. I might even have a company car and an expense account. It was what I came to London for, wasn't it?

'Of course I'd be interested.'

I didn't have to give any notice to Madame Jane, as I was freelance. I told Marjorie I'd be leaving at the end of the week. She was sad to see me go and she gave me a bag of barley twists and told me to take care of myself.

I met Mary again at SINatra's a week later; I had my bag with me. It was late and we drove through the night into the countryside outside London. I'd never heard of East Barking and it was dark when we arrived, so I couldn't see much of the place, but I began to get a bad feeling about it. The atmosphere seemed to change. Mary's attitude changed too: she wasn't the same person I met in SINatra's and I felt a sense of foreboding. But I was stuck there now.

Mary's 'house' wasn't really a house, as such. It was a flat, situated in a huge grey-and-brown building that seemed to touch the sky. I'd never heard of council estates before, let alone seen one like this. The place was littered with old newspapers and empty beer cans, and the stairwells stank of urine. The walls were covered with graffiti and the lift wasn't working, so we had to climb up endless flights of stairs to the eighth floor, past people sleeping rough on the ground.

'Don't stare at them, Tara.'

I gasped for breath before hurrying after Mary along the external landing. She was anxious to get inside as quickly as she could.

The flat looked bare, with hardly any furniture. It was freezing cold and there were clothes strewn everywhere. Used plates were piled up in the sink and the bathroom smelled of sick. There were other girls there, but they didn't say hello or anything and seemed to appear out of nowhere to look at me, then disappear just as quickly, back into the vile ambience of the place.

I felt exhausted by now and decided I'd have to stay there until I got my bearings, then I'd see what my options were.

'I really need to sleep, Mary.'

'Do as you like.'

She didn't offer me a room or anything else, so I slept in a chair that night, trying to get comfortable with my legs scrunched up and my coat over my feet, using my hands as a pillow. I could hear voices as I dozed on and off – Mary talking to one of the girls, who asked her what I was doing there.

'She'll be good for carrying the weed. She ain't staying here long.'

I resolved to get away from the place as soon as I could and make my way back to London.

The next morning, I was woken roughly by Mary. She handed me a bacon sandwich and a cup of tea.

'Get changed and freshen up when you've eaten that. We got work to do.'

There was lots of make-up in the bathroom, so I still believed that's what we were going to sell. I used some of it and some perfume, and back-combed my hair, then went back to the living room. Mary was there in her underwear, putting on a really expensive-looking dress, with a joint hanging from her lips. She put on a coat and I followed her back down the endless stairs to the car.

We seemed to drive for miles and miles, but it probably wasn't that far. We didn't speak much on the journey and I just sat watching the Essex countryside move past the window. Eventually, we came to a big country house, situated in acres of ground. There was a long drive up to it and we passed stables with horses and a kind of farmhouse with chickens and goats and a tractor.

'Be careful what you say and do.'

I didn't understand what she meant by that, but I decided to only speak if I was spoken to and to do nothing at all. That should be safe enough – shouldn't it?

I followed Mary up to the big house and she told me to take off my shoes. My feet sank into the thick carpet and it was like walking on clouds. We went through a reception area into a big lounge where a group of men were gathered. There was a short, bearded guy in the middle, surrounded by the others. They were all a lot older than me and drinking whisky. I thought: 'What, these guys sell make-up and Mary buys it from them? How strange.'

Mary gestured for me to sit down, which I did. The short guy with the beard looked over at me and I knew I'd seen him somewhere before. Then it came to me: he was the well-dressed man who was so out of place at Lucy Lightfoot's – the one Tracey wouldn't let us take a drink from.

He left the others and came across to me.

'Cat got your tongue?'

'I'm—'

'Tara, I know.'

'Mary told you?'

'It's a small world.'

That was my first introduction to Jason Ward, one of the most notorious gangsters in Essex.

The men in the centre of the room moved aside and I could see this stone table that looked like it had been carved out of a piece of a mountain and now stood there, majestic, on four oak legs. It was covered with drugs – all kinds of drugs: cannabis, cocaine, pills, heroin, everything. Of course, I didn't know what it all was at the time, but I was going to find out. The men were pouring whisky from a decanter into glasses that looked like they were made of diamonds, they glistened so brightly in the light that streamed in through long windows.

I tried to stay cool; after all, I was streetwise now and not the young naive girl on that G-Joey flight from Alderney – or so I thought.

Jason Ward asked me if I'd finished with the pole dancing.

'I think so.'

'You think so?'

'I hope so.'

'And what would you like to do instead?'

'I came to London to find fame and fortune.'

He laughed for a long time. Then he stopped and looked at me in a serious way. Then he laughed again.

'You've come to the right place.'

He said they had things to discuss and could I go outside and help Rachel with the horses.

I didn't know who Rachel was, but it turned out she was a girl of about my age. She smiled when I introduced myself, but she seemed to have a sadness about her and the smile wasn't real. It wasn't a happy smile. I was wearing Doc Martens, jeans and a hoodie and I tried not to step in the mud and dung while not getting too near the big horse-beasts, which scared me.

'How do you know Mary, Tara?'

'I met her in a club, and she offered me a job selling make-up.'

'I shouldn't be telling you this, but Mary doesn't sell make-up.'

'No?'

'No, she's a runner.'

I didn't understand. She ran in races? What kind of races? Horse races?

Rachel burst out laughing.

'She's a drugs runner ... she sells drugs, not make-up.'

The penny finally dropped: the dingy flat – all those girls – this big house – the table – the whisky – the men – the horses.

I was involved with drug dealers.

Rachel could see the panic and shock in my face.

'Jason's not such a bad guy to work for. You could do worse.'

I wanted to know more, but Mary was at the door, calling me back into the house.

When I got inside, food had been delivered and the room was filled with the most delicious, mouth-watering aromas. Jason Ward spoke to me again.

'Tikka masala?'

'Yes, please.'

I said that even though I didn't know what tikka masala was. Somebody dished up the Indian takeaway. I was starving and ate like a savage, golloping down the tikka masala and pilau rice and aloo and nan, food so beautiful and spicy I never knew existed but, now that I'd found it, I'd eat nothing else.

When I finished and was wiping my mouth with a napkin, Jason beckoned me over to sit by him on a sofa. For some reason, I didn't feel uneasy about doing that. It was like the night when he was in Lucy Lightfoot's watching me pole dance: it was that same enigmatic way he had about him – not perverted like Mervin. He started asking me a lot of questions about Alderney, who I knew on the island, was there enough space to land a helicopter?

'You know someone called Joan Allerton, Tara?'

'Yes, I know her family. I know her sister, Jennifer. She runs the local bakery and she's a really nice lady and ...'

He put up his hand to cut me off in mid-sentence. It was more information than he needed. I remembered what Mary told me on the way in, so I shut up.

'You know her husband?'

'Not really, he's from the mainland.'

'The mainland?'

'That's what we call England on Alderney.'

I was getting a bit lost with all the questions: they didn't make much sense to me. How did he know these people? Were they connected in some way? Was I here because I was from Alderney?

'You know anyone over there who can handle themselves a bit rowdy?'

'Rowdy?'

'A tough guy.'

I did know this fisherman called Skipper Grundy. He was well known on the island for drinking and brawling. I gave Jason the name of the pub where Skipper drank as he'd be able to get hold of him there. Jason Ward was pleased with the information I'd given him. He was grateful, and wanted to do something for me in return.

'How are you finding Mary's place?'

'I've only been there a night. It was cold and crowded.'

'You can stay here if you want. Plenty of room. But you'll have to earn your keep and help out in the stables.'

Mary just glared at me – I'd escaped her clutches. I breathed a sign of relief.

Living at Jason's house was really cool. I didn't see a great deal of him because he was always busy. I had my own room with no strings attached and I was fed and looked after. The house was always full of people: glamorous men and women coming and going all the time, expensive cars driving up, business being done. Everything was a bit shady and it was a fast and loose lifestyle, but I loved being there. I got on great with Rachel, she was a lovely girl. Her mother was a friend of Jason's and she had her own horse that she kept at Jason's yard. I didn't have a clue what I was doing in the stables – the hay made me itch and the horses scared me.

I stayed at Jason's for over six months, and I found out that he was interested in Alderney because Joan Allerton's husband had stolen a lot of money from him and he wanted to get it back. Alderney was a small island and everyone knew everyone else and he had no access to the community – but now I'd given him one: Skipper Grundy. This worried me and I hoped nobody would get hurt on my account, but what was done was done and I couldn't take back the information I'd given him.

One day when Rachel wasn't around, I went exploring the land around the big house. It was vast and I walked for ages until I came to this large shed. The doors were locked, but I was always inquisitive and I managed to get in through a loose panel in the side of the building. The light was dim inside and I stumbled over something. I flicked my lighter and saw with the flame that I'd tripped over a shotgun. Then I looked around and saw guns all over the place – shotguns and rifles and handguns and all sorts, along with other weapons like knives and swords and bats and crowbars. What had I got myself into? I was scared out of my wits and needed to get out of there, quickly. Then I heard this huge noise and, when I climbed back out through the loose panel, I saw a helicopter landing in a field nearby. I ran as fast as I could and hid until it got dark, then I went back to the house and crept to my room without anyone seeing me.

I grabbed my bag and left in the middle of the night.

I walked for miles and miles, without knowing where I was going. I'd forgotten how far Mary had driven me that time we came to the house from East Barking. I'd seen a film called *The Hitchhiker* back home, about a guy who got lifts by sticking his thumb out – so I did the same.

After a while, a lorry driver stopped and asked where I was going.

'I don't know.'

'I can take you as far as Brentwood.'

'OK.'

I didn't know where Brentwood was, but it was better than being here. So I climbed in and fell asleep in the warm cab.

It was very early in the morning when we got to Brentwood and the driver shook me awake. The town was big, with lots of shops and pubs, but everywhere was closed. I curled up in a doorway and tried to use my body heat to keep me warm. I must have been there for ages and the only person who passed was a road sweeper. He looked at me, said nothing, and moved on. I felt ashamed.

Once the town woke up, people started moving everywhere. I decided to do what I did when I first came to London: go into a pub and see what happened. There was a big place called the Castle – it was shaped like a castle as well, with a pointed roof and a huge black-and-white sign. I went straight to the ladies', had a wash, sprayed myself with Impulse, applied blue mascara to my eyes and back-combed my hair. I didn't have much money, so I bought a Coke at the bar. The pub was quiet at that time of the day, so I thought I'd liven it up. I found the jukebox and started dancing to the tunes.

It wasn't long before I attracted the attention of this Rick Astley lookalike who said his name was Simon. He wore a flashy waistcoat and had a posh accent. He bought me a few drinks and we played pool for a couple of hours. I found out he was a born-again Christian, whatever that meant. I told him I'd had to leave a place in the middle of the night because I was in mortal danger. He was intrigued and said I could come back to his house.

I sat with him and his mother, who taught piano, in their conservatory. She was very haughty and didn't like me at all. When Simon went to the kitchen to get us a cold drink, she asked me to leave him alone.

I had come to a decision reluctantly a bit earlier: I had to be mercenary – I couldn't face a night in that doorway.

'How much is it worth?'

'I beg your pardon?'

'How much is it worth to you for me to leave your boy alone?'

'How much do you want?'

I thought about it, but not for long.

'Two hundred pounds.'

She didn't hesitate. I should have asked for three hundred!

'All right, but you mustn't bother him any more.'

'I promise, you'll never see me again.'

She handed me the money and, when Simon came back from the kitchen, I was gone.

That was my first real experience of hustling.

Chapter 5

Learning to Hustle

So, here I was in Brentwood, Essex, with my bag and £200, not really knowing where I was or what I was going to do. The first thing was to find somewhere to sleep. Winter was approaching and the night came quick and cold. I looked for a pub, as I always did, and that's when I saw it – the Black Lamb. It was an omen, a sign from heaven. This was where I had to go, where I belonged.

The pub was run by an Irish woman who looked like Bet Lynch from *Coronation Street*. She was almost six feet tall, with a blonde beehive that made her look even more intimidating. She wore a miniskirt that was too tight, with a boob tube and big hoop earrings. A cigarette dangled from the bright red of her lips.

'What can I get yeh, me darlin'?'

'Half of lager.'

I didn't know how long my money would have to last, so the drink was just to get me through the door. She served me and was about to walk away.

'Do you know where I could get a room for the night?'

She gave me a curious look, with one eye half closed.

'A room is it yer after?'

'Yes.'

She didn't answer immediately, but studied me for a while.

'I might have one upstairs.'

I took a sip from the lager and followed her up a flight of stairs to a living room with leopard-skin chairs and an orange carpet. The woman poured herself a whisky, but didn't offer me anything.

'I'm Deirdre, by the way.'

'I'm Tara.'

'A good Irish name.'

'My father was Irish.'

A smile beamed its way across her face. I could tell she liked me already.

'Tell me this, how old are yeh?'

'Eighteen.'

I lied. Well, I was almost eighteen. She asked me a bucketful of questions, like where I came from and was I on the run and would anyone be looking for me. I told her I came out from London to see my boyfriend who worked in the Ford Motor factory, but he'd left to go up north somewhere and now I was stranded. She seemed happy with my made-up answers.

'Tell me this, Tara, are yeh a virgin?'

I thought that was rather a personal question for a complete stranger to be asking me and my mind raced back to Bruno. I didn't really know whether I was a virgin or not.

'Probably not.'

Deirdre laughed. It started as a kind of giggle, then developed into a full-blown hoot. It took her a few minutes to compose herself.

'Well, that's the best one I ever heard. I like yeh, Tara. Come with me.'

She led me up another flight of stairs to a small, single room. It had a bed and some basic furniture and the same orange carpet as the living room.

'How long will yeh be staying?'

'I'm not sure.'

'All right, I'll tell yeh what I'll do. I'll charge yeh by the night. A fiver – includes breakfast. In advance. How's that?'

Expensive, for what it was, but I gave her £5. I'd find something cheaper tomorrow. I went back down to the pub and had a few more lagers before tumbling into the bed at about 11 p.m. I immediately fell into a deep and dreamless sleep and didn't wake till 9 a.m.

When I went downstairs the next morning, Deirdre had a full Irish breakfast waiting – white pudding, soda bread, the lot. I didn't realise how hungry I was and I wolfed it down in minutes, along with a big mug of strong tea.

'Can I leave my bag in the room while I go out and decide what I'm going to do?'

'Sure yeh can, me darlin'.'

I mooched around Brentwood looking for a job and a cheaper place to live, but found nothing. I got back to the Black Lamb as it was getting dark.

Deirdre was sitting at one of the tables with a big Jamaican man. She beckoned me over.

'This is Nipper, Tara. I've been telling him about you.'

The man smiled and showed a couple of gold teeth. He had a lot of gold hanging around his neck as well, and big rings on his fingers.

'Tara's boyfriend deserted her, Nipper. She's looking for work.'

The gold teeth flashed in my direction.

'What kind of work?'

'Any kind.'

'*Any* kind?'

Nipper bought me a couple of large vodkas and later took me out in his car. We drove through a labyrinth of streets and the ambience changed. The buildings were different here – high-rise flats and graffiti and rubbish, just like the place I went to with Mary. I was starting to get worried. He stopped the car and took me into one of the flats, where some other guys were playing loud music and sniffing cocaine off a glass coffee table. They ignored me and just carried on with what they were doing.

'You want a hit, Tara?'

'Why not.'

Nipper rolled up a note and offered me a line, which I took. I immediately felt better – more confident, not so anxious. That's when I noticed the other girls in the flat – they were dressed in skimpy clothes and looked cold and nervous.

I should have known what was happening, after working in the pole-dancing clubs, but I was still young and pretty naive, and the large vodkas had gone to my head a little.

Nipper brought one of the girls over to me. Her name was Justine and he told her to show me the ropes and take me to the red light district, close to the town centre.

'This is the deal, Tara. You give me fifty per cent of what you earn and I take care of you.'

'What am I supposed to do?'

'Hookin', honey … hookin'.'

I still wasn't sure what it was he wanted me to do.

Justine whispered in my ear.

'Prostitution.'

'I'm not a prostitute!'

The gold teeth flashed again, but not in a smile. This time they were angry.

'Deirdre told me you worked in the London clubs.'

'Pole dancing!'

'Same thing as hookin'.'

'No, it's not!'

I made a dash for the door. Nipper came after me. I got out of the flat and down the steps as quick as I could. I could hear him coming behind me, shouting at me to come back.

I didn't look round, just ran and ran and ran. I didn't know where I was going, just running down this street and that street, until I thought I'd lost him.

It was late, and getting dark and cold now, and I didn't know how to get back to the Black Lamb. I thought the town centre would be safest, where there were people about. After traipsing around for a while, trying to rid myself of the effects of the vodka and cocaine, I huddled down in a doorway and tried to sleep, pulling my donkey jacket tight around me.

Gradually, the enthusiastic streets emptied of drinkers and shoppers to be replaced by the night people – alcoholics and thieves and drug addicts and pimps and pushers. Sirens sometimes squalled past like excitable harridans and doormen from the clubs hulked about, hump-backed in the shadows, looking for sex from homeless girls like me. It was a normal town during the day, but at night it was hostile and angry and unpredictable.

I tried to sleep in the well-lit doorway of a town-centre bank, but the police came along and moved me out onto the dirty, wet pavement, where I eventually closed my eyes. But it was a fitful sleep, constantly disturbed by the sounds of the night and hooded spectres leering past me in the neon lecher-light.

In fact, I hardly slept at all and was glad to see the early streaks of dawn in the sky to the east. As soon as it got light, I made my way back to the pub. It wasn't open so I waited outside until Deirdre unlocked the doors later in the morning.

'Tara, what're you doin' here?'

'I came for my bag.'

'What about Nipper?'

'Fuck Nipper ... and you!'

I dashed upstairs and grabbed my bag and pushed Deirdre to one side on the way out. The Black Lamb might've been my namesake, but it wasn't the place for me, as I'd first believed. I wasn't that black – yet.

I thought I'd better get out of Brentwood, in case Nipper came upon me, so I hitched a lift to Romford, which was about seven or eight miles away. I was back where I started, with nowhere to live, no direction in my life and very little money – which soon ran out.

I started drifting around, from Essex town to Essex town: Dagenham, Colchester, Basildon, Ilford, Canvey Island, Southend-on-Sea, East Barking, all over the county. I learned how to be resourceful, shoplifting from supermarkets, pickpocketing, skipping – which was searching in skips for food – picking up cigarette butts from the street, sleeping in doorways. It was winter and it was cold and all I had to keep me warm was my donkey jacket. I had long hair at the time and I used to wrap it around my neck like a scarf.

That's how I spent my eighteenth birthday.

Sometimes people would throw money at me; other times I'd go up to men in pubs and hustle them – get them to spend money on me with the promise of sex, but they never got what they paid for: I'd always find a way out before it got to the point of accompanying them into the public toilet, or to a cheap room, or back to their place. When I could, I'd steal their wallets and get out before they noticed.

This hustling and homeless lifestyle went on for about six months. I have to say I'm not proud of this time in my life, but I was young and alone and I had to survive the only way I knew how back then. I also had to be very careful – the pubs I frequented were gangster pubs. What I mean by that is they were used by people who worked for the likes of Jason Ward: small-time crooks and villains, burglars, robbers, drug dealers, enforcers, bodyguards, that kind of thing. If any of them caught me hustling them, I'd end up dead – or badly beaten. That's why I kept moving from place to place, so nobody ever knew who I was or could pin me down.

But I was getting tired of the constant ducking and diving.

I loved pub life, not to get drunk or anything, but just for the characters, the atmosphere, the music playing, the buzz – pubs were like my home, and the dodgy people in them were like my family.

That's where I met Joe, in the Brazen Head in Romford, Essex. Joe was rough and ready, and I liked that about him. He was a small-time gangster, not big-time like Jason Ward, but he wasn't married and had his own house. He was a lot older than me – maybe early thirties – and he looked a bit like Bruno. How strange is that? We connected because I felt protected in his company. I wanted to feel safe and he gave me that sense of security. Perhaps I was looking for a father figure and that's what attracted me to him, rather than lust. And I wanted somewhere more permanent to live – at least for a while. Joe wanted to be with me, too. He wanted to go to the pub with me, cook for me, take me for drives – life was good with him, for a while.

It wasn't long until I moved in with him and we became lovers. He was the first man I had full sexual intercourse with and I didn't like it all that much. It hurt and made me bleed and gave me stomach cramps. I really didn't know what to do, so I just lay there until he was finished. I didn't have any sexual feelings, I didn't know how to have a passionate relationship. When it was over, he got up and went to the bathroom to clean himself and left me with the smell I hated – the smell of sex. I'd shower and try to get rid of it, but it was in my nose and stayed with me for a long time afterwards.

Don't get me wrong, I really liked Joe and I know he liked me. It was fine while we were friends, but shortly after we became lovers he grew moody and possessive and started picking fights with me for no reason. He stopped taking me out and I felt increasingly isolated and realised I'd made a big mistake. But how could I get out of this situation now? I had no money and he watched me all the time. He started to become very controlling and it scared me – I mean, I'd lived with fear all through my childhood, and I didn't want to go back there again. He became obsessively jealous. He didn't like me speaking to anyone, even other women. He didn't like me going to the shops on my own either. It was getting out of control.

One rare night we went out for a drink and he insisted on driving afterwards, even though he'd had quite a few. We argued about it and he grabbed me and bundled me into the car and drove off very fast. I was screaming and trying to get out, but he wouldn't let me. Then, suddenly, the car veered off the road, crashed into a graveyard and flipped over. I can remember being thrown about inside and then blackness. I was unconscious.

I came to in hospital, not really knowing where I was or what had happened. I had broken ribs and a fractured wrist and I was covered in cuts and bruises. But it could have been a lot worse. The nurses asked me what had happened, but I said I couldn't remember because I didn't want to get Joe into trouble for drink-driving – although they probably knew that already. They were really concerned about me, because of how young I was. Maybe they thought he'd abducted me or something, I don't know. I later found out that Joe pulled me out of the wrecked car and left me in the graveyard. He rang the emergency services from a phone box and anonymously reported the accident. By the time the police interviewed him, Joe was sober and there was no alcohol in his bloodstream. He said he couldn't remember what happened and no charges were made against him.

Then they brought me a telephone and told me my mother was on the line. I couldn't believe it – how did she know where I was?

'Hello?'

'Tara?'

'Yes.'

'It's your mother here. Are you all right?'

'Yes, I'm fine.'

Apparently, they went through my bag at the hospital and found Jason Ward's number in it. They had called him and he'd put them in touch with Skipper Grundy, who was now working for Jason on Alderney. Skipper went to see my mother and told her where I was.

'Do you want me to come and get you, Tara?'

'No, I'm fine … honestly. I'm going to stay in hospital for a few days.'

'Go to Isabella's, Tara. Otherwise I'm coming to get you.'

Isabella was someone we knew who used to visit Alderney regularly. She came over with her mother on holiday and became friends with my extended family. They stayed with her grandmother, who lived not far from my grandparents. I'd go over to visit and that's how I got to know her.

She was a posh girl and always dressed the best. She seemed different from the rest of us on Alderney, coming over from London as she did. More sophisticated maybe, or more kitsch – they both seemed the same to me back then. She always had a rock-chick look: big hoop earrings, bright lipstick, spiked hair, a strange accent and plenty of curves. She loved to have fun and she was really popular on Alderney – she was one of the cool girls to hang with when I was young. She was a few years older than me, the life and soul of the party, and all the boys on Alderney were crazy about her.

My mother gave me her number and made me promise I'd call her.

I didn't tell my mother how Skipper Grundy knew where I was, or say anything about Jason Ward. I didn't ask about Joan Allerton or her husband, but I learned later that Joan died of cancer and her sister drove off a cliff in her car. They said it was suicide. Joan's husband disappeared.

It was all over with me and Joe – he could have killed us both. I didn't tell him that while I was in hospital, or when I came out, over a week later. I desperately needed a base from which to get myself back into the world, and Joe's house would have to suffice, until I was ready and could extricate myself from the relationship. In any case, they wouldn't let me out of hospital unless I had somewhere to go, and Joe's was the only place available.

But it wasn't so easy. Joe now believed he had complete control of me. He didn't try to have sex with me when I came back to live with him – I don't know whether that was because I was still injured or because he was having sex with someone else. But I didn't care, I just knew I had to get away. I was weak and still suffering from some memory loss – but I had Jason Ward's number and I remembered who he was.

After about three weeks, I was able to walk properly and the pain began to fade. I called Jason Ward from a payphone and asked him if I could borrow some money. He knew I'd been in hospital and I was surprised when he agreed to help me, considering I'd done a moonlight flit from his house.

Joe was predictable when he was sober and doing whatever it was he did: small-time crookery with his little gang. I waited for him to come home for lunch one day, and acted quite normal. I asked him for £5 so I could get meat for dinner from the local butcher, just to assure him that nothing was out of the ordinary. After I heard his car driving away, I took everything I could from the house, any cash I could find, food, clothes, toiletries – I packed everything into my bag and left, closing the door behind me. It might seem hard and unfeeling, but I was determined not to be anyone's property – and I did what I did to survive in what was becoming an ever tougher world.

I met Jason Ward in a car park and he took me round to the boot of his car. I was scared stiff in case he threw me in and drove me to a freshly dug grave in some remote wooded place.

'Why did you run away, Tara?'

'I don't know ... I wanted to go back to London.'

'So how come you ended up in a hospital in Romford?'

'Keeping bad company, I suppose.'

He put his hand on the boot to open it. My heart skipped a beat.

'We could be more than friends, if you get my meaning.'

I didn't know what to say. I never really liked Jason in that way, but I knew if I was with him I could have anything I wanted and he'd take care of me. But he wasn't a man to mess with and if he got jealous, like Joe, it would only end one way for me.

'Thanks for the offer, Jason, but I just want to get back to London for now.'

The boot of the car swung open. I half expected to see a sawn-off shotgun inside. But there was a briefcase instead. He opened it and it was like something out of a movie: the case was full of money, thousands of pounds.

'How much do you need?'

I could hardly speak for a moment or two because it took my breath away.

'A hundred pounds?'

He took £100 from the case and handed it to me, squeezing it tight into my hand.

'Tara, if you ever need anything, just call.'

I never saw Jason Ward again.

I called Isabella and asked if I could stay with her. She said yes, so I took a taxi from Romford to Fulham in London, where she lived in a big townhouse that belonged to her parents. It cost me £40 to get there, almost half of the money Jason had given me.

Another friend from Alderney was staying there at the time. Her name was Mia and she was one of the bad girls from the island, like me, so we all got on well together. Isabella said I didn't need to pay any rent and I could stay as long as I wanted. It was great, we were all young, and Isabella liked to party hard and she drank a lot.

One night we went out to a club and I met this guy called Michael, who was a bit of a wheeler dealer and a jack-of-all-trades, operating on the edges of the law. It was the summer of 1990. I was eighteen.

And I fell madly in love.

Chapter 6

Chaos in Cardiff

Michael was very handsome – tall and dark, with almond-shaped blue eyes and a beautiful wide smile. He was into a lot of things, including catwalk modelling but, unfortunately, he wasn't a great success at it. He was a restless man, finding it difficult to remain in one place for too long. If you met him you'd say he was reserved, shy even, and didn't have a lot to say around people. It was as if he didn't want people to get to know him too well, in case they might be able to control him in some way or see behind the veneer of who he was pretending to be. He was moody and had a very short temper – which I only found out later. When he drank, you had to watch what you said to him and, while not being the hardest of men, he was capable of picking a fight with anyone: he didn't care who it was and he didn't care about getting hurt. You might think someone who did modelling would be careful about getting their body broken up, but not Michael.

Why was I attracted to him? I've mostly forgotten now, but I suppose the world around me was brand new and Michael was a microcosm, a human metaphor, of what that world seemed to be: cool, charismatic, charming ... when he wanted to be. In my eyes, back then, men like him were difficult to find – enigmatic men – not the ones who revealed everything to you in the first five minutes.

Was that because they were immature, or because I was?

Michael showed me things – he liked classical music, which I'd never heard before. He played that music when we were together, like Rameau's *Les Indes galantes*, which made me feel like dancing, or the second movement of Edvard Grieg's piano concerto, which made me weep with emotion, or the waltz from Shostakovich's jazz suite, which seemed to come from an older time, long ago. Or the feeling I couldn't explain when I heard *Trois morceaux en forme de poire*, or the finale of *The Firebird*, which gave me so much hope, made me feel so alive. More than alive. Eternal. Part of everything. With him. I soared into the sky and knew what I was, what I really, really was. Without him the music wasn't the same. I tried playing it on my own, but something was missing.

He did things to me, to what was inside me. I'm not talking about sexual things, it was more than that. He made me feel like a woman inside, treated me like a woman, not like a little girl. I wanted to be treated like a woman – I could take it, even the rough stuff that was to come later. He spoke to me about things and his voice was soft and sensuous. His words were like little kisses on my ears. And he laughed at things other people didn't laugh at – didn't even think about. Things I didn't think about, until he told me. And then I thought about them all the time. He was more than a man; or maybe he wasn't, and it was just that the others were less than men. But he *taught* me things – how to live, how to love. And hate.

How to listen, and laugh. I didn't know then that he'd also teach me how to cry. That would be the next lesson.

And was that something I had to learn to be a real woman? Not a fake, sterile cypher of someone like my mother, but a woman with a deeper light, a more profound identity – with a soul that any man could float away on. A woman who needed no man to make her whole, but who could accommodate men if she felt like it. Michael would make me that kind of woman. With time.

Mia was studying at Cardiff University and she wanted me to go to Wales with her. I didn't want to, but Michael said he came from Wales and he was fed up with London and was thinking about going back there.

I probably would never have gone if it wasn't for Michael. I wanted to be with him and we agreed to go there separately and contact each other when we got settled. I can remember being on a train with Mia and the countryside travelling past – all the fields and sheep and trees – and I felt apprehensive. I was used to a fast and loose lifestyle, and I didn't know what I was letting myself in for.

Mia put me up for a few days, but she was at the university most of the time and I felt really alone, as I didn't know anyone in Cardiff. And I was completely broke. We didn't have mobiles or Facebook in those days, and I didn't know where Michael lived or even if he was back in Wales yet.

One night I decided to go into Cardiff city centre to see if I could hustle some money. There was a street called Chippy Lane – it's real name was Caroline Street, but it got the nickname Chippy Lane because of all the fast-food vendors along it – where people went after they'd been drinking, so I followed the crowd and ended up there. Anyway, I was mooching about, looking for an opportunity, when I saw Michael across the street. He was just standing there, staring over at me. I couldn't believe my eyes – I ran to him and we hugged.

That night I went back to his parents' house in Thornhill, which is a middle-class area of Cardiff. His mother took an immediate dislike to me and, when Michael wasn't listening, she whispered that her son could do a lot better than me. She was very controlling and self-opinionated, but his father was more laid-back and easy-going and seemed like a man who was prepared to put up with anything for some peace and quiet.

I knew we couldn't stay at his parents' house because Michael's mother didn't want me there, so we started looking for a place of our own. We eventually found a room in Ruby Street, which was a nice area with lots of wynds, or alleys, with names like Gold Street and Diamond Street and Copper Street, as if it was a shrine to miners who dug for jewels and precious metals or something. We had a downstairs studio flat which was kitted out really nicely.

It was to be the first of our many homes together.

I had no money and no job and Michael was paying for everything, which I didn't like. He couldn't get any modelling jobs, but he took labouring work on building sites when he needed to. We got on all right together for a while, but gradually our relationship began to get toxic. I mean he wanted to be in charge of everything: make all the decisions, go out and not come back all night and expect me to just accept it and keep my mouth shut. That was never the way I was made. We began rowing and fighting all the time and he kept threatening to throw me out – the tenancy of the flat was in his name. Then one night, things went too far and he screamed at me to leave, that we were finished. I had nowhere else to go, so I took an overdose of paracetamol and ended up in hospital.

I kept wanting to be with *Michael*, the Michael I met in London. I felt then that I belonged with him, after being blown around like thistledown. In Wales he'd become a different Michael, as if the faeries had taken the London Michael away and left this changeling in his place.

'Love' is a much maligned word, isn't it? People think sex is love, but it isn't. You love your dog or your children – that's love. The thing between a man and a woman isn't love, has nothing to do with love. It has something to do with movement and smell and taste and touch and sound and sense and light and dark and addiction and compulsion and violence and hope and despair. But it has nothing to do with love. And I wanted so badly to be loved. I didn't realise back then that sex and love were different things – I believed sex would lead to love, would transform itself into love. But now that the Michael I'd met in London was gone, sex wasn't enough and I couldn't understand what had happened.

Why did I overdose? I can't remember. Perhaps I just couldn't bear the rejection. I'd been rejected all my life and now it was happening again.

What was I doing wrong?

Again.

This time the hospital experience was horrific. They stuck a long tube down my throat and I couldn't breathe. I was gagging and trying to pull it out and they were holding me down when all this charcoal stuff came back up the tube – I think it was what they pumped into me to make me sick, to get the paracetamol back up.

When I recovered, Michael came to see me and said he was sorry and we went back to living together again. I said I can't remember why I took the overdose – but I can. It wasn't for attention or anything like that; I was just so hurt and lost and I didn't want to be in this world. It was as if nothing had meaning any more: my beautiful dream had been shattered, so why bother to go on living? I don't expect people to understand. I was very young and life had thrown me about a lot and I couldn't see anything positive to live for after the illusion of the elusive love I craved disintegrated. With the luxury of hindsight and a lot more years behind me, I know it was wrong and there's always something to live for, no matter how bad things seem.

I wanted so much for us to have a baby because I believed that would bring us back together, like before, and cement our relationship. How wonderful it would be to have a child of our own to call us 'Mum' and 'Dad' and I'd love it and look after it and it wouldn't be brought up like I was – it would be cherished. Michael wasn't interested, so we kept on fighting and making up again. We fought about everything: money, his drinking, the colour of the sky, the length of the day. When the changeling turned into an ogre and started smashing up the furniture, I still loved him – or thought I did. I believed we could still get it back, that magical time we'd had together before we came to Cardiff.

It all got too much in that little room and we eventually fell behind with the rent and got threatened by the landlord. He was a tattooist and he knew a lot of tough people, so we had to go and find somewhere else to live, fast.

We walked the streets, looking through the local papers and the adverts in shop windows, until we found another room to let. This one was on the embankment, down Riverside, which was known to be a really rough area of Cardiff. But we didn't have much choice.

Riverside embankment was a grim place. It was dark and dreary and I hated living there. It was populated by a mixture of many races and nationalities – Polish, Somali, Asian – and there were lots of gangs. As a young girl, I'd get propositioned all the time, just walking down the street. I'd laugh it off but, in truth, I was always scared of being pulled into a dark alley and raped. They knew if you were an outsider and didn't fit in, so I looked at the ground and scurried from one place to another. The water in the river was coloured green and black and it was a notorious place for suicides. Houses were boarded up with metal grids, shops were shut down, prostitutes roamed the streets and stabbings were commonplace.

We both had to claim housing benefit, to get the rent paid. In those days, you were given a giro and you could nominate someone else to cash it by entering their name on the back. Once, after we'd been arguing about Michael spending all our money on booze and drugs, he told me to go and cash his giro at the post office – as long as I had his ID, it would be all right. Then he called the police and had me arrested for fraud, saying I'd tried to rob him. I mean, what a thing to do! Why would anyone do that? Was it about control? Was the ogre showing me he could do whatever he wanted to me? I was taken to Clifton police station without really knowing why, where I was mug-shotted and fingerprinted. I was scared senseless, I thought it was something to do with the hustling. They questioned me for hours, but I was in shock and unable to answer them. I think they realised I was in a vulnerable state because, in the end, they told me Michael had made the allegation.

'Why would he do that? He gave me the giro to cash.'

I conjured up in my head what prison would be like – would I get picked on? Would there be a top dog – an alpha female? How would I survive? I was told the charges were serious and I was dealing with CID, not the regular police. They bailed me and I pleaded with Michael to drop the charges – I begged him, I cried, I said I'd do anything.

And that's exactly what he wanted, why he did it.

Control.

In the end, he went to the police station and wrote a statement, dropping the charges. I was called in and told there would be no further action. Michael should have been arrested and charged with making a false allegation but, of course, he wasn't.

That was it with Michael. I'd had enough and I vowed I was going to leave him.

Michael got a shock when I said I was leaving him. Up until then it was always him leaving me or threatening to throw me out, but now the shoe was on the other foot and he didn't like it. He went to the door as I was packing my bag and wouldn't get out of the way.

I agreed to stay because it was the easiest thing to do – that's all I can say. I was in a strange place with no friends and no money and I didn't want to have to go onto the streets hustling again. I suppose I could've tried to contact Mia, but it was a while since we'd been in touch and I probably didn't want to admit defeat – that I was a failure and couldn't hold on to anything.

After Michael persuaded me to stay, we decided it was best if we left Wales, as it seemed to be having an adverse effect on him. We got a map and closed our eyes and stuck a pin in it – Torquay, in Devon, that would be our new home.

We had just about enough money to get there, but no idea of what we were going to do when we arrived.

We headed for the touristy part of Torquay when we arrived and sat in a café, sharing a plate of chips between us. It was early winter 1990 and the nights were drawing in and getting colder. We had to find somewhere to live. We asked the manager of the café and he told us there were bedsits over on Vane Hill. Well, I don't know if you've been to Torquay, but they called it Vane *Hill* for a reason – it was like climbing Mount Snowdon.

The building was an old farmhouse, right at the top, and there was no answer when we knocked on the big blue door. We were walking around to the back when this teenaged boy sprang out from nowhere. He looked like a gypsy, scruffily dressed, with blond hair and freckles. He spoke with a broad Devon accent and we couldn't understand what he was saying for a few minutes, but once we got an ear for his words, he told us there was one bedsit left and we could have it.

The bedsit consisted of one room with a pull-down bed that sprang back up into the wall once you were finished sleeping on it. There was a gas cooker, but no other furniture, and the toilet was down the hall, shared by all the other bedsitters. Michael was able to get a job as a waiter on the waterfront, close to a casino, but it didn't pay very well.

I felt really depressed: I wanted to get a regular job, but Michael wouldn't let me. He was becoming jealous to the point of paranoia and he was afraid I'd meet someone who'd treat me like a proper human being – afraid I'd leave and that, this time, he wouldn't be able to stop me.

I tried to hustle, but it wasn't the best area for that kind of occupation – most of the people were hustling themselves, in one way or another. The young boy with the freckles was a burglar who was constantly knocking on our door, trying to sell the stuff he'd robbed.

Although Michael didn't want a baby, I wasn't on the pill and he wasn't using anything either, so I suppose it was bound to happen sooner or later. I just never expected it to be then, while we were living in a bedsit with nothing – no heating, and winter had arrived. I was living on Frosties cereal out of the box and the hunger pains were horrific. To be honest, Michael tried to make sacrifices and he'd give to me before himself – I have to say that much about him. It was early in 1991 when I found out I was pregnant. I hadn't had my period and my breasts were killing me, really tender and swollen, and I couldn't stop crying. I also suffered from really severe morning sickness – I couldn't keep anything down. I took a test and the blue line came up.

I thought Michael would go crazy and throw me out, but he didn't. He took it well and seemed to be happy, even though we had absolutely nothing.

We had each other, though; and I believed we could be a normal, happy family somehow.

Things were so hard and we just had to get money from somewhere. I hadn't spoken to my mother since she'd called me in hospital after the car accident. I didn't want to involve her in my life again, but I had nowhere else to turn. Michael had fallen out with his parents, so it was no use turning to them.

I rang Angela from a public telephone box and I had to ask the operator to reverse the charge as I didn't even have 10p to my name.

I hoped Angela would accept the call. She did – I was both shocked and happy.

'Hello, Mum.'

'Tara?'

'It's me.'

'Are you all right?'

'No. I need money ... I'm pregnant.'

I expected her to say it served me right and hang up the phone. She didn't. In fact, she sounded pleased for me and said she'd send me money for food and clothes.

I think that was one of the happiest moments of my life, when my mother wanted to help me. I ran back to the bedsit and told Michael. He was relieved, as it took some of the pressure off him.

When the money from my mother came through, Michael and I ran out to do a food shop because we were literally starving. I let Michael go in for the food, because the different smells inside were unbearable. But, despite the sickness, I was happy. Things were good again between me and Michael and we were getting on fine. He was working and I'd made contact with my mother, which was important to me for some reason – maybe because I was pregnant and needed a mother's support.

We couldn't stay living in the bedsit because it was unhealthy for both me and the baby, so we found a lovely little flat to rent in Paignton. It actually had furniture, and curtains, and a proper bed.

My mother came over from Alderney and stayed for about ten days. She helped out with the rent and bought clothes and baby things and she was really good to us. I think I loved her more then than I ever had before or have since. I remember a time when it was just me and her in the room and I was lying on the rug, watching my belly move. She smiled, and it was like sunshine had suddenly flooded in through the window. We went to bingo together, all three of us – me, Michael and my mother. We'd eat ice cream and go to the arcades and it was such a beautiful time.

One day a woman came up to my mother and pointed at me.

'Is that your daughter?'

'Yes.'

'She has the face of an angel.'

It made me cry. Here we were, the black sheep and the black lamb, together again. Only now it was different, now we were angels.

But my mother couldn't stay for ever and I knew we'd never be able to afford the flat and everything else on Michael's wages. So he got in touch with his mother, and it was decided that we'd go back to Wales.

I was angry – I didn't want his mum involved in my life or with my baby. She didn't think I was good enough for her son, so what would she think of her grandchild?

But, it was back on the train to chaos in Cardiff – where Michael would disappear into the dour *awyrgylch* – atmosphere – and the ogre would return.

His mother had suggested that we move into a hostel, as that was the only way we'd be able to get a house from the council. I'd heard horror stories about those hostels and I really didn't want to do it, but I had to face reality. The hostel she arranged for us was called the Nomad and it was located in an area called Adamsdown, close to Cardiff city centre. We had one room, with nothing in it but a microwave and a bed. I didn't know how we were going to cope.

There was a mixture of anyone and everyone living at the hostel. We had a security guard on the door and we had to sign in and out. If we weren't back by 10 p.m., we wouldn't be allowed in.

There were these public gardens that I loved to sit in, and it was there that we became acquainted with a man called George, who lived down the road from the hostel. The gardens had a bowling green and the old people would play that game all day. I loved to watch them. George was around sixty or seventy. He walked with a limp and wore a beret and a tweed jacket that smelled of mould. He saw I was pregnant and we struck up a conversation. I told him we had no cooking facilities at the hostel. He had his own house and he took in lodgers – he offered to let us use his kitchen if we did some cleaning for him. I knew we couldn't live with George or we wouldn't get housed by the council, but to be able to do our cooking and washing would be a luxury.

George's house was upside down – I mean, it was full of clutter and there was dust everywhere. The kitchen was so small you couldn't have two people in there at the same time or they'd be dancing the tango. I hoovered and dusted and Michael did the bins, but we weren't allowed upstairs: that's where the lodgers lived and they did their own thing – whatever that was. I liked George and he liked me and we'd talk for hours.

After six months in the hostel, we were allocated a council house in St Mellons, a suburb in the southeast of Cardiff. It was a new house, just built, miles from the city centre. I was ecstatic – and eight months pregnant. We never saw George again.

Chapter 7

Motherhood

I was still keeping in touch with my mother while we were living at the Nomad hostel, and she decided it would be best for the baby if Michael and I got married.

'Having a baby out of wedlock isn't a good idea, Tara.'

I felt fat, frumpy and unattractive.

'I don't want to get married, Mum.'

'Why not?'

'I look like something from the *Star Wars* cantina scene.'

But Michael agreed with her – I guess he believed it was another way to control me. I'd be 'his' wife. So it was decided. Angela flew over and took me shopping at Laura Ashley, where she bought me a royal blue maternity dress with a white collar, navy shoes with a tiny heel and she had my hair cut short into a bob.

In June 1991 I married Michael Llewellyn at the Cardiff registry office. My mother and his best man were witnesses – it was just the four of us. Afterwards, Angela paid for a meal at a Beefeater – I had calamari, everyone else had steak and chips. And that was it.

Moving to our new house was exciting for me. I'd only ever lived in one room before, or had to share, and

I wasn't used to having a whole house to myself. The council estate was just recently built, so all the houses were brand new. The fresh smell of paint and turned soil was everywhere, my baby was on the way, it was August and the sun was shining in my life.

The house had two bedrooms, with a huge living room, a bathroom and a separate toilet. There was a large garden to the back, with no grass, just topsoil. It looked like a ploughed field. But I didn't care about that. It was a palace to me.

Our house was No.1 and we were the first to move onto the estate. But soon it began to fill up and it became like a proper neighbourhood, with people and children and cars and a community. We didn't have anything in the house – nothing but bare walls and bare floors. My mother paid for grey cord carpet to be laid throughout and we were able to get a Silver Cross pram for the baby, an orange Aztec-pattern sofa to sit on, a second-hand bed and a cooker on finance, meaning on credit, which we paid off every week – with a lot of interest being added on top. We washed our clothes in the sink and I swept the carpet with a dustpan and brush.

On 14 September 1991, I started getting pains shooting through my whole body – my back, my legs, my stomach – and I thought I was going to die. I knew nothing about having a baby, so I screamed for Michael to help me. He knew even less than I did about it, but he ran down to the nearest public telephone and called an ambulance.

I was taken to Heath hospital in Cardiff, where I was given an epidural and, four hours later, my beautiful daughter, Daniella Louise was born. I was nineteen. She was a healthy baby, just under 8lbs, and I began breastfeeding straight away to get as close to her as possible, as quickly as possible.

Life was good for a while when we came home; we seemed like a normal young family. Michael was great in the beginning: he tried his hardest to be a good husband and father. But, as time went on, I could see him changing again. He was getting bored with domesticity and wanted to get back with the boys, drinking and the lifestyle that came with that. One night he came in drunk and flung me to the living-room floor when I challenged him. He started calling me an 'ugly cow' and hitting me with a stick.

He'd never actually hit me before – he smashed up the place a lot, but had never touched me. This was a new phase of his metamorphosis: Prince Charming to changeling to ogre to savage beast. My next-door neighbour heard all the banging and screaming and came round. Michael stopped hitting me and told her to mind her own business.

After that, things became strained between me and the neighbour. I tried to defend Michael, saying what he did was out of character. She said we could never be friends as long as I was with him – she had more sense than I did. I felt so ashamed, as if it was me in the wrong. I thought he hit me because he loved me, as if it was some weird demonstration of affection. I really didn't know any better and I didn't want to fail as a wife and mother, like I'd failed as a daughter.

Several months after Daniella was born, Michael wanted to move again. I didn't want to move with him, but I had no choice. Really what he was doing was shifting his violence to a different place, but he made up excuses like there were no shops or schools near us, and we had to think of Daniella. He arranged a house swap to Station Road, Llanrumney, to the northeast of Cardiff.

It wasn't a council estate, like we'd just left, it was more a suburban street and it seemed quiet enough. The house was lovely, all newly decorated inside, and the woman was prepared to leave the curtains and carpets to us. We were delighted. What she omitted to mention was that the neighbours were the roughest in Cardiff.

Our new neighbours on Station Road were a family called the Wilsons, and the matriarch's name was Debs. She was a formidable character, with a big horde about her. They were into everything – prison was an occupational hazard for them. I could see they were criminally active – they did a lot of robberies and drugs and played very loud reggae music from a ghetto blaster out the front of their house.

People were afraid to complain about them but, to be honest, they didn't bother me. I had my own problems. Michael was out all the time and, when he came home, he smashed the house up.

Then I got pregnant again. Never rains. I was happy enough about it, but Michael was furious. He told me I'd have to get rid of it. I wanted to tell my mother – at least she'd be on my side. I called her.

'Mum, I'm pregnant.'

'You'll have to have an abortion, Tara.'

'Why? I thought ...'

'You have Daniella. Another one will be too much for you.'

'I can't ...'

'You have to, Tara.'

They were both against me. Everyone was against me. What choice did I have?

I had the abortion in May 1992 – it was a Friday. Michael decided to go out drinking on the following Sunday. I found a babysitter for Daniella and went with him, even though he didn't want me to. It was like this: I had a small baby and had just had an abortion and I felt unattractive. I didn't want him to go to a pub, where I knew there would be a lot of swanky women. I couldn't stop him going, so the next best thing was to go with him, even though I clearly wasn't over the termination. We went to a pub in Llanishen, an area to the north of Cardiff and a good distance away from where we lived. Michael had arranged to meet some friends there and he didn't want me sitting with them. He threw a £10 note at me and told me to go and drink at the other side of the bar.

You're probably asking why I put up with that kind of treatment, especially someone as independent as I'd been before meeting Michael. My answer is that I was very insecure, despite my bohemian exterior. At that particular time, my hormones were all over the place and I felt vulnerable and I didn't want him to leave me. Michael was very charismatic when he wanted to be, just as he was with me in London. I knew what he could be like and how he could make a woman fall in love with him. But I also knew now about his wild temper and that it was best to conform with him when we were in a public place, as he wouldn't hesitate to cause a scene, which I didn't want. And I had a baby to think of – I couldn't just go off and do what I wanted like before. I needed Michael to help me, as I couldn't run a house and bring up Daniella on £60 a week. I was tied down. I was stuck. I was trapped. And I had to try to make the best of the hand I'd been dealt.

That night I was dressed well and my hair was pretty and, even though I really didn't want to be there, I put on a show of enjoying myself. I ordered a vodka and orange and I could see I was attracting the attention of men in the bar, especially as I was sitting on my own. Sunday hours were short and, outside afterwards, I began to get severe stomach cramps. I needed to go to the toilet, but the pub was now closed. Michael wouldn't wait for me, so I had to go and crouch behind a bush – and I noticed that blood was running down my legs. When I came out, Michael was gone – he'd deserted me and left me with no money to get a taxi home. But I had to get back to my baby, so I flagged down a car and hitched a lift as close as I could to home, and ran the rest of the way. When I got back, Michael wasn't there and I had to promise the babysitter I'd pay her double the next time. Then I got into bed with Daniella and fell asleep.

Later in the night, I heard the front door open and Michael coming drunk and hump-backed up the stairs.

'Get out of that bed, you bitch!'

My first instinct was to protect my child, so I got up and stood between her and Michael.

'I saw what you were at in the pub.'

'What was that, Michael?'

'Flirting with those guys.'

'You made me sit on my own.'

With that, he dragged me to the stairs. We were halfway down when he brought his knee up into my face.

Blood erupted from my nose. I was screaming and the baby was screaming as he dragged me further down the stairs. Then I passed out.

When I came to, Michael was sitting there, smoking a cigarette. As soon as he saw that I was awake, he launched himself at me and his hands went around my neck. He was trying to strangle me and I could feel the blood throbbing in my face. Then I heard banging on the front door and, when Michael opened it, Debs the matriarch was standing there with a big scarface guy. She looked menacing.

'Don't you think you've hit her enough?'

'What's it got to do with you?'

The big scarface guy leaned forward.

'I can make it to do with me if you want.'

Now, normally Michael wouldn't have cared how big that guy was, but I suppose he was just about sober enough to realise he was way out of his depth, so he pushed past them and disappeared into the night.

Debs took Daniella and me round to her house and called the police. They came and took me and the baby to the Royal Infirmary in Adamsdown.

As we were walking into the hospital, unbelievably, Michael jumped out from behind some bushes and tried to attack me again. The police immediately arrested him and took him away. By now, both my eyes were turning black and my nose was broken in four places. The doctors put a cast on my nose – the cast didn't work and my nose is still wonky to this day – and the police came back for me and saw me safely home.

As with most abusers, Michael returned apologising and saying it wouldn't happen again. Without the hindsight

I have now, I took him back. I was confused and didn't know what else to do.

But our relationship was truly damaged: I didn't want to sleep with him any more and I could feel a craving inside me for the independence I once had. And, once again, things got strained with the neighbours. Debs's kids started throwing stones at Michael and calling him a woman-beater. I wanted him to be gone, but I didn't want him to get badly hurt on my account, which I knew would eventually happen if we stayed in that house. The Wilsons were wild men and they used knives, and Michael would be no match for them.

It was time to move again.

We went for another swap and this time ended up in Coleford Drive, which was close to our first house in St Mellons. We were to live there for about a year and I loved that house, but I knew in my heart that Michael and I were finished, even though I didn't want to admit it and we were still living together. He was still trying to control me, he wouldn't let me go anywhere socially.

It got so bad I felt I couldn't breathe.

Then, one day, I just walked out the door.

Michael and Daniella were asleep together and I knew he'd never hurt her, but I just had to get away, even for a few hours. I looked back at the house from the bus window and tried to justify what I was doing, until the street faded into the distance and I couldn't see it any more.

All the town-centre pubs were really busy that afternoon because Wales was playing Scotland at rugby and the game was on television. I went into the Owain Glyndwr, which wasn't as packed as the others, and ordered a vodka and orange. I had zero interest in rugby, so I just sat in a secluded corner with my thoughts.

After a while, I noticed this guy in a kilt watching me. He had blond hair and blue eyes and was about three or four years older than me. I didn't encourage him, but he came over anyway and introduced himself as William. I didn't really want to talk to anyone, but I reckoned if he sat with me, it would stop the others from pestering me.

As time went on, I lost track of the hours passing and suddenly realised it was dark outside. I had to get back home. William gave me his number before I ran from the pub and down to the taxi rank.

My stomach was doing somersaults as the cab pulled up outside the house and I couldn't see any lights on. I had to break a window to get in, cutting my hand. I ran through the rooms.

'Daniella! Michael!'

But they were gone. I hailed another cab and went to Michael's parents' house. Daniella was there, but they wouldn't let me in or give her back to me. I called the police from a public telephone and they came and went inside. I cried with relief when they came back out carrying my baby and gave her to me.

Michael was reprimanded by the police and told to stay away from me.

I'd been with Michael for one and half years. Now it was finally over – or so I thought.

After a while of trying to manage on my own with a young child, I found William's telephone number and decided to call him. He invited me up to Scotland for a holiday.

I badly needed a break, so Daniella and I took the train up to a rural place near Silverburn in Midlothian.

William's house was tiny, more a cottage than a house, and he still lived with his parents. But they made us welcome and his mother kept calling me 'hen' in a broad Scottish accent. I'd never heard that term before and I thought she was talking about a pet chicken she had in the garden, even though I couldn't see one. I asked William about it.

'Where's this chicken your mother keeps on about?'

He just laughed and laughed and I didn't know what was so funny.

Over the course of a week, I enjoyed William's company. He was a gentleman and I wasn't used to gentle men. He was quiet and old-fashioned, and I was ebullient and skittish. He was benign and I was a stranger to kindness. But we got on well and, on the last day, he took me to a barn dance. It was something I'd never experienced before and it was wild, with kilts and sporrans and whisky flying. We ended up sleeping together that night.

To be honest, I didn't remember much about it. In the morning I looked at him and wished I could have all sorts of wonderful feelings for him, but I didn't. I so wanted it to be like that, but the magic wasn't there. I knew it was me, not him – he would have given me everything. I lay there in the early hours, with the light creeping over the windowsill, knowing that he loved me and wanting to be able to love him back

Our interlude in the Lowlands was over and it was time to return to Wales.

The journey home was long and, when we got back, someone had broken into the house. The place was wrecked: television smashed, sofa sawn in half, paint all over my clothes. I knew it was Michael, but there was no point calling the police, as I had no proof. It took a while for me to fix the damage and, by the time I did, I discovered I was pregnant again. This time it wasn't Michael's.

I tried to keep it hidden, but that would only work for a while, so I told them both – Michael and William. William wanted me to move to Scotland and Michael wanted me to have an abortion – after all, we were still married. I did neither.

I grew huge with the baby through 1992 and early 1993 and I developed a craving for celery and the smell of coal. I also realised I wouldn't be able to cope on my own with a toddling Daniella and a newborn baby, so I reconciled with Michael and he moved back in – but I refused to sleep with him.

I went into slow labour on 22 April 1993. It started with back pain that went on all through the night. They gave me all the drugs they could and, in the end, I gave an almighty push and my beautiful son Christopher was born, on 23 April 1993. He was 10lbs in weight and he looked like he was three months old. I couldn't breastfeed like I did with Daniella because I had mastitis and blisters forming around my nipples. I also had to have stitches, so I didn't bond with the baby straight away. Post-natal depression set in and it took me about a year to bond properly with Christopher.

Michael turned up the next day and I could tell he was on something. They'd just brought me some food and he started eating it.

'Hey, you cheeky bastard, that's mine. I've had nothing since yesterday.'

As soon as I said that, he threw the food on top of me.

'I'm not the bastard here!'

I started crying. It was visiting time and a man looked around from the next cubicle.

'What're you playing at, mate?'

Michael didn't answer him, and just walked out. Later that day I discharged myself and went home. I was bleeding and had no money for milk or nappies. I had to borrow from my neighbour, who was looking after Daniella.

With two children to raise, I thought life with Michael might get better. I mean, he had asked me if he could come back; I hadn't asked him. But it didn't get better, it got worse. Once, when it was raining, he threw me to the ground and dragged me along the road. I was covered in mud and had grit embedded in my palms. My face was so grazed I couldn't recognise myself in the mirror. Smashing up the house was his favourite pastime, and breaking the windows.

Once, we were arguing upstairs, so I scooped Daniella up into my arms and walked away. I was making my way down the stairs when he hit me on the back of the head from behind and I went flying, Daniella in my arms. I hurt my back on the stairs, trying to protect my daughter. Another time he came home in a foul mood after I'd been up all night with Daniella. I asked him to give her her bottle, but instead he threw the bottle at my head, kicked me in the leg and gave me a backhanded slap across the face – all in front of my young daughter. I was trying to get Daniella out of the room when he grabbed a knife and pinned me up against the wall. He dug the point of the knife into my throat, eyes bulging and mouth spitting.

'You fucking slag! You fucking slag! I should kill you!'

I could hear Daniella screaming and that brought him to his senses. He dropped the knife and ran from the house. I called the police and they came and took pictures of my injuries. Michael was arrested and charged with ABH and threats to kill, but he still came around and attacked me again, breaking his bail conditions, so he was arrested and put on remand until his trial.

Why did I put up with his brutality? Well, to begin with, he was 6'3" and I was 5'5". I didn't have enough strength to fight him. When he had one of his violent outbursts, I believed he could do serious damage to me, if not kill me. In my head I thought he could only get so much satisfaction out of kicking something that didn't move.

Michael was held on remand for three months, until I eventually dropped the charges against him.

Again.

Chapter 8

Sex, Drugs & Self-Control

One day, while Michael was on remand, a woman knocked on my door. Her name was Lexi and I'd heard she was a working girl. When I opened the door I could see she was really angry.

'Why are you calling me a prostitute?'

I was so shocked I couldn't even answer her. She called me a name that rhymes with 'hunt' and stormed off. This really got in my head and I knew I'd have to straighten it out. She lived at the end of the street and, later that day, I went down there.

I was really worried, as I didn't know what kind of reception I'd get. Her face was as stern as a schoolmarm's when she opened the door.

'I've never spoken badly about you, Lexi. Who told you I did?'

'Never mind who told me, is it true?'

'Of course not, I don't even know you. Whoever said it is a liar and I'll tell them to their face.'

That seemed to convince her. At the time I looked on prostitution as something dirty and horrid, that they must be really nasty people to do something like that. I associated it with badness; even though I'd come close to it a few times, I'd always managed to steer clear.

Lexi invited me in. Her house was immaculate, not what I expected. She had a beautiful, white-leather three-piece suite, a gold mirror, a huge TV and deep grey carpet throughout. We drank coffee together as if we were old friends and chatted about this and that. Lexi had a really husky voice and I told her about my experiences in London and Essex. We seemed to hit it off: I liked her candidness and she liked mine – that's how the best friendships are formed.

Lexi had a friend called Megan, who was also a working girl. She was lovely, with bright ginger hair and freckles, and we began to hang out together. I was on benefits with no money coming from Michael and two young children, so times were quite hard. One night, Megan suggested we all go for a drink to a pub called the Custom House.

'I can't afford it, Megan, sorry.'

'Don't worry about money, Tara, it's on me.'

I had a regular babysitter who I trusted, when I could afford her, so I agreed to go with them. The pub was frequented mostly by working girls and their pimps, which made me uneasy. I was being propositioned left, right and centre and I was highly offended – which is ironic, looking back now.

During the evening, Lexi took me to one side.

'Do you want to make some money, Tara?'

'Of course … but how?'

She'd got a call from a man who'd invited her to the Marriott hotel in the city centre and he had a friend. I knew what would be expected of me and I didn't want to go.

'Why don't you take Megan?'

'She's got another client.'

'Client' – that word filled me with apprehension.

'I've got to get back to the kids. The babysitter ...'

'We won't be long.'

I had no money for a taxi home, so I went with her.

It was a posh hotel, with lots of businessman types. When we got to the room, there were two Arabs waiting for us. Lexi told me to go into the bathroom with one of them, while she got on the bed with the other. The man with me was young and drunk and fumbling with my clothes. I knew I had to take control of this situation, fast.

'Money up front.'

The sound of my own voice surprised me.

'How much?'

I didn't know how much. Maybe Lexi had already given them a price. I thought if I asked for a lot of money he wouldn't want to pay up and I could leave and wait for Lexi outside.

'A hundred pounds.'

He pulled a wallet out of his back pocket and counted £100 into my hand as if it was nothing to him. I should've asked for £200 – what an idiot I was. But, having been paid, now I'd have to perform.

It was a tight fit in the small bathroom and this man was staggering all over the place. Next thing I knew he'd fallen into the bath and just lay there, laughing. He was in no fit state to have sex with anyone, so I just did a body swerve, out through the room – where the other guy was grunting on top of Lexi – and down the corridor. I took the stairs rather than wait for the lift and jumped into a taxi outside the hotel.

Lexi wasn't happy with me when we met up the next day – apparently the guy was a regular client and his friend wasn't impressed with the service. She and Megan didn't take me out with them again, but I reckoned it was an easy way to make money and perhaps I'd be able to do it on my own.

There was a corner shop in the area and the man who ran it had taken a fancy to me. His name was Tariq and he lived above the shop with his parents. I knew he had plenty of money, so I made an arrangement to go out with him one night. We had a drink and ended up going back to his place and sneaking into his bedroom so his parents wouldn't hear us. He kept trying to kiss me and I kept pulling away from him – I just wanted to get the money and go home.

'I need the money first.'

'The safe is in my parents' bedroom. Let them fall asleep .., five more minutes.'

It was hard work keeping him at bay, but I kept raising my voice and he didn't want his parents to wake up and find me there. Eventually, he tiptoed out of the room and came back with a bundle of notes.

'How much?'

'How much do you have there?'

He counted – almost £400.

'That's enough.'

I kissed him and he was like a goldfish – he was obviously a virgin. I told him I had to go, but we would have a relationship and make love when it was more convenient. I'd arrange a room for us somewhere more private.

'But I've paid you the money.'

'I make a lot of noise when I'm having sex ... your parents ...'

It was very late when Tariq drove me home and I was worried about the babysitter. As soon as the car pulled up outside the house, Michael came out the door like a crazy man. He ran around to the driver's side and started punching Tariq in the face.

The blood splattered all over me. I was screaming at the top of my voice.

'Stop! I've got money! I've got money!'

I jumped from the car and threw the notes into the air. They fluttered down like fiduciary leaves around Michael, distracting him enough for Tariq to make his escape. He drove off at high speed, swerving all over the road. I thought it would be my turn next, but Michael didn't hit me – he just gathered up the money and went back into the house.

I'd dropped the charges against him earlier that day and I knew he'd be coming out of prison; I just didn't think it would be so soon. I suppose they needed the cell for someone else. Michael had come to the house and found the babysitter there and sent her home – then he waited for me.

Next day I went round to the shop to see how Tariq was. His father told me he'd been beaten up and would have to have an operation on his eye, but he didn't connect me with the incident and there were no repercussions. In this case I did feel guilty about hustling Tariq. He was a decent enough chap and didn't deserve it. But that was me back then – young, desperate and going in the wrong direction. I never intended for him to be punched and was appalled at what Michael did, which is why I went to the shop to check on him. I never heard from Tariq again.

I convinced Michael I wasn't sleeping with anyone, just hustling them like I used to do before I met him. I had to make money some way to feed the children and a regular job just didn't pay enough. Employers expected you to work for less than a living age and I'd have to pay a child-minder out of that. He accepted my explanation because it was what he wanted to believe and the money I brought home would keep him in booze and drugs. It was like having my own live-in pimp.

And so it went on – Michael would babysit and I'd go out on the hustle.

On one occasion I met a group of builders who were working on Newport Road. They lived in lodgings close by. I pretended to fancy one of them and went back with them to carry on drinking. The only reason I was there was to rob them. I was on a mission, it was as simple as that. I took some speed, so there was no way I'd fall asleep. They were all drunk and they had work in the morning, so one by one they fell asleep, thinking I was going to have sex with their mate. I climbed into one of the bunks with him, and he fell asleep too, then I robbed every single one of them. I waited until they were deeply asleep, then I climbed out of the bunk and crawled along the floor, going through all their pockets. I took their money and blocks of weed and a leather coat.

I gave Michael the coat, spent the money on food for the kids and kept the weed for myself.

A few days later there was a knock on the door. Michael answered it. I was in the kitchen cooking tea.

'There's a guy at the door looking for his coat.'

I couldn't believe he'd found me.

'He doesn't care about the money or the weed, he just wants the leather coat.'

Maybe he was just fishing: if I admitted to having the coat, they'd know for sure it was me and maybe they'd all come round for revenge.

'Tell him I don't know anything about a coat.'

Michael was angry when the guy left. He wanted to know how he found out where we lived.

'I don't know, Michael. Maybe someone grassed me up.'

'Like who?'

'Lexi, or maybe Megan.'

'Those two prossies? How do you know them?'

That was it. We were back arguing again.

It was no use, Michael would have to go – for good.

In the course of my hustling activity, I met two girls – April and May – who were into 'blues'. A blues was a dance where it was all just black guys and women and there were lots of drugs and dancing till about seven in the morning. They usually took place in derelict buildings and there would be a proper DJ and huge sound systems. I loved dancing, especially to garage or reggae, and the more I hung out with April and May, the more I developed an attitude like them – feisty, sassy, cool as a wasp in winter.

That's when I met Maurice.

Maurice was tough-looking, with a gold tooth, and I thought he was a drug dealer. I was stranded after a dance in Newport one night, where I hadn't managed to hustle and had no money for a taxi home. My hair was short and blonde then, I was wearing a denim skirt with a cropped top and I looked good. Maurice walked with a swagger and wore beautiful clothes and he offered me a lift. He played Warren G on the way and shared a spliff with me. I told him to stop the car down the street, as I didn't want Michael to see him and go berserk again. In any case, I had a fear of black guys in those days and thought they were all criminals and dangerous gun-toters who just used women, so I wanted to keep my distance.

A few days later I was coming back from the local Tesco when I heard a car horn beeping. I looked round and it was Maurice. I was pushing a double buggy with Daniella and Christopher in it, wearing tracksuit bottoms and a puffa jacket – nothing like how I had looked a couple of nights before. He wound the car window down.

'Hey, how are you?'

'I'm good. What are you doing up this way, Maurice?'

'I've come to see a friend.'

'Oh, yes? I bet you came looking for me.'

He laughed in a likeable way.

We started seeing each other on and off, casually, when we came across each other on the street or in clubs. Nothing serious.

In the meantime, Michael and I had split up – again. He'd gone back to live with his parents and him not being around made it more convenient for me to see Maurice, without having to worry about being beaten up.

We did loads of things together for a while, Maurice and I – going to clubs and blues, smoking weed, hanging out. The sex was OK, but I was always on something when we did it, so it was artificially enhanced. I hated giving blow-jobs, but I did it to please Maurice. It was always rushed with him, because he usually had to be somewhere else. It was always in the dark, after going to a club, never in the light. I didn't want him coming back to where I lived in case Michael turned up out of the blue, and he didn't seem to want me back at his place either. So, we just did it quickly wherever we could and he always got more from it than me.

The first time we actually went out together was a strange affair. Maurice seemed reluctant when we got inside the club. He wouldn't hold my hand or dance with me but, when the DJ played a slow tune, I caught hold of him and pulled him out onto the dance floor and shuffled him around in a reluctant shimmy. Afterwards I could see he was embarrassed and he said he wanted to go.

'But I don't want to go yet, Maurice.'

'Then you'll have to find your own way home.'

Outside, he walked ahead of me and started chatting to three girls. Then he turned back and said they were friends of his who he'd known for some time.

'They want a lift.'

I was angry.

'Not with us ... not in our car.'

'*My* car, Tara.'

When we dropped them off and got back to my house, I leaned over to kiss him, but he pulled away. He said he was disappointed with my behaviour and he didn't want to see me again.

I couldn't believe it and didn't understand. I know now it was because I was a bit wild and he found it difficult to accept that. Certain guys like to be in control of their women, and Maurice wasn't in control of me – I always did my own thing. I attracted a lot of attention because I could dance as well as any black girl and they always gave me the stare because I was a white girl with a 'brother'. I didn't care and I'd stare right back at them. I'd put myself up on the stage, right in the middle of them, and Maurice didn't like that because it meant he didn't have control of me in front of his friends.

I was just a wild child and I was really hurt when he said he didn't want to see me again. He was the first black guy I'd slept with and I had real feelings for him.

Maurice didn't contact me and I began to really miss him. I told April what had happened and she suggested I go round to his place and find out what his problem was.

He lived in a block of flats in Loudoun Square, Cardiff Bay, which was a bus ride away. I pressed all the buzzers and someone eventually let me in. I climbed up three flights of stairs and went up to his door. Before knocking, I listened, and I could hear voices coming from inside. I was about to turn around and go home, but then I thought I'd come all that way ... so I tapped on the door.

Maurice opened it. When he saw me, he almost turned white. He closed the door quickly behind him and stood out on the concrete landing with me.

'What are you doing here?'

'What do you think, Maurice? I haven't heard from you.'

'I told you …'

'But I like you, Maurice … I thought you liked me.'

That look of embarrassment again. He went quiet for a moment, then he said he couldn't talk now, but he'd come and see me.

'Why can't I come in?'

'Because my son is inside … and Lisa.'

'Who's Lisa?'

'The woman I've been living with for eight years.'

You might think me a hypocrite, but something died inside me when he told me that. I know I was married to Michael, but I felt nothing for him and I would have been glad to see the back of him. The way Maurice spoke to me on that doorstep indicated that, despite sleeping with me, he still loved Lisa and he didn't love me.

I felt used. It was the end for me and Maurice.

The blues were mainly held around Bristol, which was about fifty miles away, across the Severn. I thought I had it all going on by now, that I was this bad girl. On one occasion we all went out dressed as army girls – we went to some place in St Paul's and walked down the line in front of all the women, who gave us the hard stare, but didn't try to come at us. Perhaps they thought we were real army and could do all kinds of combat stuff on them. I didn't realise how dangerous St Paul's was at the time; now I know it was infamous for crack dealing and guns. When I came out of the blues that early morning, I went into a café called the Black and White, stepping over bodies that were pranged out on crack. I didn't bother them and they didn't bother me. I just sat there in the middle of all the pipe smoke and took in the surreal *mise-en-scène*.

Another night we went to this place where fog juice was cascading everywhere and the music was deafening. I lost the girls I was with but that didn't bother me: I thought I could handle anything, walking past these Yardies, swaggering, swinging my hips, getting myself noticed. Then this guy grabbed me and held my arm really tight. I tried to prise myself away from him, but he wouldn't let go. He started walking, pulling me with him, whispering in my ear.

'You make a fuss, I slit ya throat, gel.'

He was smiling at people as we walked through the crowd and they all made way for him. It was then I noticed he had no fingers on his left hand.

He pushed me up the steps and outside into the night. We moved towards a white van and he threw me into the back of it, then he jumped into the driver's seat and we took off. I tried to get out, but the doors were locked. He never said a word, just looked straight ahead at the road. I was banging the sides of the van, hoping he'd be pulled over by the police, but he wasn't.

After about ten minutes he came to a halt in a dark, deserted street and opened the van door. He put a finger to his lips to indicate that I shouldn't make a noise. He dragged me into this dark house and pushed me up the stairs and into a bedroom.

'I need to go to the toilet.'

My voice was hoarse with fear. He grunted and pointed towards a door. I went into the bathroom, but I knew he was standing outside, waiting for me. When I emerged, he flung me up against a wall – I could taste the whisky on his breath, see the desire in his eyes. He pulled my arm up tight against my back and tried to undress me with the hand that had no fingers. I knew he was going to rape me.

Suddenly there was this noise – it was a kind of 'ping' and all the power went off. It took him by surprise and he didn't know what was happening. I did.

'What be dat?'

'Power's gone off.'

'Why?'

'Someone didn't pay the bill.'

'Cyan we fix it? I want see ya.'

'Sure, let me go and I'll do it.'

'Be quick.'

As soon as he let me go, I was gone down the stairs and out through the front door. I could hear him stumbling after me in the dark and I ran and ran and ran, even though I didn't know where I was or where I was running to. Down a lane, through another lane, into some woods and out the other side, until I came to a main road where I was able to hail a taxi.

I told April about it the next day and she said the fingerless guy was Jake the Snake, and he was a much-feared man in the Bristol area. He had a couple of brothers who were also notorious and as feared as he was. She told me not to report the incident to the police and to be careful, because he'd be after me now.

'It would've been better just to let him have you, Tara.'

No way! But it really shook me up and it put me off going to the blues again.

Some time later, I was out looking for someone to hustle and I decided to go to a club called Buzz in Cardiff. I was inside looking around when, suddenly, I felt this iron grip on my arm. I turned around and it was him – Jake the Snake. I froze.

'I bin lookin' fi ya, bitch.'

'Do I know you?'

'Get down da cellar!'

I hoped someone would help me, but nobody was interested in getting involved. Either they didn't realise what was happening or they just turned a blind eye. I knew I couldn't let him get me into the cellar, so I started struggling as we got closer and closer to the stone steps leading down there. It was no use – I imagine his right hand had developed extra strength on account of him having no fingers on the left.

Anyway, because I was dragging my feet, one of my shoes came off and he let me bend down to pick it up. I immediately hurled it at this girl who was dancing with her back to me. It hit her hard and she turned towards me with a furious face.

'Who threw that?'

'I did, you skanky whore!'

She came at me, along with several of her friends and, within seconds, all hell broke loose, with boyfriends and bouncers getting involved. The Snake was forced to let go of me in the melee and I made my escape out onto the street and away home.

I had to get this guy off my back, so I told Maurice about him. Maurice had a big family and they 'knew some people', if you get my meaning. I didn't know if he would agree to help me, after the way we'd parted, but he was my only option. To my surprise, Maurice went to see the Snake and pointed out the possible consequences – was it worth it for a white skettle? It could have escalated into an all-out gang war. But it didn't. The Snake saw sense and left me alone from then on.

There was a gypsy family living close to me at Coleford Drive and I started having problems with them. It started when one of the men came knocking on my door, asking if I had a spare cigarette. His wife then got it into her head that we were having an affair and the whole family began threatening me. They'd be outside my house, all of them, calling me out to fight them. Now, I could hold my corner with most people, but there was no way I was going out to have a street fight with a family of gypsies. It got very bad and I started smoking a lot of weed to keep myself calm. I was also taking a lot of speed at the clubs I went to in the evenings and, between the weed and the speed, I was starting to freak out a bit. The police recommended to the council that I be moved, for my own safety. I didn't want to go, as I'd made some friends in the area, but the housing officer said it was an emergency transfer and I had no choice.

The housing officer was called Malcolme Azikiwe. I asked him to move me somewhere nice and he said he would, if I went out with him. I knew he had the power to place me in a derelict house in some really bad area, so I went for a drink with him in the city centre. When he dropped me home, he was kissing and groping me in the car, but I got him off me by promising that, when I moved, we could see each other regularly. Shortly after that I got a new house in a place called Fairwater, which was a district in the northwest of the city. Of course, I never did go out with the housing officer again and he knew if I reported him he'd lose his job. A hustle for a hustle – I thought that was more than fair.

The new house was lovely, a semi-detached on top of a hill. And the next-door neighbours seemed pleasant enough. The best thing was Michael didn't know I'd moved there. Peace and quiet – how wonderful. It didn't last long – a little boy from down the road stole Daniella's bicycle and she was crying her eyes out. I had to go and see his mother. Her name was Janet and she was a big, ferocious woman. I had my work cut out. We had a blazing row and I took back the bike. She threatened to batter me and I told her she could try. After that, I kept my children away from hers. I used to see lots of different cars outside her house and I knew she was into something. I mean, if you mention the word 'gangster', most people think of men. But there are women gangsters, too.

I divorced Michael in 1994 and that's how he found out where I was. I did all the legwork and cited unreasonable behaviour as grounds. The papers were served to him by court bailiffs which meant the divorce could proceed without him being able to contest it. I had good grounds – police records of the beatings – and the judge awarded a decree nisi. A couple of months later I got my decree absolute. But Michael now knew I was at Fairwater and he turned up again.

I couldn't believe it, he was like a bad penny. He said he'd changed, and I felt sorry for him because he didn't have anywhere else to go: his parents had thrown him out, and he was Daniella's father after all. I said he could stay but it wouldn't be as man and wife. There would be no sex and I'd be allowed to live my own life.

He agreed to my terms and I thought that maybe he really had changed. But he hadn't. Once he got his feet through the door, the violence soon started up again, ending, one night, when he threw a big pot of minced beef and gravy all over me and the kitchen floor.

Janet, my arch enemy, heard the commotion and came across. She took me and the children over to her place and that was the beginning of a formidable friendship. We would become a force to be reckoned with in the criminal sorority.

Chapter 9

Partners in Crime

You don't just become friends with someone overnight, at least not in the criminal world. It takes time, people have to learn that they can trust you. Janet and I would go for a drink together, our children would play together and we were both into making money whatever way we could. Michael was back, coming and going as he pleased, and I couldn't get rid of him. He started hitting me again and calling me names in front of people. He got violent if I asked him to leave. He didn't care if I called the police – he'd just get lost for a while and come back again sooner or later.

Taking speed became a regular thing for me. I couldn't seem to do without it and I lost a lot of weight. Michael would come in drunk and I'd take speed to be awake when he came in and be ready for him. At one time I was on speed for three days straight, with no sleeping and no eating. In the end I was hallucinating through lack of sleep and I had to stop for a while.

It was the summer of 1995. Janet and I were sitting out front watching the children playing, when this guy called Labron turned up. He was a big-time drug dealer and really handsome, at least I thought he was – tall, with black curly hair, and full of charisma. We hit it off straight away and started seeing each other. One night he gave me this tablet and we had sex. It was the best sex I'd ever had, not because Labron was a great stud or anything, but the drug he gave me made it extraordinary.

Labron and I hung out together at a club called Winston's. It was upmarket and the place where all the good-looking, sharp men went. The music was fabulous and I loved to dance there.

One night, Labron asked me to hold his jacket and I could see a cellophane bag with lots of tablets like the one he'd given me in it. I knew they were called mollys, a slang name for ecstasy, and he was selling them in the clubs. I supposed he wouldn't miss a couple, so I dropped one straight away and put another in my pocket. I'd only taken ecstasy that one time before and, after a while, I could feel myself coming up on the drug. My neck went all tingly, my eyes were wide and I felt euphoric. I had this amazing feeling of love for everyone around me and I couldn't wait to get to the club to start dancing. But, as we got close to the door, I saw the bouncers looking at me and I started to feel paranoid and anxious.

'I don't want to go in.'

'Why not?'

'I want to go home.'

We got into a taxi and I was losing it by now. Labron looked at me as if I was crazy.

'What's wrong with you, Tara?'

'I can't breathe. Stop the taxi!'

I was screaming for the cab to stop and let me out. When it did, I ran into a nearby convenience store and grabbed a Mars bar and a bottle of Lucozade. I don't know if it was the sugar or the glucose that helped, but I felt a bit calmer after that and, when I got home, I put on some music and danced all through the night.

Next day I felt really sluggish, so I thought I'd take the other E to get myself back up. Within minutes of dropping the ecstasy, I felt sick. My heart was racing and I was pacing up and down, up and down, non-stop. I started burning up. The whites of my eyes went yellow and I had to get some weed to bring myself back down. I went across to Janet's and found some friends of Labron's there. They were all smoking weed and I joined in – it turned into a drinking session that ended up back at my house and went on for most of the night.

Next morning, Labron banged on my door. When I answered it, he slapped me full force across the face.

'Slag!'

I was holding my son Christopher at the time and couldn't protect myself. Michael came in shortly after and I asked him to mind the children for a few minutes. I grabbed a knife from the kitchen and followed Labron across the street to Janet's and tried to stab him. I was like a raging bull – who did this man think he was, that he could hit me while I had my son in my arms?

I had the knife to his neck and was jabbing the point of it at his throat.

'If you ever come near me again, I'll kill you!'

My eyes were bulging and he knew I meant business. I expected the police to be called, but they weren't – probably because he was a known drug dealer and didn't want attention of that kind drawn to himself.

But it was the end of me and Labron.

Michael was drinking all his money away as usual and the hustling was getting dangerous on my own, after the close shave with Jake the Snake. So Janet and I decided to team up.

Our first 'victim' was a receptionist at the Marriott hotel. She'd heard Janet did dodgy stuff and she contacted her. The receptionist wanted Janet to work a scam with her chequebook. I said I'd help. She gave us a list of merchandise she wanted, along with the chequebook and card, and said she'd report them stolen after twenty-four hours. That way she'd get refunded for everything that was spent and she'd have the goods as well. In return, we could take a few bits for ourselves. Basically, she was asking us to take all the risks and she'd take most of the spoils. I thought that was out of order.

'Let's rinse her, Janet.'

Well, there wasn't a shop in Cardiff we didn't hit. We got stuff for our children, stuff for our houses, clothes for ourselves, cigarettes, alcohol, food – everything. We even hired a van and got Michael to drive it, so we could load up all the merchandise we bought. I was the one signing the cheques, as I believed I could forge the receptionist's signature better than Janet and, anyway, she'd already been to prison for fraud.

We were almost done and decided to go into one final shop, while Michael waited outside in the van. I signed the cheque, and the snooty woman at the cash register sniffed when she looked at it.

'The signatures don't match up.'

'What are you talking about?

'I'll have to call the bank.'

Janet and I looked at each other – we'd have to brazen it out.

'Listen, honey, my hair doesn't match two days in a row.'

With that, I snatched the card and cheque back from her and we sashayed towards the exit, leaving the goods on the counter. There was a security guard at the door and I was sure he was going to stop us. He stuck his arm out as we approached and I thought, 'We've had it now.' But he just opened the door for us and wished us a nice day.

When the Marriott hotel receptionist came round for her merchandise, we told her to get lost and gave her back her card and the cheque stubs. She wasn't happy about being turned over, but there was nothing she could do about it, without admitting her part in the scam.

That expedition cemented the friendship between Janet and me – we were now partners in crime.

There was a woman who used to come round the estate who worked for Provident, a credit company that loaned money to poor people who couldn't get it from a bank, at high interest rates. I was having a coffee with Janet when she told me this woman and her husband had enquired about having a threesome with me.

'A threesome?'

'You know, Tara, kinky sex.'

Look, at this stage in my life I wasn't a shrinking violet or anything, but for someone to presume they could proposition me like that made me very angry. I didn't even know them. Who or what did they think I was? We drew up a plan to hustle them. I told Michael I had to go out to make some money, so he agreed to babysit. Then we took the woman and her husband to a pub with live music and got them both drunk on mixtures – mixing different spirits together. At closing time, we suggested we go back to their house for a party and they thought the threesome was on. We even got a group of strangers from the pub to join us so we could blame them for what was going to happen.

Back at the house, Janet kept them all occupied and plied them with more booze, while I ransacked the place. I took the woman's Provident money, which was about £200, her benefit book, two tubs of barbiturates and a big bottle of expensive perfume. Once I had the loot, I signalled to Janet and we made our excuses and left. The husband didn't want us to go but we said 'some other time' and did the body swerve through the door.

Next morning, we quickly got to town with the benefit book. All I had to do was forge her signature on the back, a sample of which Janet had, and we could use it four times at different post offices. We made about £600 altogether.

Later that day, the woman came to Janet's.

'I got robbed last night.'

'Oh, no! It must've been those people from the pub.'

We consoled her and took her home. While we were there, I robbed her again.

Then there was this woman in the street who didn't like me and was running me down to Janet behind my back.

'Invite her over for coffee, Janet.'

She did and, while the woman was there, I climbed over her back fence and got into her house. I stole all her jewellery and sold it to the local pawn shop for £300.

I have to say that, now, I regret becoming involved in that sort of petty crime. But, at the time, I felt no remorse for the people I was hustling. The way I saw it was, they would do the same thing to me, given half a chance. I suppose it was the succession of criminal environments I was living in. Crime was rampant because it was the only way to make ends meet in a greedy society that didn't value people like us. And, if you weren't a part of it, you'd be a victim of it – one or the other. There was no in-between. It's no excuse, I know – and I spend my time now helping people who are casualties of deprivation and despair. People of the street, who have nothing. People who are now as I once was. But I'm writing this as I saw it then, through the eyes of a young woman who was trying to survive in a world with no safety nets, no bank-of-mum-and-dad to bail her out, no lifeline to grab on to when things got tough.

By now, the speed was becoming a real problem for me and I was addicted. On one occasion I got a gram and wrapped it in a Rizla and bombed it. The rush hit me hard. I had tingles all down my body like electric shocks – I'd never experienced this before on it. I felt really ill – it was the worst experience ever, and I just couldn't get myself together no matter what I did.

I grabbed the children and ran across to Janet's, bursting through her door and shouting.

'Call an ambulance, I'm having a heart attack!'

'Don't be ridiculous, Tara.'

'I am, I'm dying.'

I ran up her stairs and jumped under a cold shower. A few minutes later I could see flashing blue lights outside the window. The ambulance people came and checked my pulse: it was eighty-five.

Janet spoke to them.

'Is she dying?'

'She might, if we don't get her to hospital.'

They wheeled me out in a chair, soaking wet, mascara running down my face, looking like a complete junkie, through the crowd of people that had gathered outside in the street.

They took me to the Royal Infirmary in Adamsdown, where I was put on a drip and left on a trolley in a corridor. Everyone who passed by looked at me as if I was a drug-crazed creature who had inflicted this on herself and deserved no sympathy – and that included the nurses.

After a couple of hours I'd calmed down and my heartrate had returned to normal, so I got off the trolley and walked out, with the drip still in my arm. I flagged down a taxi and was surprised when he stopped and let me get in – I mean, I must have looked like something from *Night of the Living Dead*. Only problem was, I had no money to pay him and neither did Janet. He ended up accepting the engagement ring Michael had bought me before we got married.

I collected my children from Janet and went home. When I pulled the drip out of my arm, blood spurted everywhere and I had a hard time stopping it.

That episode really frightened me, and I knew I had to cut back on the speed.

Easier said than done. I started to have bad withdrawal symptoms – it was the worst pain ever. It would start with cramps in my legs and arms, then I'd get the sweats and the shakes. I couldn't eat and my mouth was covered in ulcers because I was constantly chewing gum and gurning. I was short of breath and had chest pains and bad panic attacks. I couldn't go out because the paranoia was horrific – I was constantly thinking people were out to get me. I was aggressive and suffered from severe exhaustion, mainly because, on the speed, I didn't sleep for days on end.

After a while, I couldn't take it any longer – I had to have a hit. I phoned my supplier, a guy called John Jones. He looked like Dolph Lundgren from *Rocky IV* – same height and build and hairstyle, except he spoke with a wide Welsh accent, which ruined the illusion. I still had the barbiturates I hustled from the Provident woman and I asked John what he'd trade me for them.

'A seven bag.'

'All right.'

A seven bag was seven grams in a bag for £35 – which was the cheapest way to buy speed, as a single gram bag cost £10. Half price. I knew the downers I was swopping it for were worth more than that on the street, because everyone wanted them due to doctors prescribing them left, right and centre – people were getting hooked on them and couldn't get enough. But right then I was in no mood to haggle – I just needed a fix.

John was going to ring me back with a time and venue to pick up the speed, but I missed the call and did a 1471. A voice I didn't recognise answered.

'Yes?'

I was cautious. 'You just rang me.'

'No, you just rang me.'

I was really feeling the withdrawal, my mouth was dry, I couldn't breathe, I was getting disorientated and going into panic mode. But, somehow, the disembodied voice on the other end of the line seemed to soothe me. We worked out that John had called me from this guy's phone. His name was Luther.

'You don't sound well, Tara.'

'I'm not.'

'Well, I'm a doctor. Come over and I'll check you out.'

After that incongruous introduction, Luther and I started communicating a lot by phone and I got to like him, even though I'd never met him. He seemed so calm and I was so strung out. We arranged a rendezvous. He gave me a time and place and I turned up and waited. It wasn't long before this big, rough-looking guy approached me.

'You Tara?'

He wasn't Welsh. He sounded Brummie.

'No.'

He started to walk away. I called after him.

'Only kidding.'

He turned and I could tell from his expression that he didn't have a sense of humour. I decided not to joke with him again. The Brummie's name was Stan and he took me round the corner to where a red sports car was parked.

Luther was in the car, wearing shades. He was in his thirties, with spiky hair and a large nose.

And that's how I met my second husband.

Luther and I got on really well. I knew he was a big-time gangster, but I didn't care. He was just such a change from Michael's mania – so laid-back, like nothing fazed him. We talked a lot and eventually I told him about my situation with Michael and how I couldn't get rid of him. He offered to send some people around to 'deal with the problem'.

I said no.

After an afternoon in a pub with Stan and Janet, Luther invited us back to his house. It was in a really posh area called Llandough, on the corner of a big hill. It was the kind of area where professional people lived – doctors and lawyers and the like. All the houses had beautiful gardens, with expensive cars parked outside. Luther's house was huge – it looked like the kind of place only a celebrity or a gangster could afford. The ceilings inside were high and white, the rooms were enormous and there was a jacuzzi and all sorts of other things that belonged in the mansions of the rich and famous.

Right then, standing in the middle of that fabulous place, I whispered to Janet.

'This house is going to be mine and my children's.'

As time went on, I spent more and more time with Luther, but I never found out much about him. He was calm and laid-back, but really secretive about what he did. Sometimes I saw behind the facade, when he raised his voice on the phone.

'Listen here, you motherfucker, do you want the Milkybar Kid to come round and play?'

I didn't know who the Milkybar Kid was, but he didn't sound like the kind of person you'd want coming round to your house uninvited.

One night I was with Luther in his house when Stan, who really didn't have a sense of humour, stormed in.

He grabbed me by the arm and forced me up against the wall.

'Your friend made a fool out of me tonight and now I'm gonna kill you.'

He pulled out a handgun and held it to my head. I was petrified and almost wet myself with fear. I waited for Luther to say something, but he didn't. Still with the pistol to my head, Stan pulled out a stun-gun. The blue lights from the prongs were so close to my face I could hardly see.

Luther finally spoke. 'Leave the girl alone, Stan, it's not her fault.'

Stan turned away from me for a moment and that was enough – I was gone, hyperventilating all the way home. It turned out later that Stan was on crack cocaine that night. He and Janet had gone to a club and Stan got paranoid about some guy and hit Janet, so she left him. That's when he came to Luther's to take it out on me.

Luther made him apologise and promise it wouldn't happen again. I decided to give them both the benefit of the doubt and agreed to go back to seeing Luther.

One night I got ready and was just on my way out when Michael grabbed me and ripped all my clothes off and punched me in the eye.

'You walk out of this house, Tara, and I'll set fire to it.'

I didn't go that night, but the next time I saw Luther he asked me to marry him. My children hadn't met him at this stage – I couldn't take that risk because of Michael. But I instinctvely knew, from the time I'd spent with him, that he was basically a decent man and would be good to them. I'd told Luther I divorced Michael in 1994, but he kept coming back because he never really accepted the fact that we were no longer man and wife. This was an opportunity to finally make him face up to reality. I had a choice: I could have Luther send the Milkybar Kid round to see Michael, or I could get married again.

The registry office date was set for 31 October 1996 – Halloween. Michael knew nothing about it and I asked him if he'd take the children out trick-or-treating for the day. When he left I got ready – I wore a long black dress, with platform shoes, and my hair was cut in a pixie style, with long wispy sides and short at the back. Janet and Stan were witnesses. There was a party afterwards full of Luther's friends – all the hard-men gangsters of South Wales and even further afield. Stan was there, and a guy called Budgie, who'd just come out of the French Foreign Legion, and another guy called Hobbs, who had a reputation for being handy with a knife. It was inevitable that a fight would break out, which it did. Luther just sat in a corner while they were banging and beating on each other – not what I expected for my wedding night. Then he signalled and we left with two of his bodyguards and climbed into a limousine.

The limousine drove me to my house and Luther waited outside while I went to the door. Michael opened it and looked me up and down.

'Where the fuck have you been?'

'I've been getting married.'

His face was a picture – as if he'd been hit on the side of the head with a cricket bat.

'You can keep the house and furniture, Michael. I just want the children.'

Before he realised just what was happening, I collected Daniella and Christopher and we all got into the limo and drove off.

I didn't even look back.

Chapter 10

Gangster's Girl

Luther was a handsome Welshman: he was 6'4" with reddish ginger hair and a lean frame. He was always immaculately dressed and his calm exterior had the ability to make me feel safe, no matter what was happening around me. He was always more of a peacemaker than what most people would imagine a big-time gangster and drug dealer to be. He was a genuinely honest man, if that's not a contradiction in terms when describing a career criminal. He was a very generous man and one of the sharpest people I'd ever met, with a strong, capable mind. I really grew to love him: not for what he could give me, but as a truly genuine person. I'm sure he loved me as well – he was more than a husband: he was my trusted best friend and my safety net in an unpredictable world. He was always there for me. He would always put me and my children before himself and you can't say that about many men.

Life was a lot different from anything I'd previously known after I married Luther. Of course, everyone thought I'd married him for his money and, while an element of that might have been true when I first met him and saw his house, it certainly wasn't true after I really got to know him and my children and I settled in with him.

I moved straight into the big house after we got married. It was a truly wonderful place – huge rooms, thick carpets, full-length curtains, cinema-sized TV screens with total surround sound, marble fireplaces and chandeliers. The bedrooms were like those you'd find in a five-star hotel. Luther had the children's rooms professionally decorated: Christopher's wallpaper glowed in the dark, with a moon and planets and stars, and Daniella's was all in pink, with ballerinas. Another room was converted into a playroom for them, with all their toys.

The back garden was large, but overgrown, so I had builders in to pave it all and we had a treehouse built for the children with a slide and swings, which they loved. Luther was a very rich man by the time I met him and he offered to buy me a brand-new sports car. I declined and put the money to use renovating an extension that was off the living room, and not being used for anything. I had dark oak flooring laid and burnt orange wallpaper and velvet curtains hung. I installed reclining chairs and a cocktail bar, with a pure wool Indian carpet as a centrepiece to set it all off.

The house was a palace and I was in my element as its queen.

It was located just down the road from Penarth Marina, where I could take the children to see the boats. There was a large shopping centre, the doctor's surgery was a five-minute walk away and the schools were also close by. Perfect.

I enrolled Daniella and Christopher in one of the local schools, but the other mothers were a little wary of me. I'd always fitted in where the streets had scruffy kids and abandoned shopping trolleys and burnt-out cars, but here

I was considered flashy, ersatz, kitschy. I was over-the-top – the way I dressed, the way I walked, the way I looked at people. But I didn't allow their derisive stares to bother me.

I did make one friend. Her name was Nicky and she was a couple of years older than me, tall and willowy, with the most amazing hair cascading down her back. She worked in a local supermarket and it turned out her son was in the same class at school as Daniella.

We soon became good friends and Nicky was one of the kindest people I'd ever met. She was totally opposite to me, completely straight, while I was bent and crooked and twisted. She wasn't one for confrontations and didn't put much store in money or materialism. We were chalk and cheese, north and south, black and white, but she never judged me, even though she knew I was broken in many respects. Maybe that's why we got on so well – they say opposites attract, don't they?

Over time, we forged a close relationship and Nicky came to be one of the few people I truly trusted – and the only one I trusted to look after my children. Her door was always open and she was there for me emotionally. We spoke to each other every day and we're still good friends, despite losing touch a little at times. I think I made her laugh when I spoke about my exploits and she gave me back the gift of love, keeping me stable at times when everything else was out of focus.

Then, one night, Stan and some other men brought Luther home in a bad way. He'd been hit on the head with something and his shirt was covered in blood. I was traumatised for a moment and in a state of shock.

'Oh my God.'

Then I instinctively reached for the phone. Luther knocked it from my hand.

'Who are you ringing, Tara?'

'An ambulance ... oh my God ...'

'No ambulance.'

Apparently, Luther was set upon in an alley when he went to meet someone he had business with. He'd left Stan and his other associates behind because he needed to do it alone. When he didn't come back, they went to look for him and found him in a pool of blood. He made it clear he couldn't go to hospital because there would be too many questions to answer.

They knew a dodgy doctor or veterinary surgeon or somebody who knew a bit about medicine and he came round. That's when I saw that Luther had been stabbed in the stomach, which made me panic even more. Luther told the others to take me out of the room while the dodgy doctor stopped the bleeding and stitched him up. He left some antibiotics and said when he was leaving that Luther would need to be looked after and there was no one else to do that except me.

Luther was very weak for a matter of months and I had to do everything for him – washing, feeding and dressing him. I got a limited amount of sleep because the dodgy doctor said he thought Luther's spleen had been damaged and he could die if it got infected. I woke at every little sound during the night and gave him the antibiotics and painkillers at regular intervals. I was with him 24/7, as well as running the house and taking care of the children.

If anyone came to the door, I'd panic in case it was the people who'd hurt him. Neither Luther nor Stan nor anyone else would tell me who did it or why and I was petrified they'd come back to finish the job. What if my children were in the house? Would they hurt them too? I was jumping at every little noise – worrying myself sick. I wasn't a trained nurse and, after months of coping, I think my body just burned out and I had a nervous breakdown. I was physically and mentally exhausted.

It began with a horrendous panic attack and a fixation with dying, and I couldn't leave the house. I wanted to cry, but I couldn't let Luther see me bawling, as I was trying to stay strong for him. Things got worse and I couldn't even take the children to school – I used to send them in a taxi. I didn't know what was wrong with me and I spent a lot of the time in bed, thinking I was going to die. At one point I thought my throat was swelling up and I couldn't breathe, and I had a noise in my head that wouldn't go away.

The state of my mental health worsened and I wouldn't come out of the bedroom. In the end, Luther called a doctor (a legitimate one this time), who came to the house and diagnosed an anxiety disorder. He gave me this little round blue tablet – it was 10ml of Valium.

It took all my madness away, but it was the beginning of my love affair with the drug, which was to last twenty years.

Luther recovered and, as time went by, I came to realise just what a big-time player Luther was. I mean, *really* big-time. He orchestrated deals abroad as well as in the UK and, although he was very secretive about what he did and rarely involved me, all kinds of people would turn up at the house at any time, totally unannounced, and some of them were extremely dangerous looking.

One evening I heard a banging on the door and when I opened it, a group of policemen forced their way past me and into the living room, where Luther was meeting with some men. I could see the men reach towards the insides of their jackets, but Luther shook his head. He was cool with the police.

'You have a warrant, I presume?'

The sergeant in charge came right across to Luther and stood over him.

'You going to cooperate, Morgan?'

Morgan was Luther's surname and now my married name.

'Not really.'

'What if we chuck a few kilos around this room and arrest you?'

'Go ahead, I have witnesses.'

I was standing close to the sergeant and he turned to me.

'Who're you?'

'I'm his wife.'

The sergeant smirked and turned back to Luther.

'What if I arrest her, take her down the station, see what she knows?'

Luther stayed calm.

'Take her.'

I was frantic now.

'No, Luther, don't let them take me.'

'Don't worry, Tara, I'll have a brief there for you in no time.'

It was Luther's way of calling the sergeant's bluff. The police left without me. I had to sit down, because my legs were shaking.

Although Luther was as cool as an icicle in a deep-freeze, most of his friends were completely crazy. I told you about Stan, and Budgie from the French Foreign Legion and Hobbs the knife-man; well, there was another guy called Nutty Norman who lived up to his nickname, and a man called Paul West, who was a complete psychopath – and they were just the regular houseguests. Luther always tried to protect me and keep me out of harm's way, but there were occasions when things got scary.

One night Luther was out somewhere and I heard a car pull up outside. When I looked through the window, I saw a taxi driving away and two really rough-looking men approaching the door. I thought they might be the men who attacked Luther, so I phoned him in a panic.

'Let them in, Tara.'

I did as he said and they sat in the living room without speaking. One of them had a big slash scar across his throat and the other looked as if he could crack a coconut with his forehead. I was nervous.

'Luther won't be long.'

No response.

'How long have you known him … my husband, I mean?'

Scar-Neck answered. 'A thousand years.'

'That's a long time.'

I laughed. They didn't. 'No sense of humour, just like Stan,' I thought.

Luther seemed to be taking for ever and the atmosphere was taut as a tripwire. I couldn't stop staring at the guy's neck. The words came out of their own accord, without me consciously speaking them.

'What happened to your neck?'

Silence. Coconut-Crusher eventually answered for Scar-Neck.

'His ex-wife tried to saw his head off with a Moulinex.'

For those of you who don't know, a Moulinex is a brand of electric kitchen knife that people use for carving the Sunday roast. Maybe they did have a sense of humour. But I was glad when Luther finally arrived home.

The one who really frightened me was Paul West. He and his wife Daisy came to the house for drinks from time to time. She kept looking at the floor all the time because he used to beat her badly and she was terrified of him. But I liked her, perhaps because I knew what it was like to be living with an abuser, from my years with Michael. Paul and Daisy came over one evening because he had business with Luther. So we wouldn't be in the way and the men could discuss what they wanted in private, I suggested that Daisy and I should go and get some cakes for tea. I asked what they fancied; Luther said he didn't care, but Paul wanted a custard slice. By the time we got to the bakers, they'd sold out of custard slices, so I just grabbed a box of jam doughnuts.

When we got back, Paul went berserk and threw the box of doughnuts across the room, screaming: 'In the land of the blind, the one-eyed man is king!'

Whatever that was supposed to mean? Daisy just put her head down and stared at the floor, but this was my house and I wasn't going to put up with that kind of behaviour.

'Why don't you chill out, Paul? You're lucky we brought you back anything.'

He spoke to Luther, even though he was looking directly at me. 'Sort your bird out, Luther, before I kill her stone dead.'

Luther stepped between us. 'Tara, you need to cool down. Paul, you need to leave.'

Luther didn't do business with him after that and I heard Daisy eventually left him. They say he set fire to their house and stood on the roof as it was burning.

The year 1997 was a great year. Money was no object and we were living an extravagant lifestyle. The children were in an amazing school and we'd eat at the best restaurants. Jewellers would come to the house and I'd just pick whatever I wanted – life was as good as it gets. I wanted to share my good luck with those less fortunate and I'd go into town and pick up homeless people and take them back to the house for a bath and some food. Luther would despair of me, but I knew what it was like to have nowhere to go and, after ranting at me about security, he'd try to understand what I was doing. Over the years, I had always seemed to attract people who'd led hard lives and been abused, violated and exploited, and I always had an overwhelming desire to help those people if I was in a position to. When I was with Luther I had both the means and the opportunity and, although he didn't like it, he didn't stop me either.

Luther promised to buy me a new car if I passed my driving test. Learning to drive was a typical episode in the life of Tara – I drove my instructor to the point of suicide. Back in 1997, they used their own cars and I really didn't have a clue what I was doing. The man's name was Bob and he'd get so stressed.

'Tara, for God's sake, you're going to burn my clutch out!'

On the test itself, I went straight through a red light and the examiner was holding on for dear life. Then I went over a roundabout and got in the wrong lane at a junction and caused chaos for the other motorists. I thought I'd done well and turned to the examiner at the end. His hands were trembling.

'Have I passed?'

'Is the sky green?'

I had to take the driving test five times and, in the end, Luther paid the examiner to pass me as he couldn't cope with my carrying on after failing. He also paid the theory paper examiner to check my answers, which were all wrong, and change them to the right answers.

That Christmas I decorated the whole house like Santa's grotto and bought presents for everyone. It was 23 December and someone was knocking on the door. I opened it to see this guy wearing a long green coat, a beanie hat and a substantial beard. I thought, 'Are you kidding me?'

'Father Christmas come early?'

'And you must be the infamous Tara.'

'Infamous?'

He just grinned.

'Is Luther in?'

The man's name was Larry and he was from London. He was on the run after escaping from Belmarsh Prison and Luther invited him to stay for the holidays. What could I say? It was Christmas after all.

A few weeks later, and Larry was still living with us. People were coming to the house to see him and he was selling them cocaine. I couldn't believe the brass neck of the man – he wasn't paying any rent, was eating everything in the kitchen, his room was like a rat-hole because he never cleaned it, and now he was abusing our hospitality by dealing drugs from our house, where my children lived. He had to go!

Before I could persuade Luther to throw him out, we were raided by the police in the early hours of one winter morning. They surrounded the house, front and back, and they were armed. I heard noises outside and I looked through the window and saw them.

'Luther, Luther, wake up ... Police, they're everywhere.'

'Go to the kids, Tara.'

They came in and handcuffed Larry, then they searched the whole house. One of them was the same sergeant who had threatened to plant cocaine and arrest me that previous time.

'You can go to prison for harbouring a fugitive, you know.'

I tried to stay calm, for the sake of the children.

'Fugitive?'

'Your houseguest.'

But Larry had made an arrangement with Luther that, if he got caught, he'd swear we didn't know he was on the run. They didn't arrest us, but it was a close thing.

Then, one day, Luther became seriously ill; because his spleen was damaged when he was attacked and stabbed, it became enlarged and ruptured. He was vomiting and had diarrhoea, and beads of cold sweat broke out all over his body. I went with him in the ambulance and they put him on a drip at the hospital. But he had caught an infection and ended up having to have his spleen removed and the infection spread right through his body.

I was a mess – I thought he was going to die under the anaesthetic because he was more at risk than the average person due to his injury which meant that his immune system wasn't functioning as it should have been. I was inconsolable, sobbing and telling him how much I loved him.

The operation was a success and he didn't die, but he had to stay in hospital for almost a year. I went to see him every day.

Chapter 11

Emotional Breakdown

While Luther was in hospital, my role as his go-between grew. Luther never liked to show he was vulnerable. Physically, he was fragile after the attack, but mentally he was really tough and people in the underworld respected him for his resilience and for never showing weakness. So, while he was in hospital, he had to keep that tenacious exterior intact. That's where I came in.

The first thing he asked me to do was deliver some money to Birmingham. It was £20,000 and I was the only one he trusted with it. I don't know who I delivered the money to, all I know is his name was Shane and his face had been recently slashed from his eye socket to his chin. Luther told me not to pass any remarks.

'Whatever you do, don't mention his face, Tara.'

It was a long drive up the M5 and Luther sent one of his bodyguards with me for protection. We parked the car on a narrow street in the Northfield area and I knocked at the door of the address Luther had given me.

As soon as Shane opened the door, the first words out of my mouth were the taboo ones: 'It doesn't look that bad.'

Shane gave me a hard stare for a moment, then he started to laugh. 'Fair play, missus, you're a game bird.'

But Luther didn't see the funny side. He was angry with me when I got back and told me it could've gone the other way and I might have a facial slash to match Shane's if it had.

The other thing that happened while Luther was in hospital was that certain people who may have been resentful of my relationship with him decided they could push me around and intimidate me. One particular woman was Susan – she was tough and had a reputation for violence, along with a strong personality and a lot of followers. When she saw me on the street she blocked my way and wouldn't let me pass. Then she and two of her friends began to elbow me to see if I'd react. I didn't, because that would have given them an excuse to beat me up. The next time we met was the same, and the time after.

I didn't want to tell Luther, as he had enough on his plate, trying to recover and run things from hospital, so I decided to join a local martial arts club and learn how to fight properly.

The instructor looked me up and down. 'What do you want to get out of this, Tara?'

'I want to beat three women up.'

Apparently, that was a good enough reason.

I started training and I surprised myself by how good I was at it. It seemed to come naturally to me and everyone was impressed.

A few weeks later Susan and her two friends were on the street again, waiting for me to try to get past them. I stayed calm. Susan was right in my face, smirking at me, venom in her eyes. I slammed her so hard she went flying and I was instantly on top of her, pounding her in the head and body. Her friends dragged me off and then backed away. I invited them to come on if they wanted some of the same, but they didn't fancy fighting me. I let them pick Susan up from the ground and take her away. There were no more problems with the girl-gangsters after that, and no more intimidation from anyone else either – the word got around: I was hard. And I had to be, in that world. It was sink or swim, and I intended to stay swimming for as long as possible, and for as far as possible. You have to understand, this was a self-defence thing – a self-preservation thing. Once the violence began, adrenaline took over and rationality went out the window.

I kept up the martial arts training and got better and better. It gave me confidence and made me feel strong, enough to handle anything that came my way.

One afternoon I went to the school to pick up the children and Michael was standing there, a bag of sweets in his hand. I glared at him.

'Tara, please ... I just want to see the kids.'

'No!'

'I've changed, Tara. Can I at least give them the sweets?'

'No!'

I bundled Daniella and Christopher into the car and drove off. Later on I started to worry. What if he tried to take the children from me? After all, they were living in the house of a known gangster who had been raided by police on a number of occasions. He could use the argument that they were exposed to danger.

Michael was back living with his parents, so I rang him there.

'What do you think you're doing, Michael?'

'I just want to see the kids, that's all.'

'Why now, after all this time?'

'I miss them, Tara. I'm in a stable relationship with someone now.'

In the end, I decided it was probably better to give in to him. After all, he was Daniella's father and he had a right to see her.

It went well for a while, but this was Michael and it couldn't last. He'd had the children for the weekend and when he brought them back he complained that Christopher had nits in his hair. I was fuming.

'He didn't have them when you picked him up.'

With that, Christopher rubbed his hair against Michael.

'Daddy's going to get nits.'

I couldn't believe my eyes when Michael roughly elbowed him away.

I jumped to my feet. 'So now you're a child-beater as well as a woman-beater!'

It got really nasty. Michael threatened to throw me through the window. I screamed at him to get out. That was it, I wasn't going to let him have the children again after displaying that he was capable of using violence towards them.

I may have been feeling strong with my martial arts training and I wasn't physically afraid of Michael any more, but I didn't think I could deal with this on my own – so I told Luther. The next day Michael was picked up by a few heavies and thrown into the back of a van.

He was told what would happen to him if he ever came near me or the children again.

He never did.

I'd fallen out with my mother because she wanted the children to stay with her on Alderney for a holiday, but I wouldn't allow that as I didn't know who she might have living with her. I'd stayed in touch with my aunt Christine over the years and one summer morning in 1998, I was on the phone to her, having a fairly typical conversation, when she asked me a question completely out of the blue.

'What happened between you and Bruno, Tara?'

I don't know why, but emotion welled up inside me. It was as if someone else blurted out the answer, some child-voice inside me.

'He abused me when I was little.'

'I knew he beat you, Tara ...'

'He sexually abused me, too.'

The trauma of actually saying those words was huge. When I was a child I'd got used to it and thought it was me, part of *me*. I didn't understand that it was wrong and vile, and I'd put it out of my mind. But now, actually saying it like that was like admitting to myself that it had happened. And it shouldn't have.

There was silence on the other end of the phone.

'You do believe me, don't you?'

She did – I think she already knew and just wanted me to say it.

After she hung up, I wanted to tell all my family on Alderney about the abuse. After all, it was why I was so wild. It was why I became a pole dancer and a hustler and a lot of other things besides. I wanted them to understand and support me. I wanted them to love me. If they knew the truth, they would love me – wouldn't they?

I rang them all: my aunts, my cousins, crying down the phone to them – please see me. See me. See me, please!

They were matter-of-fact about it. My mother hung up on me. Christine had already called my aunt Sylvia – she listened to me but said very little in reply.

'I have to go now, Tara.'

She didn't want a scandal on the island involving her sister, my mother.

Cousin Adele listened too.

'I hope he didn't touch me, Tara.'

I think she would have known if he did.

'I believe you, Tara, but it was when you were a kid.'

As if I'd fallen over and grazed my knee, but it had healed and I should forget about it now I was grown up.

I felt let-down. Again. They should have protected me from Bruno back then, but they hadn't. Now they were rejecting me again. It felt like they blamed me, that what happened was my fault and now that I was talking about it, admitting it, it was worse than when I just kept it to myself. I was the dirty one, the bad one, the one who had embarrassed them and was now embarrassing them again.

I didn't want this family any more – I wanted a new family.

I wanted my father.

I knew my father's name and I knew he loved the song 'Galway Bay', but that's all. So I rang up Galway Radio and they let me put out an appeal live on the air for him to contact me. That very same night, my father rang me and I spoke to him for the first time in almost twenty-five years. He told me he'd never forgotten me, but he just couldn't reason with my mother. I understood that.

I found out I had a half-sister and two half-brothers, the oldest of whom was serving a twenty-year prison sentence for murder. My father was living in Dublin and I desperately wanted to go and see him, and for my children to meet their grandfather.

I booked a flight, but before it was time to go, I was contacted by some cousins on my father's side. They told me that my father had run off with his brother's wife, their mother. They were grown up now, and told me my father had been arrested for sexually assaulting them when they were young. He was charged but they were pressured into withdrawing their statements by the family, so no trial or conviction ever took place. They said he was a pig of a man who used to beat them severely and hose them down with cold water. They never had decent clothes to wear and they hated him.

He wasn't a Heathcliff or a Roibin, like I imagined – he was another Bruno.

I was devastated. I cancelled the tickets to Dublin. Instead, I went to visit my half-sister, Orla, who lived in Berkhamsted, Hertfordshire, to see if what I'd been told was true. Orla had a daughter called Clara who was about six. It was intense meeting a family I never knew I had, after growing up as an only child.

At dinner that evening, Orla showed me a picture of my father.

'He doesn't look like a child abuser.'

I said it in all innocence, but there was immediate silence at the table. Orla's partner wanted to know what I meant, because they had sent Clara over to Ireland on holiday once.

Orla dragged me into the kitchen and said her partner had lots of high-level connections and he could take Clara away from her if he found out our father was a child abuser.

It was like there was this big, black secret hidden for years and years and they just lived with it, even though they knew it was wrong – exactly like my mother's family on Alderney. Maybe they thought it would just go away, but then I came along and blew it all up. I was supposed to stay for a week but, after that, Orla asked me to leave. She said I'd betrayed the family – the family I'd lost and found and now lost again.

Luther was out of hospital by now and, when I got home, I was an emotional mess. I started drinking heavily to dull the pain in my heart and took Valium to make myself sleep. Luther suggested I go and visit my half-brother in prison, to see what he had to say about my father. He was in a high-security jail called Full Sutton in Yorkshire and Luther arranged for me to see him.

I sat at a table opposite my half-brother. He showed no remorse for his crime. I brought the conversation round to our father.

'I'd rather be where I am than where he is.'

I didn't ask him what he meant by that. I mean, here was a dangerous man who was looking at a lot of prison time. I didn't want to pry too deeply, in case that might upset him and maybe get him into trouble in prison.

He asked me if I'd visit again. 'Only next time wear a short skirt and don't forget the brown parcel.'

I didn't know what he meant, but Luther explained he wanted me to plug brown heroin up inside my vagina and, when I visited, remove it and pass it to him.

I didn't visit again.

The experiences with both sides of my family had left me deeply traumatised.

I just wanted to keep drinking and drinking.

One night I was out drinking heavily and I decided to drive home. Luther usually had one of his men accompany me, but this time I was on my own. Someone was lying on the ground in the car park, probably drunk, and I accidentally reversed over their legs. I could hear a crunching sound, but I didn't get out to see what it was – I just drove away from the scene like a cat with a can tied to its tail. Then I crashed into some parked cars. I managed to crawl from the wreckage and rang Luther to have me picked up. The police came shortly after I got in, but Luther hid me and told them someone had taken the keys without his permission. He didn't know who. The car was towed to the police pound and they were waiting to have the airbags tested for DNA and fingerprints.

I was petrified, as I knew I'd go to jail – I'd crushed someone's legs and left the scene of an accident and then smashed several cars up. What was I becoming? I wanted to give myself up – to take what was coming to me but, if I did, what would happen to my children? I was in a maelstrom of guilt and remorse and confusion.

As ever, Luther came to my rescue. He paid someone a lot of money to climb into the police pound wearing a balaclava and petrol bomb the car – that got rid of all the evidence.

Next morning Luther rang the pound. 'Hello, this is Luther Morgan. Could I send someone down to collect my kids' PE kits from the boot of the car?'

'Hold on a moment, I'll go and check.'

Luther winked at me while he was waiting.

'I'm terribly sorry, sir, it seems there's been a fire and your car's been destroyed.'

'What? I can't believe you're telling me my car isn't even safe in the police pound!'

'I'm sorry, sir.'

'What about compensation for the PE kits?'

Luther and his friends had a good laugh about it, but I didn't think it was funny.

After that, instead of drinking, I just sat around and got stoned. Nothing made me happy any more. Luther tried to drag me out of my depression.

'Why don't you find something to do?'

'Like what?'

'I don't know. You're always saying how much you regret leaving school so early. Go back to college.'

'What about the children?'

'Do a course that fits around them. Hire a nanny. Whatever.'

So, at the beginning of 1999, I enrolled at Barry College, which was about nine miles south of Cardiff, to take a fitness course and become a personal trainer.

And that's where I met Owen.

Owen was ten years younger than me. I'd been with Luther for three years and I was trying to emerge from the depression and emotional breakdown brought on by reconnecting with both sides of my family. I still loved

Luther, but I needed someone to holds hands with, someone to put their arms around me and give me a reassuring hug, someone to tell me I was a normal, worthwhile person, not the result of the union between two desperately dysfunctional people – something unnatural and dark, the spawn of the black sheep and the even blacker pooka.

I wasn't happy, and Luther was busy with his business, back in charge now that he was out of hospital. It didn't help that he was always surrounded by people – friends or henchmen or bodyguards or dodgy deal-makers. I felt isolated, marginalised.

I'm not saying it was Luther's fault our relationship was deteriorating: it was mine. The problem was that I needed some indefinable expression of belonging that had been missing from my life since I was born. Most of the time I was able to get by without it, but now and then the longing for that love came over me and I searched for something that I wouldn't find until much later in my life.

I felt alone when I began my course at Barry College. I was in a group, but couldn't really interact with them. Owen was also part of the group, but seemed alone, like me, usually sitting in a corner on his own during lectures. He was very young and very handsome, with olive skin and black hair and eyes. We had to introduce ourselves and say where we were from, and I discovered that Owen lived quite close to me. It was a long way out to Barry and he had to catch buses back and forth, so I offered him a lift, as I was driving that way anyway. He accepted and I started picking him up. He didn't speak much and it was usually me making the conversation. I found out that his father was a violent alcoholic and Owen and his mother had moved around a lot, through a series of refuges. Because we both felt abandoned as children, it formed a kind of kinship between us – a kindred spirit thing of mutual understanding and affliction.

The weeks turned into months at Barry College and I was struggling with the theoretical side of the course. The physical side was fine, as I was fit enough from my martial arts training, but some of the student-centred coursework was giving me problems. Owen offered to help me in exchange for the free lifts I was giving him.

One Friday afternoon I went around to his house. I can categorically assure you that neither of us had any ulterior motive in mind but, as we sat there together, a fleeting look of longing occupied the space between us and we kissed. It wasn't a passionate kiss, just a brief acknowledgement of each other's presence. It happened very quickly and ended just as quickly. I pulled away and hurried from the house.

Over that weekend, I experienced dreadful feelings of guilt and kept telling myself that it was a silly mistake. I resolved to tell Owen on Monday that I wouldn't be able to offer him a lift any more.

But that's not the way things turned out. And I had no idea then that a single kiss would result in divorce from Luther.

Chapter 12

Despair & Destitution

Monday came and Owen was standing on the corner. I was determined to drive past but, at the last moment, I couldn't do it and I pulled over to pick him up. Neither of us spoke about the kiss on our way to college. In fact, we hardly spoke at all and a stealthy silence established itself inside the car.

The week went on and towards the end of it, I knew something had to be said. I drove Owen to a pub and ordered a couple of beers.

'Let's talk, Owen.'

'I love you, Tara.'

'What?'

'I've loved you since we first met.'

This was ridiculous, he was just a boy. But now that he'd expressed his affection, I realised I had strong feelings for him too, feelings that had developed slowly, like seeds in the soil that were now ready to burst into bloom. We talked and talked and it seemed to me that Owen was what I was looking for to put my life back on track.

I couldn't go behind Luther's back and deceive him after all he'd done for me and my children so, that night, I told him there was someone else in my life.

Luther already knew things were strained between us and I think he was actually relieved it was over. He had enough to deal with without me in a constant state of depression and he didn't take the news as badly as I thought he would.

'I don't want anything from you, Luther, you've given me enough.'

'You can keep the car.'

'Thank you ... for everything.'

'Can I see the kids sometime?'

'Of course, they love you so much.'

Daniella and Christopher were young and they both took the break-up well. I don't think they really understood what was happening and I didn't go into detail with them. I didn't tell Luther who Owen was either, just in case. No matter what, he was a gangster and there were plenty of people who owed him favours – they might unwittingly try to come after Owen without Luther's knowledge, thinking it would be what he wanted. In fact, Luther didn't ask me who it was, and I don't think 'who' mattered that much to him; it was just the fact that it had happened and our marriage was over. When we finally parted, I could have had half of everything he owned, but I voluntarily walked away with nothing.

I had to find somewhere to live with Owen, so we both quit college. He had to get a job because the luxurious lifestyle with Luther was gone. I wanted to stay in the area so the children's schooling wouldn't be disrupted and we found a place in Glebe Street. It was a private rent and I was lucky to find it. I remember going to see the owner and begging him to let me have it and promising I'd be an ideal tenant. The house was a bit grim – it was a terraced property in an old street. There was a Chinese takeaway next door and a pub across the road. The interior was awful, after what I'd been used to. It had threadbare carpets throughout, a tiny kitchen and an even tinier bathroom, three small bedrooms and a few paving slabs for a garden. I cried when I saw the place and wondered how on earth we were going to live there. All right, I know I'd lived in worse places with Michael, but I'd become used to a better standard of living and my children had had a taste of the good life, living in a beautiful house. That's what upset me most – by leaving Luther for Owen, I'd taken away their golden time. How selfish of me!

But Luther made it his business to find out where the children would be moving to and, when he did, he insisted on having the house completely renovated. He got builders in to knock down walls and enlarge the rooms, he had the place completely recarpeted and repainted and, in the end, it looked half decent and habitable. He also paid the rent for six months in advance and he was paying me £250 per month in child maintenance, which was more than Michael ever did.

I have to say here that I will always be grateful to Luther for being the real man he was and not a silly, whinging boy. I will always have love in my heart for him and I will never forget or regret the time we had together.

The new millennium came and, along with it, a new life for me. I panicked for a while after leaving Luther because my safety net was gone and I was with a boy who was young and immature and kept going back to his mother. I soon realised I'd made a big mistake and I rang Luther and told him so. He said there was no way we could get back together now and it would be better all round if we divorced. That was a fair comment: I was in a situation of my own making, and now I'd have to live with it.

Don't get me wrong, I did believe I loved Owen, in the same way you can believe you love someone who you think is a reflection of yourself. It wasn't real love.

My divorce from Luther came through in 2001 and, immediately, Owen wanted us to get married. I didn't, but he said he felt insecure as things were and I finally agreed, just to keep him happy.

I married Owen in July 2001. I was twenty-nine and he was nineteen – he was my third husband in ten years. I wore a long pink dress with roses all down the back, with a garland of flowers in my hair. My friend Nicky was my maid of honour. Daniella was almost ten and she wore a white fairy dress to be my bridesmaid. Christopher was eight and wore jeans and a blue checked shirt – he looked a proper little man. We married at Cardiff registry office, with the reception at a pub called the Oyster Catcher afterwards. There was a wedding cake and balloons and music and we put £300 behind the bar for drinks. Owen didn't tell his parents he was marrying me, but some of our friends came along and everyone had a good time. We'd been given a wedding present of a voucher to stay at the Marriott hotel for one night and that was our honeymoon. On the way there we stopped off at a club. I was still in my wedding dress, which attracted a lot of attention. Owen grabbed me by the arm.

'We're going to the hotel, now!'

'I want to stay for a while, Owen.'

But he wouldn't have it and we went to the Marriott. We were only just married and already it was going wrong. I fell asleep and the wedding night was never consummated, as they say in historical novels.

And so I settled into this new life, looking after Daniella and Christopher and being a wife to Owen. He worked at whatever he could find and trained at the gym to become a professional boxer. I trained with him – I was at the gym a lot doing hardcore circuits.

Owen was very controlling – not in a direct way like Michael, and he was never violent or physically abusive – but in a coy, childish way. It was almost as if I was looking after three children. For instance, he liked to go out with his younger friends and didn't want to take me with him. He said I was trouble when I went out. It was probably because of the age difference. Young women in the group would say sarcastic things and one night this girl came and sat on his lap. I pushed her off and she glared at me.

'Who do you think you are? I've known Owen since we were kids.'

A group of them started to form around me. I'd just had artificial nails put on, they were bright red. I flashed them in this girl's face.

'I'm his wife, that's who I am.'

She took a swing at me and I ducked. The next thing, she went flying. Two of the nails came off and were stuck in her head. She was screaming like a banshee and her friends started to crowd me. I assumed a martial arts stance and they backed off. Owen grabbed my arm and pulled me out of the place, before the police arrived.

As far as sex was concerned, it was good insofar as I was physically attracted to Owen, although a lot of the time I preferred drinking to having sex. He was a very handsome young man and his mother constantly reminded him of that. I always felt I was in competition with her. She never liked me – here I was, ten years older than her son with two children from other men. She believed he could have done much better than me and that I had ruined his life. We'd started rowing a lot and, when we did, Owen would run home to his mother. The cracks were appearing in our relationship.

I still had a raging Valium addiction. Whenever we argued, Owen would use this against me and call me a 'blue-head', which is a slang term for a Valium addict. My periods were also very irregular and my mood swings were all over the place.

Then I got pregnant.

I didn't realise I was pregnant until I was getting on for three months. I knew I couldn't keep it – my situation was precarious, and the constant bickering was wearing me down. Money was very scarce because Owen wasn't earning a lot and every little thing got blown out of all proportion, like it does when you quibble with a sulky adolescent. I was totally detached from the life growing inside me. I had no connection with it. I didn't want it. They gave me an emergency appointment at Heath hospital for a scan to determine just how far gone I was. I told the nurse I wasn't sure if I was going to keep the baby and she turned the screen away so I couldn't see it. She told me if I wanted an abortion I had to take this little white tablet straight away and then be back in two days.

'Can I have time to think about it?'

'There's no time. You're too far gone.'

'I can't make that kind of decision now, lying here.'

'If you don't take the tablet right now, you can't have a termination.'

The nurse stood over me with the white tablet and a glass of water.

I swallowed it.

My legs were like jelly as I stumbled out of the examination room. I made it to my car and just sat there in a state of inert confusion. There was a clock on the dashboard, but I couldn't see the time. Time, in fact, had stood still. The earth no longer spun on its axis. Everything outside the car may have been moving, but I'd become inanimate, waiting for my own personal Godot.

I stayed like that until a policeman knocked on the window.

'Are you all right in there?'

I didn't respond, just looked straight ahead, as if in a trance.

'Can I get you some help? Would you like me to fetch a doctor or a nurse?'

I heard the words vaguely, distantly, coming towards me in slow motion down a long echo chamber. The policeman tried to open the car door.

'Did you hear what I said, miss?'

His face appeared inside the car, materialising out of an obscure haze. I stirred in the driver's seat, nodded my head – tried to bring reality back from where it had fled to.

'I'm all right, officer. I'm all right now.'

I started the engine and drove away.

My eyes were puffy and swollen from crying when I got home. Owen asked me what was wrong.

'I had a scan. The baby's dead.'

He didn't say anything. I think he was relieved. I had a banging headache and all I wanted to do was sleep, but I couldn't. I had this dead baby inside my belly and it would be there for another two days.

On Thursday morning I was admitted to the abortion clinic. Nicky came with me. The first thing they gave me was another tablet. They explained that the first one was to separate the placenta from the womb and the second was to get labour going. I took the second tablet and a nurse told me not to look down.

'What do you mean?'

'When you need to push, go to the lavatory and place a bedpan underneath you and don't look down.'

I didn't understand, but they said it was to prevent the foetus from going into the toilet and it wouldn't be good for me to see it. They then put suppositories up me to soften the cervix and induce labour. I was in sheer agony, screaming and screaming. The labour pains lasted over five hours and when the urge to push finally came, I ran to the toilet with the bedpan. I felt something coming away and I didn't look down. A nurse quickly took the bedpan away. There was blood all over the floor as I staggered back to the delivery room.

The hospital wanted me to stay in overnight, but I just had to get home to my living children. I slept in the same bed with them that night.

I thought Owen would take the next day off work to look after me, but he didn't. Not that it mattered much – I had no feelings left for him now and I don't believe he had feelings left for me. The marriage was over. When he came home that evening, I told him I wanted a divorce. He wasn't bothered – we'd grown so far apart that he just went along with whatever I wanted. I cited 'irreconcilable differences' and he was more than willing to sign the papers.

I was sure his mother was influencing him so, while the divorce was being finalised, I said he'd have to go and live with her. I knew she'd be glad to know it was over between us and that there were no grandchildren to make it messy.

It was the beginning of 2002 and we'd been married for less than a year.

With Owen gone and Luther no longer paying me any money – he'd met a new woman who put a stop to it – things were really tough and I was soon destitute. I had to think of a way to make some quick cash. I saw an ad in the *South Wales Echo* – it was right at the back of the paper in a square box and it said: 'Looking for beautiful women to join our exclusive team,' something like that. It was a massage parlour called The Ambassador and, although I didn't consider myself to be beautiful, I thought I'd give it a try. I mean, how difficult could it be? I was no angel, I'd hustled and pole danced and lived with gangsters. All right, I knew the place wouldn't be a massage parlour in the strictest sense of the term and there would probably be 'extras' involved, but I'd done private dancing at SINatra's for the gropers and the gawpers, could this be any worse? I went along for an interview.

I didn't know what to expect, so I wore a little grey T-shirt and matching shorts. I looked nothing like the girl I was in the pole-dancing clubs – I didn't have a tan and I wore no make-up, I wasn't very confident and I walked about with my head down.

I was shown into a room where a group of women was sitting. They were all in their underwear, eating or reading or watching television. They looked me up and down when I entered, as if they were sizing up the competition.

The manageress was called Gloria and she was a short woman in her forties, with dyed blonde hair, huge breasts, loads of make-up and high heels to make her look taller and more intimidating. She said they had regular clients and one of them always tested the new girls out.

'Will you be OK with that, Tara?'

'Sure.'

I wondered what kind of a test it could be – I had no experience as a masseuse, but I believed I could bluff my way. In reality, I was way out of my depth but I didn't know it. However, once into the sex industry, there was no way back out.

'You do know this isn't just about massage, don't you, Tara?'

'Of course, I've been around.'

She called this man in. He was about fifty and big and burly – he looked like a farmer to me. He wore an old man's vest and light brown trousers. He had squinty eyes and a huge beard. Gloria must have reckoned if I could handle this one, I could handle anything – that's what I thought to myself as he sniffed around me like a big hairy dog.

The man led me into another room. It had a double bed and an en-suite shower and not much else. I didn't know what I was supposed to do, but I was ready to take my cue from him. His voice was gruff.

'Take off your clothes and lie down.'

What? Shouldn't I be saying that to him? Who was doing the massage here? I was confused, but I did what he said, not wanting to appear stupid. Maybe there was a technique to this that I didn't know about. He got undressed at the same time and I could see he had a huge penis that was getting bigger all the time. He told me to put a condom on it, which was beside the bed.

Believe it or not, I didn't know how to do that. I mean, I was on the pill when in relationships, so I didn't realise there was a knack to putting a condom on an erect penis.

Before I knew it, the farmer was on top of me and ramming his gigantic erection up into my vagina. It was really painful and I started to bleed, but that didn't put him off. I wanted to cry, but I stopped myself. I just lay there, looking at the little clock on the wall and waiting for it to be over. It was like I went totally dead inside – no feeling and no emotion.

'I can tell you're a new girl, nice and tight.'

It seemed I was underneath him for a lifetime, while he grunted like a hog. He kept licking me and I could smell his breath, almost taste it. The bed was creaking and my head was banging against the wall. Finally, he let out an almighty groan and ejaculated.

It stank. He stank. I got up quickly while he disposed of the condom and I ran straight into the shower. I stood there under the lukewarm spray for ages and when I came out, he was gone.

I was broken in now, and I felt different. I was different. I was no longer Tara the hustler, Tara the pole dancer, Tara the gangster's girl.

Now I was Tara the prostitute.

Was that what I wanted to be? Was it what I had to be? I don't know – even now, looking back.

Chapter 13

Massage Parlours & Brothels

I got the job and went to work at The Ambassador in early 2002. I contacted my friend Nicky, as she was the only person I really trusted with my children, and she was happy to look after them for me when they weren't at school. Luther still took them on some weekends and, if I was really stuck, I would phone my old regular babysitter and pay her well for her time. I didn't like leaving my children with anyone other than Nicky when I had to work at night.

You could argue that I should have found a daytime job at Tesco or Sainsbury's – worked for minimum wage and accepted my mundane lot in life. That wasn't me – that wasn't Tara. I was like a firecracker back then, burning from both ends. I picked my kids up from school when I wasn't working, and during holidays they went to Bears Club, which had lots of fun-filled activities. I looked at it as if I was working in a normal job like many mothers do. I told them I was selling cosmetics and sometimes I had to travel long distances and stay in hotels overnight. Thankfully, they believed me.

The Ambassador was a massage parlour in name only, purely for legal reasons – but really it was a brothel. There were leather suites in the reception areas and all the rooms had fancy names – like the Gold Room and the Amber Room and the Rose Room. Every room had an en suite and a double bed, the towels were wrapped in the shape of hearts and there was baby oil, talc and nappy sacks on the side tables, along with the condoms. To start with I didn't know what the nappy sacks were for, but I learned later they were for disposing of the used condoms. Sweet aromas of jasmine and sandalwood wafted everywhere and nondescript muzak emerged discreetly from hidden speakers.

When a woman went into a room with a client, it would be written down on a sheet: 'Lucy in the Amber Room for 1 hour.' I was given a price list as if it was a menu: handjob £20; blow-job £40; missionary £70 with no kissing; 69er £80. Extras could be negotiated in the room and I learned quickly not to tell Gloria or the other girls if I did. I had to give half of what I earned to the receptionist at the end of each shift. She'd put it in a kind of plastic tube thing along with my name and it would go in the safe. The shifts were 10 a.m. till 10 p.m. and 10 p.m. till 6 a.m. The busiest times were weekends, month-ends and Christmas – maybe some guys got vouchers as presents. Who knows? The place was very regimented: if you missed a shift, you had to pay a fine of £30 and if you missed more than three, you were out the door with no way back in.

When a client came to The Ambassador, we had no idea what he was going to want. I remember when I first started there, the receptionist called out, 'Punter!' and all the women started fussing about, getting their hair straight and pushing up their breasts, slapping on lipstick and spraying perfume. Then they strutted out as if they were on a catwalk, while the client sat there with a drink and decided which one to pick. I thought this was very demeaning and it took me some time to get used to parading myself like a pea hen at a Miss Poultry contest. But I learned how to switch off and not show emotion and it became very mechanical after a while.

We all had working names – mine was Whitney. There would normally be about nine girls to a shift. No two women looked alike on a shift – some black, some white, blonde, brunette, auburn, etc. The Ambassador catered for all tastes, with the ages of the women ranging from eighteen to sixty. The oldest woman there was a grandmother, but she was very elegant and always very busy. I'd say most of the women were my age – they didn't employ many young girls because they wanted women who were mature about the work and who wouldn't cause any problems for them – women who were reliable and able to handle it. They also catered for all different tastes in body size: most of the girls were curvy with big breasts and big bottoms; I was one of the leanest women there. Also different nationalities: Polish, Bulgarian, Romanian, Welsh and English.

I didn't have a slender beach-body any more, and I had that birthmark on my left breast that looked like a love-bite – when I took off my bra their eyes would automatically be drawn there. I was so self-conscious I'd make excuses and try to laugh it off.

'What a place to have a birthmark in this business, ha ha.'

We came in and went out the side entrance, into an alley, not onto the main road. There was to be no smoking inside, the rooms had to be stripped and made ready for the next girl after use, stockings only to be worn – no bare legs unless specifically asked for – and no fraternising outside work.

I found the other women I worked with to be very detached, and reticent. They didn't speak about their personal lives and it was almost impossible to strike up a meaningful conversation with any of them. I didn't know if that was because of The Ambassador's stringent rules or if it was just the way they were. They were all more experienced sex workers than I was, so I suppose that impassiveness came with time, as you became desensitised to what you were doing. I wasn't completely there yet.

The women at The Ambassador were very well 'presented'. They were all immaculately dressed and extremely professional. The massage parlour-cum-brothel was regarded as a high-class establishment, or so Gloria kept saying. I rarely saw her after that first 'interview': the day-to-day running of The Ambassador was usually left to the receptionist. On one occasion I had a heavy period and didn't want to work, but Gloria called and said she needed me to come in, everything would be fine. She took me to a chemist across the road and bought a baby sponge. She told me to boil it so it was sterile, then squat and push it as far up inside me as possible – it would absorb the blood and nothing would show while I was working. On another occasion she told me she had been a working girl herself once – she had used the money she made wisely and set up The Ambassador, which was now well established and paid for a luxurious lifestyle. Then she winked and said the big money was in going 'bareback' with clients, which meant having sex without a condom.

I was horrified at the thought of doing it with complete strangers without protection. 'What about HIV? What about STDs?'

'You get yourself checked out every month at the clap clinic.'

'But, there's no cure for HIV.'

'Life's full of risks, Tara.'

That was one I wasn't prepared to take. But I was learning the tricks of the trade.

The clientele at The Ambassador was pretty upmarket – you had to be a member to gain access. Most of them had money and seemed sophisticated, if that's not another contradiction in terms. I mean, you'd imagine men like that could get women anywhere and wouldn't have to use a brothel, but I suppose it was easier than having to pick someone up in a bar or club and then having to book a room in a hotel. Most of them were married and they didn't want a relationship or any complications, just sex. Others wanted the kind of sex they couldn't get from a wife or girlfriend.

I was making money at The Ambassador, but it wasn't great. On average, I'd take home about £400 a week, but that would mean working up to fifty hours and leaving my children with Nicky for long periods. I'd get sore, I'd get tired; I'd get urinary infections and cold sores from being run down. I was also changing as a person and becoming inured to things around me – I could feel the hardness coming on me like a protective covering. Another thing I didn't like was being told what to do – they were always on my case at The Ambassador about cleaning. If we were quiet, we had to clean the parlour and the reception areas and it really annoyed me. I wasn't there to be dusting skirting boards and not getting paid for it. I reckoned there had to be other brothels around, so I started looking in the local papers.

In actual fact, there were lots of them, all in the vicinity of The Ambassador – City Road and Albany Road, the two main streets in the centre of Cardiff. But I couldn't tell which were upmarket and which were rough trade.

In the end I took a chance on an establishment called Lovejoy's on Albany Road. It was just opening up and everything was brand new. I auditioned for the owners, who'd come down from Scotland, in a local café. I was dressed in a business suit with black high heels and bright red lipstick. The men were a lot older than me and I knew I had to sell myself to them and let them see I was a strong, independent woman who could take control, and not be some wilting wallflower.

'Would you like something to eat with your coffee, Tara?'

'Sure, a bacon and egg sandwich … two eggs.'

I got on well with them after that.

They took me round to see the parlour. It had two sitting rooms – one for the clients and the other for the girls – and a kitchen/launderette at the back. It was situated at the back of a large car park – ideal for the clients to discreetly come in the back way. There was a hallway and a glass panel for the receptionist to sit behind, as if she was selling stamps in a post office. Upstairs, there were only three rooms – the master room, the double room and the single room. It wasn't nearly as big as The Ambassador, but it didn't have as many rules and regulations either. You could pretty much do and wear what you wanted, which suited me.

'Do I get the job?'

'Let's go upstairs and give you a test run.'

It looked like I was going to have to perform again to get the job, but I wasn't going to do it for free, like I had with the big farmer at The Ambassador.

I went upstairs with one of them and he didn't have a condom; neither were the showers working yet. I was matter-of-fact.

'I'm on shift in an hour, so I can't get all sweaty.'

'So, what do you recommend, Tara?'

'A handjob. That's all that's on offer today.'

'OK.'

He lay on the bed and I remember how grotesque it all seemed, with my hand going up and down on his penis – up and down, up and down. I didn't want him ejaculating over my suit, so I positioned it to go all over his belly. After a lot of grunting and groaning and me joining in with my own sound effects, Mount Vesuvius erupted. I wiped my hand on the bed.

'That'll be thirty pounds, please.'

He looked at me in surprise, then laughed and paid up.

'You've got the job.'

I left The Ambassador, and my shifts at Lovejoy's started immediately afterwards, with the working name of Natasha. The receptionist was a black women who looked like Whoopi Goldberg: she had a vibrancy about her and a carefree attitude and we hit it off straight away. She took me through to the sitting room to meet the other girls. They ranged from nineteen to mid-thirties and they were a lot friendlier than the women at The Ambassador. The place had a much more relaxed atmosphere but, even so, I had to find out who the alpha females were – who were going to be the busy girls – who were my main competition for clients. Lovejoy's was open 24/7, so they took on as many girls as they could, and we could fit in as many clients as we wanted: the more we serviced, the more money we made. It was a bit all over the place really, but I had more freedom to do what I wanted. You could smoke inside as well; I lived on cans of diet Coke, Red Bull and Regal Blue cigarettes. You had to buy your own condoms at Lovejoy's, but a woman from the Royal Infirmary came round all the parlours giving sex health advice and free condoms, and I was always first in the queue for the freebies.

I really liked working at Lovejoy's. The clients were mostly all right and, if you didn't like the look of someone, you could pass and they'd pick another girl. We had some good laughs with the weird guys. This one man came in with something under his coat that bulged. It was too big to be his penis and he paid for two girls, me and Aneta. I was worried he was one of those crazy prostitute killers and maybe it was a gun or a machete under there. The receptionist patted him down and said it wasn't a weapon.

'It's soft, girls.'

Aneta was Polish and much bigger than me, so I reckoned if it got rough we could deal with him between us – me with my martial arts and her with her thunder thighs. When we got to the room I stood by the door in case I had to make a quick body swerve. Aneta acted all professional and asked him what he wanted. He opened his coat and two pairs of stretch jeans fell out. We looked at each other, confused.

'I want you girls to put them on.'

Mostly they asked us to take our clothes off; this was a novelty.

'Really?'

'Yes.'

It was a real effort getting into the jeans, even for me, as they were skin tight and looked like they'd been spray painted on. Aneta's belly hung out over hers and she looked like a Japanese sumo.

'Now rassel.'

'What?'

'I want you to rassel on the floor.'

He meant 'wrestle'. I was trying not to laugh as Aneta and I rolled around the room. I was on top of her, then she was on top of me, we were doing roly-polys around the floor, all the time trying not to burst into hoots of laughter. Meanwhile, the guy had stripped naked and was masturbating feverishly. It was like some bizarre circus act that went on for half an hour, after which I was exhausted.

It wasn't all fun, of course. One of the girls went bareback, as suggested to me by Gloria at The Ambassador, to make the extra money. She caught chlamydia and had to go to the clap clinic for antibiotics. When the receptionist found out, she got fired; word would go around the other parlours and it would be very difficult for her to get rehired anywhere. I mean, the rumour of an STD in a massage parlour was the kiss of death for that establishment. The clients would go elsewhere and the place would go dark. I wasn't up for the bareback idea in the first place, but that really put me off.

One time no girls turned up for the Sunday shift, except me and the receptionist – and there was no way she was going to turn any tricks.

'Let's just close up, Tara.'

'No, I can work the parlour on my own.'

'I don't think so.'

'I can. If they want me, they'll just have to get in line.'

And so it began. Suddenly there was a rush on – client after client. I was up and down the stairs like a whore's knickers, if you'll pardon the pun. Two guys showed up at once and I made them an offer they couldn't refuse.

'Normally you'd get charged extra for this, but I'll do you both at the same time, or if one of you wants to watch, you'll get a free sex show.'

I ended up doing them both together, riding one and masturbating the other. They ejaculated in unison. Synchronisation. I serviced fifteen men that night and made myself over a thousand pounds.

The council moved me from the terraced house in Glebe Street to a maisonette on Stanwell Street, close to where Daniella and Christopher went to school. The place needed decorating so I decided to look for a loan. Now, don't forget, this was 2002 and the banks were flinging money at everybody. Anybody could get a loan, even a working girl from a brothel, so I thought I'd get a piece of the action. I wore the shortest skirt possible without getting arrested, a check Burberry shirt, cut off at the sleeves, and a pair of knee-length white patent boots – very sixties and very sexy. My hair was cropped short and dyed strawberry-blonde. I had a deep tan and oozed confidence.

The loans guy asked me why I wanted the money and I said for home improvements. I was rubbing my knee against him and fluttering my eyelashes. He asked me about my earnings and I said I was a professional masseuse, with an income of £40,000 per annum. He agreed to loan me £25,000. I asked for a banker's draft, as I needed to pay the builders cash and, sure enough, three days later, I went in and they handed me a big brown envelope full of money. I took it home and hid it in the breadbin. I made myself a big joint and got very stoned – then I couldn't sleep. Thoughts kept running through my head – paranoia, guilt. Next day, I gave the money back to the bank.

'I've been left some money in a will, so I don't need the loan now.'

That night I couldn't sleep again. What had I done? Had I lost my mind? So I went back to the bank the following day.

'The legacy wasn't as much as I thought, so can I have the loan back?'

I didn't tell the bank I was moving and they had no way of finding out where I went. The way I looked at things back then was, if they were stupid enough to fall for the hustle, then they deserved everything they got – especially the ones with money. They had nice comfortable lives, while my children and I were living on the edge. I just did what I thought I had to do, that's all.

The icing on the cake was that my decree absolute from Owen came through. I was a free woman again, I had a new home and a lot of money. I decided to take the children on holiday to Palma Nova in Majorca, while the decorators were tarting up the maisonette.

I didn't go back to Lovejoy's after the holiday, probably because I could never settle anywhere for too long and I always liked to be moving on. I'd heard about this parlour called Josephine's that was smaller than The Ambassador and not as busy as Lovejoy's. It was an opportunity to build up the clientele and I could see myself eventually running the place if I played my cards right. Alright, the parlour was grim and full of a kind of latent despair, but I never looked at anything as a complete write-off – there was always opportunity, if you knew where to find it. I was a good organiser and leader – I could be the alpha female in that place as long as I stayed off alcohol and drugs.

I called the owner and she asked me to come down for an interview. The place looked very dingy from the outside and it was just as dingy on the inside. The carpets and furniture were worn and threadbare, and the television in the sitting room didn't work. There were chairs that didn't match and rickety stairs with no bannister. The rooms looked like the inside of a homeless shelter and the beds dipped in the middle from overuse. The showers were so temperamental you never knew if you'd get scalded or frostbite. The curtains were damp and the bedcoverings looked like they could get up and walk out on their own. I was having second thoughts.

The owner's name was Belle. She was tall and blonde and in her early fifties. She said everything would be getting fixed, people had let her down, stuff was on order, etc. The girls were rough trade too, and I could tell they didn't want me muscling in on their territory. Some were from outside the area, like Newport and Swansea, while some had addiction problems with alcohol and drugs. Others were loud and foul-mouthed and some were reclusive, morose, almost misanthropic. Some had been abused and some were being pimped. None of them were there to make friends, but they were there to make money – just like me.

I decided to give it a shot, mainly because there didn't seem to be any ridiculous rules or regulations. I could always leave if things got too sketchy.

The parlour itself was in a different league to what I was used to. There was no management routine, no security, and the girls did everything for themselves. It was bizarre, rather than disorganised, but fascinating in a weird way that appealed to my kaleidoscopic nature. When I turned up for my first shift, the girls were drinking alcohol openly. This was unheard of for me – the other parlours had strict no-drinking policies, as we had to be at our best for the clients. Here it just looked like a group of half-naked women having a drink and a chat, rather than a professional establishment.

The clientele was as rough as the place itself because Belle didn't care who came through the doors, as long as they could pay. There was no dress code and they could be drunk or stoned – if they had a pulse, Belle let them in. For her it was a matter of quantity, not quality.

I kept a low profile on that first shift, as some of the girls had regulars and I didn't want to tread on their toes. One of the girls working that night was called Gemma – she was withdrawn and plain-looking and the clients didn't pick her. I was making enough money and I felt sorry for her. I always tried to put myself in other people's shoes so I could understand how they felt. The routine with the cash and plastic tube things was fairly slipshod, like the rest of the place, so I offered her £20 from every client, the money I should be giving to Belle, so she'd have something to show at the end of the shift. It meant Belle would still take her percentage of what I had left, but I didn't care. Gemma was really grateful as now she had about £200 in earnings without having to perform for it.

'You mustn't tell anyone, Gemma.'

'I won't.'

'If Belle finds out …'

'I won't tell, Tara.'

But she did.

Belle asked to see me – she was in the kitchen with a new bread-making machine. I mean, baking bread in a massage parlour that was falling to pieces …? Weren't there enough things rising in here without dough as well?

'I have to suspend you, Tara.'

'What for?'

'Did you give Gemma the shift money?'

'Yes, but you didn't lose out. You got your cut from both of us.'

'That's not the point, Tara. If she's not earning, I have to know about it.'

She suspended me for two weeks and I spent all that time with Daniella and Christopher. I wasn't going to go back to Josephine's long-term after that, but other parlours would know I was suspended and I had to clean the slate.

Some weeks later, I noticed there was an increasing level of drugs being taken by the working girls at Josephine's. I went to see Belle.

'If we get a bust, Belle, I'll be arrested and so will you. I have children to think about.'

What I didn't know then was, it was Belle who supplied the girls with ecstasy and cocaine. The next thing I knew, this wild woman called Bianca was coming at me, screeching and calling me a 'grass'.

'I'm gonna tear your hair out, you bitch!'

I stayed calm.

'Shouldn't we step outside first?'

I was fitter than this girl and I knew martial arts. She knew that, too. After a lot of name-calling and posturing, she backed down. But things were not working out as I expected at Josephine's.

The final act in this sordid drama came a couple of nights later. A client came in and asked for 'watersports', which meant he wanted someone to urinate on him. He chose me because I was relatively new and he wanted to try me out. I hadn't done that kind of thing before and didn't want to do it then, either.

Belle twisted my arm. 'You don't have to have sex, Tara. Just squat over him and think of England.'

'It's perverted.'

'I might have to suspend you again.'

It was worth £200 and that's what persuaded me in the end. I took the client to one of the rooms and placed some towels on the floor. He got undressed and lay down and I squatted over his face. All I could see through my legs was him looking up at me and I just couldn't urinate, no matter how hard I tried. He started to get frustrated.

'If you can't do it, find someone who can!'

I didn't want to lose the £200, having come this far.

'Let's play a game.'

'What kind of game?'

'You close your eyes and wait for it.'

I jumped off him and went to the nearest toilet, where one of the other girls was just about to take a pee. I grabbed a bottle from the washstand.

'I need your pee.'

'What are you talking about, Tara?'

'Pee in this bottle … please.'

She did and I quickly ran back to the room.

'Are you ready?'

He was as eager as a kid at Christmas.

'Yes. Yes.'

'Keep your eyes closed and it will all come out.'

He did and I poured the bottle of urine over him, then squatted back down.

'What a gush that was.'

He paid up. Another satisfied customer.

I had almost finished cleaning the room when I heard a commotion downstairs – screaming and shouting and the sound of glass breaking. I rushed down to a scene of carnage. One of the girl's pimps had turned up and was smashing everything in the parlour, including the windows. When she had tried to stop him, he had punched her and she was out cold on the floor. The others were all clucking around like constipated chickens, including Belle, and the clients were running out of the door like fleas off a dead dog.

I got some cold water and flicked it on the girl's face, gently tapping her cheek with my hand till she came to. Then we carried her out to my car and I drove her to hospital. I made sure someone was seeing to her and then I left – I didn't fancy sticking around to explain what had happened.

Josephine's got closed down after that and I was out of a job.

I decided to take some time off.

Chapter 14

Hell's Angel

The maisonette on Stanwell Street was above another maisonette and the people who lived there weren't very welcoming towards me and my children. I did make friends with a woman called Michelle who lived close by and who had children the same age as mine, and who was living on her own, like me. She liked to drink and had a garden, which I didn't, and we used to sit out there with our watermelon-flavour Bacardi Breezers during the early summer evenings of 2003.

Then, one day, I was in a supermarket doing some shopping and I needed something from the top shelf which I couldn't reach. I was stretching up when this muscular arm came over my shoulder and brought the item down for me. I turned around to see a man of about forty, wearing a sleeveless T-shirt, army shorts and heavy biker boots. He was bald and covered in tattoos and looked like a tough guy – the kind of man a woman should avoid. But that was never my way, was it?

'Thank you.'

'You're welcome.'

His accent was English and polite, not what I expected to emerge from such a rough exterior. I could see he worked out, so I thought I'd use that to extract more information.

'Do you train?'

'I used to, over at Cogan leisure centre.'

'Me, too. I did martial arts there.'

'Well then, we're practically friends already.'

I offered him my hand. 'I'm Tara.'

'And I'm Axel. Well, David really … Axel's my Angel name.'

'Angel?'

'As in Hells. Why don't we get caffeined up?'

He seemed educated, well-spoken and articulate, in contrast with his appearance, and that intrigued me. So we went for a coffee and chatted about this and that and exchanged phone numbers.

A few days later I got a call, late in the evening.

'Hey, Tara.'

'Hey.'

'It's me, Axel. Can I come over?'

I didn't like men coming to where I lived with my children. I was hesitant.

'It's late.'

'Just a cup of tea, nothing else.'

I gave him my address and he came over.

We had some tea and talked some more. This time the conversation was deeper. He told me he'd lived in Surrey for most of his life and that accounted for his accent. He'd come to Wales for a festival with his Hells Angels 'chapter' and stayed. He was living with a woman called Jackie, but he didn't love her. I wondered why he felt it necessary to divulge that – that he didn't love her – but I felt he was just being open and transparent, which

I liked. In return, I told him some things about myself, including the fact that I was a working girl – in the biblical sense of the term. That didn't seem to faze him and he went on to say he'd been in prison for attempted murder: a friend of his had crossed the Hells Angels and he was told he had to kill the man. He almost killed the guy, but couldn't go through with it and did the time instead. Afterwards it meant he was forced to leave the chapter or be killed himself.

It sounds ridiculous now, but it seemed as if we were somehow kindred spirits. The sound of his voice mesmerised me. I felt as if this was a man who had kindness inside him, but who could still protect a woman like me from the wild world she was living in.

A few days later Axel was back, telling me he'd finished with Jackie, the woman he was living with but didn't love.

'Why?'

'Because I like you, Tara, and I can't be unfaithful to her.'

Alarm bells started ringing – had he assumed he could move in with me after a night of conversation and a pot of tea?

I didn't need to worry.

'I'm moving in with a friend, until I can get sorted out.'

We began to spend a lot of time together after that. Daniella and Christopher met him and liked him and he took them for days out. He wasn't a drinker and he wasn't into drugs, either, so I felt a sense of security when I was with him. We went training together, out for meals; he even took me to meet some of his family and I could tell they thought a lot of him, which put me even more at ease. Eventually, after a matter of months, we decided to be a matter and he moved into the maisonette with me.

As I said, the neighbours underneath weren't very friendly and they'd bang on their ceiling with a broom handle for the slightest of reasons: if the children were playing, or I had the radio on, or if Michelle came round for a drink. I didn't want trouble with them because it was an introductory tenancy, which meant a trial period for a year. If there were complaints, then I could be kicked out.

Axel loved to cook for us and his meals were amazing. Shortly after he moved in, he was using a food blender and the broom handle banging began.

'What's that noise, Tara?'

'It's the neighbours downstairs. They don't like me.'

His expression changed in front of my eyes. He looked demonic and he began swearing loudly. Then he charged down the stairs and started banging on their door. 'Get out here and I'll kill you!'

I came after him and pulled him away before they called the police. I felt sick to my stomach and had a panic attack, worrying about getting evicted. The same thing happened a few days later, and it started to affect my health: I stopped eating and started having more panic attacks. I lost lots of weight and was constantly on the verge of a nervous breadkown.

That's when I began spending a lot of time at Michelle's – just to get out of the way with the children. One drink would lead to another and Axel would start ringing me to come home, which I usually did.

One evening I didn't get home quickly enough and, when I eventually came through the door, he grabbed me by the throat and pinned me against the wall.

'Are you trying to make a monkey out of me, Tara?'

I couldn't breathe, let alone speak. My lips were turning blue when he finally released me and I fell to the floor, gasping. The next day he was full of apologies and said it was the pressure of living in the maisonette with the hostile neighbours underneath.

Axel stayed really nice to me after that and we decided to get married. This wasn't an impulsive thing, like with Owen. In fact, I don't know who proposed to who or if anyone proposed at all – I think we just discussed it over the course of several weeks and came to a mutual agreement, or perhaps we did it for more security with the tenancy.

Husband number four.

My dress was purple and silver with a long fishtail and Axel's suit was purple and grey. Can you imagine? I ordered limousines with big purple bows on and hired a fancy marquee in the grounds of a hotel for the reception, with a three-course sit-down meal. Axel's speech was endearing, full of wit and charm, and we danced the night away until the early hours. We didn't have a honeymoon and, when we got back home, I was more than a bit tipsy.

'Did you have to drink so much, Tara?'

'What are you talking about?'

'You could barely walk at the end.'

One word led to another and Axel took off his wedding ring and chewed it until it was all mangled up. I threw mine over the balcony of the maisonette and we slept separately that night. Déjà vu – I should have seen the trend, but I was too drunk.

I never really knew what Axel did for a living. He'd go off somewhere and, when he came back, he'd have money. I didn't ask where it came from, but I knew it couldn't be anything legal. We were still getting pressure from the neighbours and I found it hard to relax, which put a strain on the embryonic marriage. This infuriated Axel and I began spending yet more time at Michelle's to keep out of his way, sometimes even sleeping over there with the children.

The final straw was when one of Luther's old enemies moved into the block next door. His name was Matt the Hat because he always wore this ridiculous *Flower Pot Men* headpiece. He met me on the street shortly after he moved in with his gangster girlfriend.

'How's the spleen-less scumbag?'

I went up nose-to-nose with him.

'How's your paedophile father?'

I told Axel about him, but he just said he couldn't afford for the police to be coming round at the moment: I knew it was because he was criminally active, but I thought it was ironic, considering he was the one threatening the neighbours.

'Don't cause any problems, Tara.'

It was Daniella's twelfth birthday in September 2003 and we were all going out to celebrate. When we got down to the street, Matt the Hat's girlfriend was standing there. She sneered at me and called me a slag. This was in front of my children and I was furious, but I decided to ignore her. Even so, it played on my mind all evening. Afterwards, some friends of Axel's came back with us for a drink. As Axel stayed sober, he decided to drive them home later. He warned me on the way out.

'Don't go next door, Tara.'

I nodded my head in agreement but, as soon as they left, I was round there banging on the door and calling her out. This woman had been verbally abusing me for weeks and I'd ignored her. Now she'd insulted me in front of my daughter on her birthday. She'd upset my children and it had been festering in my mind all day. She'd gone too far. We ended up on the green in front of the maisonettes and I got her hair locked round one fist and gave it to her in the face with the other. This woman was a fighter and no pushover, and Matt the Hat was standing on the balcony in his shorts and absurd billycock, cheering her on.

I just started getting the better of her when this fist came flying over her shoulder and caught me square in the eye. It was the Hat, who'd come down to help his girlfriend out.

By the time Axel got back, I was sitting on the ground with a black eye and the place was swarming with police. I got arrested and so did Matt the Hat. We spent the night in the cells, but no charges were brought due to no witness statements being forthcoming.

Axel waited for Matt the Hat a few nights later and put a knife to his throat. 'I'll kill you if you hit Tara again.'

Matt got the message. But the pressure of living there was taking its toll. I was drinking every night to take the edge off my anxiety and taking Valium to get through the days.

Then, one day, Axel disappeared. I tried ringing him but got no answer, tried his friends and family, but no one had seen him. I was worried – Matt the Hat had friends. I contacted Luther to see if he knew anything. Nothing. Days went by and still nothing. I couldn't go to the police because they'd want too much information about Axel and, if he was all right, I might inadvertently drop him in it.

I started drinking even more heavily.

Days turned into weeks. Still nothing. I left the children with Nicky and went down to the docks, to see if I could find him. It was a rough place where the Hells Angels hung out and the women were wild, but I didn't care. I had to find out what had happened to him.

I was trawling around the bars, asking questions and smoking joints to keep my courage up, when this guy came over to me.

'You're gonna get tuned if you keep on, girl.'

Which meant I was going to get beaten up, maybe killed. The atmosphere in this place was charged. They were all smoking crack and you could chew on the tension.

'You better go.'

I took his advice and got in my car and left the area.

On the way home I was pulled over by the police. I wasn't drunk, as I'd only had one glass of wine, but I was stoned from the amount of weed I'd smoked.

'How can I help you, officers?'

'You were swerving all over the road.'

'What's a little swerving between friends?'

'You need to come with us.'

They put me in the back of a van and took me to the station. Smoking marijuana always gave me the munchies and now I was hungry. I gave the desk sergeant a stupid smile.

'Could you run out and get me a chicken sandwich?'

He wasn't amused. They wanted to breathalyse me, but the weed was really kicking in and I started to laugh and couldn't blow into the machine. The more they told me to stop laughing, the more hysterical I became, until I was rolling around on the floor, holding my sides. In the end they stamped a form with 'Failure to Respond'.

I woke up in a cell on a blue vinyl-covered mattress with no pillow. I was dehydrated and had a banging headache. It wasn't funny any more. I'd lose my driving licence and my house. I'd already lost my fourth husband. How could anybody be that careless? Everything was falling to pieces around me.

They charged me with drink driving.

Two months after Axel had disappeared, I was sitting indoors, listening to fireworks going off – it was Bonfire Night – and asking myself what everybody had to be so bloody happy about, when the phone rang.

'Hello.'

'It's me.'

'Axel?! Where are you?'

'Listen, Tara, I'm not coming back to that fascist area. I've found us a place in Splott.'

Splott was one of the roughest areas in Cardiff at that time. It was close to where the street prostitutes worked, and their pimps and other criminals controlled the area. You had to be tough to live there – I was, but my children weren't. I'd tried to shelter them from real hardship and, even when my life was going haywire, I always tried to make theirs as normal as possible.

I put Daniella and Christopher into the car and drove to where he said he'd meet me. When I arrived, he was standing there with open arms, as if he'd just been down the road to get a pint of milk.

'Where have you been, Axel?'

'On business.'

'You could have called me.'

'I couldn't.'

I pursued the matter until it was pointless – I just couldn't get a straight answer from him. I later found out he'd been in hiding because someone was trying to kill him – probably the friend he was sent to kill by the Hells Angels. Now the 'problem' had been solved and he'd found this little bedsit with a mattress, a sofa and a television – nothing else, not even a cooker or a washing machine. There was a tiny communal bathroom down the hall that we had to share with the other tenants of the building.

'You don't expect us to live here, do you?'

'It's just temporary.'

I was glad he was back and I still wanted to be with him, but the children's school was up in Penarth and I was soon to be in court on the drink-driving charge. I had no money and Christmas was on the way – things couldn't get any worse. Or so I thought. I remembered I had a couple of cheque books that the bank had given me with the loan, so I stayed with Axel until they were all used up. I had a guarantee card which I showed when I wrote a cheque. I always made it look very formal and filled out the stub even though I knew it would bounce because there was no money in the account. We ate out or got takeaways and bought new clothes for the children and never went back to the same place twice. But it couldn't last for ever and we were soon back where we started.

Axel knew I worked the parlours and, once the cheques were gone, he brought home a newspaper and said he'd seen ads looking for girls. One of them was Lovejoy's, where I'd worked before, so I rang them and was able to get a shift straight away. Axel didn't seem to mind me working and he said he'd babysit while I was doing it.

So, I started back at Lovejoy's.

At first Axel was fine with it – he'd drive me over there and take the children to school and pick me up afterwards. But it didn't take long for cracks to appear in the facade. I suppose it's difficult to ask your husband to accept that you're going out every day and having sex with other men; I could understand that – but it was his idea in the first place, and I wouldn't have done it without his approval. He'd start arguments for no reason and call me a prostitute, and even worse. Then, one night, as I was coming up the steps to the bedsit, he suddenly opened the door and kicked me back down. Then he emptied my working bag on top of me – all my underwear, shoes, condoms, calling me every name he could think of in front of passers-by.

That's when the love went out of me, and the light of reality came in. It was as if I'd been hypnotised by him, but that kick brought me out of my trance.

After that, I spent as much time in the parlour as possible, working back-to-back shifts, seventy hours a week. I rarely saw the children: they were looked after either by Nicky, my babysitter or Axel, and I was still drinking heavily. Then my case came to court and

I pleaded not guilty. The police said I swerved over a roundabout and barely missed an oncoming car. They made it sound much worse than it actually was and I was found guilty and banned from driving for eighteen months, with a £200 fine.

I was now dependent on Axel for transportation: to get to work, to get the children to school, and shopping – everything. It was hellish. He had complete control over me. If I didn't get home from Lovejoy's when he wanted me to, he'd come down there and play up and threaten to burn the place down. Then, when we got home, he'd become violent. I had black eyes, split lips, footprints on my stomach and gashes on my head. If I fought back, it only made things worse – once he hit me so hard with the back of his hand he knocked me out. And he didn't care who was watching – even the children. I'd cover the bruises with make-up when I was working and dose myself with painkillers. There were times I couldn't let a guy lie on top of me and I'd have to say I'd pulled a muscle or make some other such excuse.

Things finally came to a head on Christmas Eve, 2003. It was awful: we had a bare tree with no decorations and no food because I'd spent all the money I earned at the parlour on presents for Daniella and Christopher. This started an argument which carried on into the following day. The children only had Pot Noodles for Christmas dinner, and it was heart-breaking for me. They didn't complain, as they had their presents, but it just wasn't right.

Between this, the beatings, the drinking and the Valium, my life was spiralling out of control. But I was only half aware of what was happening – I was like a zombie in a twilight world. Then Axel started again:

'Why did you spend all the money on presents, Tara?'

'Why don't *you* earn some instead of poncing off me all the time?'

With that, he started to hit me and, when I fell down, he began kicking me all over. Daniella and Christopher were screaming at him to leave me alone and that distracted him enough for me to get to my feet. I grabbed the keys and bundled the children out and into the car. He came after us.

'If you drive that car, Tara, I'm calling the police.'

Before I could start the engine, he smashed the driver's window in on top of me with a baseball bat – then the windscreen, then the rest of the windows. All with the children inside. He dragged me out of the car and back into the bedsit, with the children coming crying behind.

Next morning, I was cut and bruised and my ribs hurt like hell. When I looked outside, the car Luther had bought for me was all smashed up and Axel was nowhere to be seen. That's when I completely lost it. I began to break everything in the bedsit, which was little enough. The windows and the television were the first things to go, I pulled the curtains down and slashed the mattress with a knife. I'd had enough and I didn't care any more: I wasn't going to make my children live in that hovel any longer. They looked so sad, standing in the midst of all this chaos.

It was time to take them back to the maisonette in Penarth, away from the mad mayhem. It was the only thing to do. First, I went to the hospital to get my injuries checked. I didn't give my real name, but they X-rayed me and said I had two cracked ribs. They asked me if I had anyone at home to look after me, because I needed complete rest to heal. I lied and said I had.

We weren't long back there when Axel came after us, all apologetic as usual and saying how much he loved me and it was me working at the parlour that made him so angry, even though it was his idea in the first place.

'What about my car, Axel? You smashed it up ... and me, also.'

'I'm sorry, Tara. I'll get you another car.'

'Come back when you've got one, then.'

And I slammed the door in his face.

A couple of days later he turned up with an almost new red Proton Saga SV. I didn't know where he got it from and I didn't ask.

'Can I come back now ... please?'

Like a fool, I let him in.

Nobody bothered us back at the maisonette for all of five minutes, then it was back to the broom-banging again. They wanted us out, that was clear. I had a meeting with the housing officer and I took Axel along. I said we were a growing family now and the children needed rooms of their own – we needed something bigger than a two-bedroom maisonette with nasty neighbours. They gave us a three-bedroom house in Splott with a garden, which was close to the town centre. The children would have to change schools, as I couldn't drive now, but Daniella had already moved to a secondary comprehensive and she was having problems with Matt the Hat's daughter there, and Christopher was due to move up after the holidays, so they were both OK about going to a new school. In reality, I wasn't given a choice – it was either accept the house in Splott or be evicted and on the street.

Axel went to the traveller site down Rover Way, where he had some friends, and borrowed an old pick-up truck. He chucked all my furniture and stuff over the balcony into it and covered it over with a tarpaulin. Then off we went in our gypsy wagon with our meagre belongings in the back, to our new home in Splott.

Chapter 15

Fighting on the Streets

When we first drove into Spruce Close in Splott, it looked nice enough, even if it was in a housing estate where they put troublemakers who wouldn't be tolerated anywhere else. The house itself was a different matter. All the walls were painted dark blue and covered in grease stains. It was a three-storey town house, with a small kitchen and large dining room on the ground floor, the living room and main bedroom on the first floor, and the bathroom and two smaller bedrooms on the second floor. There were no carpets or curtains and no appliances of any kind. I didn't know what we were going to do: I'd blown all our money on the wedding and stuff for the children and supporting Axel, and there was nothing left.

Daniella and Christopher got into a local school, which was one of the roughest schools in Cardiff – I didn't know how they were going to cope. The house itself backed onto a big roundabout where street prostitutes worked. It was chaos at night when we were trying to sleep and there was so much noise from the punters pulling up and the pimps shouting and the girls screeching. If they weren't making a commotion round the back, they were doing business out the front, right underneath my daughter's bedroom window. Daniella would come down and tell me about the loud voices in the street and I'd go out there and tell them to move away.

'Or what?'

This girl wouldn't move. She had lipstick smeared all over her face and her eyes glared at me through thick mascara.

'Or I'll move you.'

With that, she tried to hit me. Bad mistake, as I had raging PMT on that particular occasion. I grabbed her hair and kneed her straight in the face. That's when two pimps came out of nowhere and tried to pull me off her, without success. Then she bit me and the shock loosened my grip – the pimps were able to get her away.

You might think I was being a hypocrite, as I was a working girl myself. But I plied my trade in the brothels and didn't bother the general public. It was all behind closed doors and out of sight. That probably won't make it any less squalid to the moralistic, but in my opinion back then, it was professional and not antisocial in any way. In fact, we were performing a service to the public, offering relief to men who might otherwise be roaming the streets raping and ravishing.

After the bite, my finger swelled up like a balloon and I had to go to hospital for a tetanus jab.

It wouldn't be the last of my encounters with the street prostitutes.

I had to start making money fast, so I could get the house into a liveable condition and buy groceries and take care of the children. I considered going back into the parlours, but I wanted a better way, a cleaner way. Having seen how the street girls operated close up and knowing I was just one step above them, I believed there had to be another way to do what I did best. That's when I decided to try an escort agency.

It had already been suggested to me by a client in one of the parlours, who said I was too pretty for a brothel. The first company I tried was called the Bayswater Agency – the name had an exclusive ring to it and conjured up images of five-star hotels in London, with sophisticated, well-spoken men. I knew I could hold my own in that kind of company, as I'd come from a rich family on Alderney and knew how to mix with money, even if I never actually had any.

The owner was called Wylie, a slender man with a mop of tight curly hair. He wore young, fashionable clothes, even though he was in his late forties. I had to go to his big house in a secluded part of the valleys for an interview. I drove there, even though I was banned – I had no choice.

Wylie told me the agency operated throughout the UK, not just in Cardiff, and asked if travelling to meet clients would be a problem for me. I lied and said no. He took pictures of me to go on the agency website and told me I'd get more work if they could see my face.

'Would that be OK, Tara?'

'Sure.'

The house was actually a farm, with acres of land around it, and the place was full of beautiful women. He said the agency's clientele ranged from businessmen to politicians and celebrity types and I'd have to be discreet, as some of those people were in the public eye.

When I worked the parlours, it was a separate charge for each sex act, but this was one set fee for everything. I could arrange the fee with the client, depending on what was required. I had to pay £30 a head to the agency and the rest of the money was mine. The agency's cut was deposited into a bank account at regular intervals and they checked with the client to make sure the 'service' was good. This was ideal for me, as most of the work took place in five-star hotels. I needed to look the part and get a smart, sexy business suit and a decent car. I still had the Proton Saga, but it was hardly appropriate. Driving would be a big problem because of the ban, so I naively decided to use disguises whenever I went out.

It was about this time that I found out that Axel had been previously diagnosed as psychotic. I'd seen him take tablets sometimes, but I never asked what they were for and assumed they were amphetamines or something similar. Then, one evening in the spring of 2004, a street prostitute and a punter were going at it among the communal bins close to the house. I shouted at them.

'Hey, what do you think you're doing?'

'What does it look like?'

Axel came out and spoke to the guy.

'Listen, I haven't got a problem with what you're doing, but not in front of the kids.'

'Your kids should be in bed, mate.'

With that, Axel went into the house and came back out with an iron bar. He smashed the punter's kneecaps and left him screaming on the ground. I called an ambulance, which came and took the man away. The police also came and asked who did it, but the prostitute was gone and no one would say.

Later, I remarked to Axel that he didn't need to be so violent. He'd hurt the man badly and he could have ended up in jail.

'It's my head, Tara, it gets screwed up sometimes. That's why the doc gives me the pills.'

'What pills?'

'The ones I take … olanzapine … amitriptyline … After I was diagnosed.'

'Diagnosed as what?'

'Psychotic.'

The man I had first met was charming and generous. He never swore or drank or took drugs. He was always reading books and was never violent. The man I married turned out to be someone else and now he was telling me he was a psychopath.

One day Christopher came in and said some women outside were swearing and shouting. I asked which women and he said the ones coming out of a campervan that was parked in the entrance to Spruce Close.

A pimp had set his girls up in the camper and they were operating out of it. Axel went down there with a crowbar and threatened to smash the van up if the pimp didn't move it, which he did. But the next day it was back again, so Axel went down again and this time he did smash it up, with the pimp and all his girls screaming inside it. Then he came back and sat in front of the television with his cup of tea, as if nothing had happened. That certainly wasn't normal behaviour.

When I thought about it, I realised he never expressed real remorse for anything he did.

At one time, when I was stressed with anxiety, he wanted me to see a psychiatrist and then tried to have me sectioned – so he could control me even more than he was already. Then, when I tried to stop drinking, he'd bring home alcohol and encourage me to have it – again, that was a control thing.

I'd married someone I didn't know at all: a vile, evil man who brainwashed me to the point of paranoia – so much so that, when we finally parted, I was too scared to change my mobile number for ten years, because he'd told me he'd never leave me.

'I'll kill you first, Tara.'

And I believed he was capable of doing it.

One weekend I suggested we do something different. He immediately turned into Norman Bates.

'You want to do something different? I'll give you something different!'

He drew the curtains, turned the television off, unplugged the landline phone and held me and the children hostage in the living room, making us sit there in the dark.

'How's this for something different?'

I'd had a few vodkas and he was frightening Daniella and Christopher.

'Go and dig up your dead mother, why don't you?'

He had told me once that his mother had been a prostitute when she was alive. I didn't know whether it was true or not, but I was angry, defending my children, trying to usher them upstairs. I wanted to hit back at him for doing this to us.

'She's no better than me. No, actually, she is – she's dead.'

He flung me against the wall so hard I lost my breath. I tried to call the police from my mobile but he grabbed my phone off me and smashed it over my head. Blood spurted out everywhere and I was covered in it. The police turned up, not because I managed to call them, but because a neighbour had. Axel was charged with GBH and sentenced to six months in Swansea prison.

You're probably thinking it was my own fault, that I should never have married him so quickly after meeting him – and you'd be right to think that. I'm making no excuses for the bad decisions I made, except that he beguiled me when I should have known better. I didn't know better, because I was always looking for that elusive closeness and attachment I'd never had. I thought the men I met would bring that sense of belonging with them, but they didn't. I really didn't even know what it was, because I'd never experienced it. So this was the life I was leading, fighting in the street, fighting with Axel, fighting my demons with Valium, which was ravaging me inside. I was also drinking a lot of vodka – it was cheap and it got me where I wanted to go. Quickly.

No matter how bad things became or how low I felt, I still always tried to help people when I could. For instance, a family called Jones lived on the estate and they weren't really cut out for a place like Splott. One day I saw Margaret Jones by her car, looking down at her tyres, which had been slashed. It turned out that this family had been the target of local bullies for about five years and their lives were being made hell on earth. They'd been subjected to awful abuse – windows smashed, stone-throwing, name-calling – and the police had done nothing about it. It upset me and weighed heavily on my mind – I was always for the underdog, having been one myself and knowing what it was like. This bullying wasn't going to stop by just asking or pleading – sometimes you had to fight fire with fire. I asked Margaret and her husband if they wanted my help. They were unsure at first, as they didn't want to bring any more trouble on themselves. They were afraid.

'Trust me, Margaret, I'm your friend. I can promise they'll never bully you again.'

The ringleader was a man called Johnny Black, who used to sell a draw on the corner of the street – he was selling weed to schoolkids, thinking he was something special and up there with the big dogs when, in fact, he was nothing but lowlife. Anyway, Johnny loved his car – a metallic black Fiesta Zetec with a personalised number plate. It was his pride and joy and he was forever polishing it. After making the agreement with the Joneses, I went over one night and threw white gloss paint on it, so it looked like a dappled cow. Next morning, you could have heard Johnny screaming in China. But I wasn't finished. The following night, I paid a couple of Axel's Hells Angel friends to set fire to it. And, while it was burning and Johnny was pulling his hair out and jumping about like a demented flea, I walked over and stood watching, so he knew it was me.

Two months later he moved away and the Jones family had no more trouble. Margaret gave me a huge hug.

'You're an angel, Tara, God sent you to help me.'

Then there was Jade, a young girl of about twelve, Daniella's age, who was always roaming the streets. One day in the summer of 2004 Daniella brought Jade to our house and asked me to look at her hair, which was all knotted. When I checked it, I saw the hair was matted from not being washed. She reminded me of myself, all those years ago, when I was a child – the wild waif of Alderney. When I looked more closely, I noticed that Jade had marks on her neck.

'Where did those marks come from, Jade?'

'My mother attacked me when she was drunk ... I haven't been back.'

'Where have you been sleeping?'

'Bus shelters.'

Jade had brothers and a sister, but their father was gone and their mother was a serious alcoholic, so the children mostly had to fend for themselves. I asked her if she wanted to stay.

'Yes, please.'

I went to her house to tell her mother, but the woman was drunk and shouting abuse, so I left and bought Jade some pyjamas, socks, underwear and toiletries and settled her in. A couple of hours later the police turned up – her mother had reported her missing and wanted her back. I explained what was going on, but it made no difference to the police: they insisted that Jade had to go home. On the way out, I whispered in the girl's ear.

'If anything happens, and I mean anything, you come back. I don't care what time it is.'

I couldn't sleep that night and, at about 2 a.m., I heard a gentle knocking on the door. It was Jade – she was back, with her face marked and patches of her hair pulled out. I took her into bed with me and cuddled her all night.

Next morning I called the police. The same sergeant who had taken Jade away turned up.

'You're not taking her this time, she's not going back there. Look at her face.'

The police went to the mother's house and arrested her, but she was so drunk she couldn't be interviewed.

Jade stayed with me for three months, before Social Services came and took her away. It was so sad when we had to say goodbye. We cried. I gave her my pink McKenzie coat which had a fur collar. She was adopted by a lovely family from Ely and I'm still in contact with her. In fact, I had a text from her recently which said: 'Thank you for helping me when I couldn't help myself. I really do appreciate everything you did.' That was so nice – it reassured me that there is some love in this world.

Experiences like these eventually made me realise my role in life was to help others – it would be the only way I'd find true fulfilment.

But not yet.

With Axel in prison, I had more freedom to be an escort. It was a step up from the brothels, which were a step up from the street. I felt safe with Axel locked up and I was glad I'd finished working in the parlours, at least for a while. I knew I could go back to them if the escorting didn't work out.

Wylie called me with my first job. It was a friend of his called Charlie who always checked out the new girls and I was to meet him at the big house in the valleys – a test run for me, to see if I was fit for it. After the rough customers at Josephine's, I was fit for anything.

I wore sheer black underwear and a wraparound black office dress. I had my supply of condoms, so off I drove to Wylie's place – with no licence.

I knew I had to appear confident, even though I didn't feel it. But I needn't have worried: when I got to the farm, I found this little guy sitting there in a pair of shorts with an air of anticipation. He paid me £180 for an hour and only wanted straight sex. I just wanted the money and to get it over with. Charlie didn't last very long, maybe about a minute, but I still got paid for the hour. It was the quickest money I'd ever made. He was a good friend of Wylie's and had a big ego so, afterwards, I tried to make him feel like he'd had his money's worth by lying and telling him how good he was. I handed over £30 to Wylie and Charlie gave me a good review – I was on the payroll and my escort name was Natasha, like it had been at Lovejoys. Wylie said he'd be in touch with the next client and I should make sure I was available.

As it turned out, I was different from other escort girls because I had a very forceful personality. The clients were used to pliant, eager-to-please women and they got a surprise when I arrived. I was strong-willed and independent and would take the lead instead of waiting for them to do it. I wouldn't do anything extreme; in fact, I was pretty basic in what I offered. My menu was three positions: behind, on top or missionary. That was it. Take it or leave it. No kissing, no extras, no oral, no role-playing and definitely no butt plugs or rabbits or handcuffs or love rings or dildos or strap-ons or swinging from the chandelier. I was never anything special in bed; in fact, most of the time I'd just lie there like a sack of potatoes and turn my head away, just making the right noises until it was over.

I know this is going to sound absolutely ridiculous, but as time went by I found it strange being away from Axel. I knew what he was and how violent he could be, but we had grown together in a weird sort of way. It's difficult to explain and I'm sure only women who have been in this kind of relationship will understand but, over time, he'd isolated me from everyone and now here I was, on my own, down in Splott, without his protection. I was living in a dangerous, turbulent world and he was my safety net. When he went to prison for beating me up, I told myself that Axel and I were over and I hadn't intended having anything further to do with him. In fact, I resolved to get divorced as soon as possible. I certainly didn't intend to go and see him in prison – but in the end I did.

It started with him writing me a letter, which he was very good at – he wrote poetry under the pseudonym of the Magician – telling me I was the love of his life, etc., etc.. Then I phoned him and eventually took the children to visit him.

We caught a train down to Swansea. The visit overwhelmed us, as we'd never been inside a prison before. I regretted bringing Daniella and Christopher, but neither Nicky nor my regular babysitter had been available and I didn't want to leave them with just anyone in Splott. We were searched and sniffer dogs were all over us, then we had to go through interminable doors and barred gates, then wait in a queue while they brought the prisoners up. Axel stuck out like a sore thumb, even in a place like that – a big man with a bald head and piercing blue eyes. There was a play area for the children and I sat opposite him. We didn't speak about what had happened to get him in there and he seemed genuinely happy to see me. The time went quickly and I didn't tell him I was escorting: he was so unpredictable I wasn't sure how he'd react.

Better to leave that until he got out.

Chapter 16

Escorting

Wylie had an extensive client list and they all wanted to meet the new girl. The problem was safety – in the brothels there were always other people about, but with escorting, I was going to places on my own to meet with total strangers.

It would only take one serial killer.

After Charlie, Wylie connected me with this politician who was in his sixties: a nice man who didn't want sex, just company. He picked me up at the bottom of my road and we drove to a restaurant for dinner, which was convenient for me as I was still banned from driving. He was quite stout and had a white beard and his glasses were perched on the end of his nose. We talked about books and music and art and it took me back to my conversations with Elisabeth Beresford when I was a young girl on Alderney. When the meal was over, he paid me and took me home. I can't mention his name for obvious reasons, but he became a regular and he used to call me his number one girl. I actually liked being with him – even though he didn't want sex, he was more 'normal' than many of the Bayswater clients.

Once I got used to it, I became more comfortable with escorting. Most of the men were middle-aged and well-to-do and not a single serial killer amongst them. I was usually hired for an hour and paid well for my time.

One night I got a call from Wylie: he wanted me to meet a girl called Kristina outside the Marriott hotel in Cardiff, because two men who were in town for the rugby wanted some company.

Kristina was wearing trousers with a white blouse. My heart sank, as I always took great pride in my appearance.

'You look like a waitress, honey.'

She was wearing mid-heel sandals and her blouse kept popping open.

'You do know where we are, don't you, Kristina?'

'What d'you mean?'

'It's the Marriott, not some B&B on Newport Road.'

'I know that.'

'Well, sort yourself out and don't scuff your feet when you walk.'

She was taken aback that I'd spoken to her in that tone, but I looked the part and I didn't want to be shown up.

When the hotel room door opened, I was surprised. They were young, good-looking men and not the usual midlife-crisis types. They had a lot of cocaine on the table and plenty of alcohol. They were polite and said we could help ourselves to whatever we wanted, which I declined. I was driving on a ban and the last thing I wanted was to attract unwanted attention from the police. If I was caught, I'd be joining Axel in prison and what would happen to my children then? The men just paid for straight sex and that was fine with me.

Kristina went into the bathroom with one and I got onto the bed with the other. My one had taken a lot of cocaine and drunk a lot as well, and he was taking for ever to come. I just lay there listening to the grunting and groaning and, after an eternity, the hour they paid for was over.

I always tried to be careful telling punters the time was up, because some clients could get angry and want their money back if they hadn't ejaculated. This one was all right about it. I tapped on the bathroom door.

'I'm done, Kristina. See you.'

Then I left. I phoned Wylie and told him everything went fine and I'd deposit his money in the morning.

It wasn't always that easy.

The next client wanted to meet in a hotel in Newport. I asked Wylie for his name and number, so I could give him a call. I liked to hear the sound of their voices on the phone before I met them.

'No name and no number, Tara.'

'Married, eh?'

Wylie gave me a description and told me to meet the man in the hotel bar. He was short and burly, with red hair and freckles, wearing a blue shirt and chinos. He was in his thirties and handsome enough in his own particular way, and I wondered why he needed to hire an escort. He didn't offer me a drink or try to make much conversation – just wanted to get to the room as quickly as possible.

'Give me ten minutes, then come up to room 203.'

I waited, then went up. I knocked on the door. No answer. I knocked again, still no answer. I was beginning to think he didn't like the look of me and had done a body swerve, when he opened the door. I had to blink and look again – he was wearing a pink bra, a leather miniskirt, tights and red high heels.

'Come in.'

I had to compose myself and try not to look as startled as I obviously was. After coming all this way, I wanted his money, but not at any cost. He started speaking in a high-pitched voice, asking me which kind of skirt I preferred – the netball skirt or the school skirt? Then he produced a large strap-on penis and wanted me to be the man and use it on him.

No way!

'Look, I don't specialise in this ...'

His voice returned to normal and he looked deflated. 'Why did Wylie send you, then?'

I didn't know. I had to leave without being paid. I was angry and called my boss. 'Why did you send me, Wylie? You know I'm not into that stuff.'

'I'm sorry, Tara. Look, I have someone else for you, so the night won't be a complete waste.'

'Not another perv, I hope?'

'No, he just wants to take pictures of you in your underwear.'

He gave me a number and I rang this man called George. He said he was married and wanted to pay me £400 to take some pictures. Was this too good to be true? I was wary, especially after the strap-on guy earlier.

We arranged to meet in a pub close to Cardiff prison, where all the lawyers used to drink – I reckoned that should be safe enough. George was a wealthy businessman in his fifties. He had a big black moustache and black hair without any hint of grey, which made me think it was dyed. He wore a check shirt and jeans that were a little too tight, so his belly hung out over the waistband, and old-fashioned boots.

George turned out to be very clever at what he did, but not streetwise at all. He was lonely and his wife was a bit of a tyrant, from the sound of things. After chatting for a while, it was time to talk turkey.

'Where do you want to take the pictures?'

'In my car.'

'Car' was an understatement – it was a huge five-seater off-road Toyota Land Cruiser. We drove to a secluded lay-by and he produced the latest thing in camera equipment. He asked me to strip to my underwear and look seductive.

'I'm not stripping in a car in a lay-by. If the police come, I'll be arrested for indecent exposure.'

'Don't worry, I'll be quick.'

And he was. He took lots of pictures and then paid me the £400.

George was one of those men who wanted to save me from myself. I always told the clients I was single, if they asked, and George wanted to see me again.

'Just call Wylie and arrange it.'

'No, no, Natasha, I'd like to see you privately, not through the agency.'

I didn't want that – it would make things too complicated. He was married and so was I, even though he didn't know it. Axel would be out soon and I didn't want any trouble.

'I'm afraid that's not possible, George.'

He started the engine and we drove back towards town. He was quiet on the way and I could see he was thinking.

'What can I do for you, Natasha?'

'I beg your pardon?'

'I'd like to do something for you … anything you want.'

My old Proton car was getting past its sell-by date and was worn out from all the travelling. I needed to replace it, but couldn't afford to. I thought I'd test his offer.

'You could buy me a new car.'

I didn't expect him to agree.

'Will you meet me privately if I do?'

It was an offer I couldn't refuse.

True to his word, George called me the next day and we arranged to meet at a garage, where I traded in the Proton for an almost-new orange Vauxhall Corsa. It cost George £2,500, but he didn't seem to mind because he had lots of money and that amount was small potatoes to him. I was a bit worried about what he'd expect in return for that kind of generosity, but I really needed the car. You'll probably have guessed by now that I was always one for doing things on the spur of the moment and worrying about the consequences afterwards.

My next client had rented a cottage in the village of Sully, seven miles southeast of Cardiff, and wanted to meet there. He seemed sweet enough on the phone and that put me at ease – I was always wary of the growly ones. As I got out of the car in Sully I could hear this loud guitar music. The guy who opened the cottage door was an American in his forties.

'Hey, come in. I'm just chillin'. You wanna drink? A smoke?'

'No, thanks. Just a diet Coke for me.'

He told me he was a film director and his latest movie had been very successful. Just like my politician, he didn't want sex, just company.

'You're real pretty, Natasha, so why ya doin' this kinda work?'

Another one – I'd heard it so many times.

'Give me a starring role in your next movie, then.'

He just laughed. I don't know whether he was a film director or not, but I sat with him for two hours, watching him get stoned and listening to him play his electric guitar. Easy money.

Life was good when I was escorting. I got to spend lots of time with the children, I wasn't drinking so much and I was earning plenty. The Valium addiction was still bad, but I'd yet to realise it was an addiction.

Axel was due for release in a few days' time and I promised to pick him up. The day before, I drove up to Clifton Street for fish and chips. When I was driving back, I saw this girl in her early twenties standing on the corner all alone. She was tall with long black ringlets and she looked so forlorn. I stopped the car and rolled down the window.

'What's your name, honey?'

'October.'

'Really? Well, you must know how dangerous it is round here.'

'I know.'

I held the car door open for her and was surprised when she got in.

She was a working street girl and I asked her why she wasn't in one of the parlours, where it was safer – she was certainly pretty enough. She said she had fallen pregnant to a punter and her father had thrown her out. She'd had an abortion, but now she was living rough. No parlour would take her on without a fixed address. It was a bad situation.

I brought her home and fed her and gave her some money to stop her having to go out again – even if it was only for that one night. I told her I was a working girl myself, but escorting instead of being on the street corner – not that there was really much difference.

I would have let her stay longer if Axel hadn't been coming home the following day. I was sad about it because, even though I had fights with the street girls for making noise, it broke my heart to hear them being heckled and called names by idiots in passing cars. Next morning I gave her £100 and said I hoped I would see her again.

I never did.

In the years after my encounter with October, I often tried to help the street girls and, when I couldn't get them to give up what they were doing, I'd try to get them into the parlours where at least they'd be warm, and safe from predators and pimps. These girls were beautiful human beings, not sordid objects to be used and abused. It was mostly their addiction to hard drugs that forced them onto the streets in the first place.

It was an hour's drive to Swansea prison. I dropped Daniella and Christopher off at school and got there for about 10 a.m. Axel was already outside waiting. He was wearing a leather jacket, blue jeans and Timberland boots, and he gave me a big bear hug. I was hoping things would be different now that he'd spent some time in prison for hitting me.

'Nice motor, Tara, where did that come from?'

I had to tell him I was working again, but not back in the parlours. I played it down – it was only a few hours a week and the money was great. His reaction was cordial, as I reassured him I didn't want to be with anyone else, it was just a job to me. I didn't tell him about George or how he bought the car for me. We went for breakfast and then spent the next three hours in bed.

Sex with Axel was never that spectacular. He was pretty basic in his needs and nothing really moved the earth for him. I suppose that was due to the psychosis.

I was getting a bit bored with the Bayswater Agency. When you're a new girl, all the clients want to try you out and see what you're made of and you can make a lot of money. After a while, though, you're not a new girl any more and others are coming in, so trade falls off a bit. As well as that, George was asking to see me privately and get the returns on what he had paid for – the orange Vauxhall. He could only escape very rarely and even then not for long, which suited me.

I didn't realise how many escort agencies there were until I started looking seriously. One of them caught my eye: it was called Park Lane Escorts – they all had names of upmarket London areas, as if that made them chic or something. Park Lane Escorts didn't want to interview me and they didn't seem to care what I looked like: the fact that I had experience was enough for them.

After Axel was home for a while, he began thinking how we could make even more money. He drew up a plan: I'd sign up with as many agencies as I could. He'd drive me to the venues and I would get the money from the client and run, without having to perform. They couldn't go to the police and we could hit as many as possible in a night.

I don't know why I agreed to this; eventually, it was bound to go bad because the clients who'd been ripped off would complain to the agencies and I'd get blacklisted.

Axel had an answer for that.

'You can change your name and appearance and sign up as someone else.'

The first victim was in a Travelodge in Bristol. It took us an hour to drive there. The man wanted me for six hours and was willing to pay £1,000. I never went to these rendezvous dressed as a hooker: I always wore a formal business suit, so my children never suspected anything and believed I was a cosmetics salesperson.

I knocked on the door and this average-looking man opened it. His name was Jimmy. I sat on the bed and exposed a bit of leg to get him hot under the collar.

'Do you know the routine, Jimmy?'

'No, not really.'

'Money up front, then I'm all yours for six hours.'

'OK.'

'Oh, and you need to sign this contract.'

I produced a formal-looking document that I'd composed, just to make it look legitimate. Jimmy just wanted to get on with it. He signed and gave me the money.

'Can you pour me a drink, Jimmy?'

'Sure.'

I engaged him in conversation while he was pouring. I needed to find out who he was, whether he was criminally active or had any connections. If he was a gangster I could be in big trouble for what I was about to do. He turned out to be an ordinary man who'd had a big win on the horses.

'And it looks like I've got another winner with you, Natasha.'

'You certainly have, Jimmy. Let me get my equipment from the car.'

'Equipment?'

'Of course. We need to be inventive if we're going to last six hours.'

I could see the excitement in his eyes. Outside, I jumped into the car and told Axel to put his foot down.

Jimmy complained to the agency. I told them he'd been a con-man who'd had no money and wanted to pay me at the end of a six-hour session.

'I wasn't falling for that, so I left. It was a wasted journey.'

The agency apologised to me for the inconvenience. I bought bicycles for the children with the money: pink and purple for Daniella, blue and silver for Christopher. Those bikes were the best presents they'd ever had.

The next one was a contractor who was down from Liverpool and staying in a hotel in Cardiff. I called him and told him I wasn't familiar with the area and could we meet upstairs in the BHS café. He agreed. I entered the St David's Dewi Sant shopping centre and went up the escalator to the café. He was already there and we sat and chatted over a cup of coffee. I always made a point of asking for the money up front, so he handed over £200. I sat there flirting with him, putting him at ease. Then my phone rang, just as I knew it would – it was Axel.

'I'm sorry, I have to take this call. I hope you don't mind?'

I walked around for a minute, just talking randomly into the phone, getting closer to the escalator. Then my high heels were in my hand and I was barefoot down the steps, two at a time. Axel was waiting outside with the car and we sped off. I expected the guy to call the agency to complain, and I had an excuse ready, but he didn't.

It was crazy and reckless, but it was also exciting, and I was hooked on the adrenaline of doing this and getting away with it. But I knew it was just a matter of time before I either got caught by the client and beaten up, or the agencies realised what I was doing and blacklisted me.

The next job was at the Hilton in Cardiff and the client wanted a guy and a girl. Was I up for it? He was willing to pay £500. It was 7 a.m. and Axel didn't want to be my getaway driver, so I went alone. The agency called and said the male escort would be late, so could I just get the ball rolling until he arrived. Perfect. The client was already in a bathrobe when I got there – he said he'd been at a casino all night and now he just wanted to relax.

'Where's the guy?'

'He's just finding a parking space,' I lied. 'He won't be long.'

The money was on a side table by the bed, but I didn't want to just grab it and make a body swerve for the door. I took off my jacket and blouse.

'What's your name?'

'Jake.'

'What are you into, Jake?'

'What about a bit of bondage?'

So I tied him, spread-eagled, to the bed with his socks and tie, then I looked at my mobile.

'My phone's gone dead, he won't know the room number. I'll have to go and meet him.'

I covered his erection with my blouse, put my jacket back on and turned up the collar. Then I discreetly lifted the money and made my exit. It had taken just half an hour. I was even back home in time to take Daniella and Christopher to school.

The agency rang me later that day, after the client managed to free himself and complain. This time they weren't falling for my excuses and I was sacked. I didn't care, as I was still registered with others.

The next call was to a secluded farm over the Severn Bridge in South Gloucestershire. The client was an established actor. Well, Axel and I decided to put on a little performance of our own. The actor paid me up front, then made me a cup of tea. He put on some Johann Strauss and waltzed me around the lounge and into the bedroom. He was just getting down to business when Axel came crashing through the door.

'Where's my wife?'

The actor's expression was one of horror when he saw this big, bald Hells Angel-type coming at him. I got between the two of them and looked all penitent.

'I'm sorry, honey. I'm sorry.'

Axel played along with the charade.

'Is this guy your boyfriend, Natasha?'

'No! She's a hooker ...'

'Are you calling my wife a whore?'

The actor almost defecated on the bed and tried to hide under the sheets. Axel marched me outside and into the car. We laughed all the way home. But I got sacked from that agency as well – and word was getting around that I was ripping clients off.

And there was still the little matter of George, who hadn't been getting his money's worth for the Vauxhall Corsa. His wife was away for the day and he insisted on seeing me in a room he'd booked at the Radisson hotel. Axel wanted to know if I was meeting another client and if I needed him to come with me. I didn't want him to know about George.

'No, I'm just going for a drink with Nicky.'

George and I drank champagne and he took more pictures of me in my underwear. I didn't notice the time passing or how much champagne I was drinking, until I suddenly realised I was more than a bit tipsy.

'I have to go now, George.'

'Can't you stay a bit longer?'

'No, I don't feel well.'

The interior of the hotel was like a maze and George offered to walk me down to the lobby. I was hanging off his arm and giggling and he was in high spirits, too. Then I saw Axel at the reception desk – his face looked grim. He grabbed me and pushed George away, almost knocking him over. As soon as we got outside, he gave me a backhander and split my lip. Blood dripped down onto my stockings. He started kicking me towards the car and punched me a few times.

'Get in the car.'

'No!'

He grabbed me and threw me in onto the passenger seat and drove off at high speed.

I slept with Daniella that night. I'd had enough of this treatment and, next morning, after the children went to school, we had an almighty row. A man from Carpetright was there to lay a new stair carpet and Axel poured a tin of gloss paint all over it. I picked up the carpet layer's hammer and smashed Axel over the head. The workman was terrified and didn't know what to do, but if he hadn't been there, I'm sure Axel would have killed me. Instead, he stormed out of the house, jumping into my car and driving off at speed. What I didn't know was that he'd changed the car's log book into his name.

I was glad to be rid of him and I never wanted to see him again. But Axel wasn't the type to go quietly – he began a campaign of harassment and intimidation. I found out he was living with some of his old Hells Angels friends, not far away, and I began to get really nasty notes from him pushed through my letterbox. Then my internet cable got severed. Nicky even received a threat, saying if she stayed friends with me her house would be burned down with her children inside. A van with blacked-out windows tried to run over me in the street and then parked up outside my house at various times of the day and night. I found out later that Axel was able to get into the house while I was sleeping and that he'd sit there, watching me.

But the thing that annoyed me most was him taking my car. I needed it to work, so I rang him and told him I wanted it back.

'It's not your car any more, Tara.'

'It is, George bought it for me.'

I realised I shouldn't have mentioned that name as soon as it came out of my mouth.

'Who's George?'

Silence.

'Is he the guy you were with at the Radisson?'

I hung up. The next day I went over to where he was living and banged on the door. Axel came out and spat in my face. He got into the car and I ripped the wing mirror off as he tried to drive away. Then I picked up a brick and threw it through the window of the house he was living in. Axel stopped the car. I started to run. He came after me and rugby-tackled me to the ground, then he started to hit me. I tried to cover my head and face with my arms, but he kept on punching. Someone must have called the police because they turned up and pulled him off me. I was in a bad way. Axel pointed to the broken window and said he wanted me charged with criminal damage.

What about what he'd done to me?

We were both arrested and put in separate cells at the police station. I was crying and in a lot of pain – Axel was like a wild man, growling at the police when they tried to go near him. I was released without charge at 6 a.m. the following morning; Axel was detained.

After about two hours' sleep, the police were at my door, requesting a statement from me. I had a cracked rib, a fractured hand, two black eyes, clumps of hair ripped out and lumps and cuts all over my head. The police took photographs and also took a statement from Nicky.

Axel was charged with three counts of GBH and threats to kill. He was bailed, but not allowed to make contact with either me or Nicky.

I didn't hear anything from Axel until the following week. There was a knock on the door. When I opened it, Axel was standing there, in clear violation of the court order.

'Don't forget, Tara, I know where you are.'

Then he turned and walked away. I knew that, even though police patrolled the area, if he wanted to get me, he could.

A couple of days later the phone rang. A strange voice, sounding husky, on the other end of the line.

'I'm gonna throw acid in your face, you slag.'

I called the Crown Prosecution Service and said I wanted to drop the charges against Axel. They wouldn't allow it, saying they'd subpoena me and Nicky if necessary. In the end, though, it didn't matter because Axel went on the run and didn't turn up for trial, so now there was a warrant out for his arrest.

That was the lifestyle which had become normality for me – the dysfunction of daily living.

The only good thing was, I got my car back.

Chapter 17

Blackmail

It took me a while to recover from the beating Axel gave me, and I was now blacklisted by most of the agencies. I needed to make some money and deluded myself that George was my only option – he was infatuated with me and he was very wealthy. I decided to go back to hustling, and George was the obvious target. I didn't really feel anything for him, even though he was always a perfect gentleman and a lot better than most of the men I'd been with.

I started having coffee with him every Thursday, which was when his tyrant wife allowed him out, and planting the seeds of the scam. I had decided to hit him for £20,000, which I knew he could well afford.

I suggested he could leave his wife and I could buy all kinds of erotic underwear to pose for him in and we could have a free life together. At first he didn't bite – how could he leave his family? No, it was better the way it was. But I kept chipping away at him, enticing him, talking about suspenders and babydolls and corsets and crotchless knickers until he couldn't resist it any longer. When I had him worked up into a frenzy, I reminded him of Axel.

'That crazy man at the hotel?'

'Yes, George, he's very dangerous. He thinks he owns me.'

'Oh God …'

'But I can get rid of him for good.'

'How?'

'I can buy my freedom from him.'

In my heart, I didn't think he'd fall for it, it sounded so soap-opera and clichéd, but I suppose if you're not streetwise and you want something bad enough, you'll convince yourself it's genuine.

The following Friday my phone rang – it was George, and he wanted to meet me. He picked me up in his big Land Cruiser and handed me an envelope. There was £500 inside. I was disappointed.

'It's not enough, George. I told you he wants twenty thousand.'

'You misunderstand, Natasha, this is just a deposit. I've set up an express transfer and you'll receive the rest in your bank account on Monday.'

'Oh, George, thank you so much.'

'Let's go and celebrate.'

We went to a pub and George had a Guinness and I had several glasses of wine. I sat on his knee and let him put his hand up my skirt and I hugged him and told him I loved him.

I had to keep him on the hook until the cash cleared on Monday.

We kept in touch by phone over the weekend and I was worried all the time. I never quite deserted the religion I was brought up in at school, or maybe it never totally left me, and I always prayed when I committed a crime and didn't want to get caught.

'Lamb of God, who taketh away the sins of the world, have mercy on me.'

I'm sure lots of people have done that – go to God when things get rough, when there's no one else to turn to.

Monday arrived. I went to the bank and, sure enough, £19,500 had been transferred by banker's draft to the account I'd set up specially. I told them I needed to take it all out to put into a trust fund for my children. Nothing went wrong and the cashier helped me to put the money into a holdall.

When I emerged from the bank, Axel was behind me, wearing a disguise. He grabbed the holdall and looked inside. He'd been stalking me and knew all about the hustle.

'I want in on this, Tara, or I'll blow it for you.'

What could I do?

'I need to get out of the country for a while, Tara. Let's take a trip to Turkey.'

So I booked a holiday for us and the children to Marmaris. Axel had two passports, one in a false name, so it wasn't a problem for him to get in and out of the country in disguise, even though he was a wanted man.

In the meantime, George kept ringing me and I kept putting him off, saying I had a lot of things to sort out and I needed a few more days.

The weather was beautiful when we arrived in Turkey and it was great to be away from the greyness of Splott and the catastrophe of my life there. The resort was called Club Aliza, with swimming pools and water slides and colourful bars and boat rides and safari trips. Daniella and Christopher were ecstatic and money was no constraint. I just spent and spent on them – anything they wanted.

One day I was relaxing on the beach while the children enjoyed the paddle boats. Axel had gone off somewhere and I hoped he wouldn't come back. But he did – and he had my name tattooed on the side of his face, in a Celtic design. It started above his left eyebrow and ended on his cheekbone, just under his left eye – a bit like the boxer, Mike Tyson's.

I was horrified.

'My God, Axel, why have you done that?'

'Because I love you, Tara.'

But it wasn't because he loved me, it was because he wanted to tell the world he owned me. I felt sick.

Later that night we were in one of the bars and got into conversation with a couple called Stephen and Shayla. Shayla was beautiful, with long red hair and green eyes, and she was an escort like me. We had quite a lot to drink and then took the children back to the rooms. Axel fell into a deep sleep, as he wasn't a big drinker, but I stayed awake, listening to the night outside the window. Then I heard a soft tapping on the door.

'Who is it?'

'Shayla.'

She pulled me out into the corridor when I opened up, and kissed me.

'You want to have an adventure, Tara?'

I quickly threw on some clothes and we ran with arms linked down the main thoroughfare, as if we'd just been set free from some dark dungeon. We drank lots of shots and danced on lots of bars and ended up making love on the beach.

I'd been with women before, but Shayla was something different, probably because she was an escort herself. She was sophisticated in a daring kind of way and she understood me, Tara – who I really was. We seemed to have a connection.

Neither of us wanted a complicated, on-going relationship, just a night of wonder and bliss. I wasn't disappointed, it was one of the best times of my life. I never saw Shayla again after that.

We stayed in Turkey for a month and, when we got back to England, I'd spent most of the money I'd hustled from George, with nothing to show for it.

As soon as the flight landed, Axel and I were arguing again. He insisted on driving and he locked the doors and put his foot down. We were travelling at a hundred miles an hour and he said he was going to drive into a wall and kill everybody. The children were traumatised and I told them to keep quiet or none of us would get out of the car alive. Within minutes, Axel had calmed down and slowed down – it was bizarre how he could have these uncontrollable rages and then be so calm afterwards.

Axel was still a wanted man, but now he had this hold over me – he knew I'd hustled George, and he could blackmail me. I had to let him move back in, too, even though, if he was caught in my house, I'd be arrested for harbouring a fugitive. But I had no choice. Axel was a very clever psychopath and could easily manipulate people. He was very plausible and reasonable when he wanted to be and could harm me greatly if he communicated with George or the police, or both, anonymously. My children were always my first concern, even in the midst of the mayhem of my wild and unpredictable life, and I couldn't risk going to prison and losing them.

It wasn't long before I got a call from George, which I was expecting. But I hadn't thought things through – I wasn't bothered about anything except the money and now that was almost gone.

'Natasha, my darling, where have you been?'

I didn't know what to say. I told him I couldn't talk right then and I'd call him back. Axel wanted to know who was on the phone.

'The man I hustled.'

'The one who bought you the car?'

'Yes.'

'How much is he worth?'

'I don't know ... a lot.'

'Let's do him for more.'

I didn't want to, but Axel had the upper hand. Besides, I thought if he implicated himself in the hustle, then he wouldn't be able to have this hold over me.

I called George back. I told him someone had found out about the £20,000 and had kidnapped me and abused me until I handed it over. Now they wanted another £10,000 or they were going to hurt me some more.

'Who are these people, Natasha?'

'Pimps. They see me as their property and you're trying to steal me from them.'

He didn't fall for the story and I didn't blame him.

'Listen, Natasha, I suggest you work it off for them. It shouldn't take you long to earn ten thousand ... a few months, maybe?'

That angered me, even though I had no right to be angry. But it was clear that George saw me as an object, not a real person – the object of his fantasy. I doubted if he ever really intended to leave his family for me but, for the sum of £20,000, he could buy the object of his fantasy, just as he could buy a new car or an extension to his house.

I spoke to Axel before asking George to meet me and he drew up a plan. I chose a quaint little pub called Sophie's Lodge which was off the beaten track and had huge bay windows where people could be seen from the outside. George was happy with that. Thursday was his day off from his wife and we met and sat in one of the bay windows. It was bright inside and dark outside and I pulled George close and kissed him passionately. This took him by surprise, but not as much as when I took his hand and shoved it up my skirt. Out of the corner of my eye, I could just see the silhouette of Axel outside in the grounds, with a camcorder. When he finished filming George and me in a clinch, he panned round for the registration of George's Land Cruiser. Then my phone rang.

'I have enough. Let's go.'

I told George it was an emergency and left quickly.

Back home, Axel and I looked at the 'evidence' – it was conclusive. I also had some of the pictures George took of me in my underwear, which had the PRNU pattern, the fingerprint of a camera.

We burned everything onto a disc and left things to settle for a few days. Then I rang George again. I told him the pimps were dangerous people and if they didn't get their money, there was going to be big trouble.

'They don't know me, Natasha, you'll just have to deal with it.'

'One of them knows you, George.'

'The crazy man at the hotel?'

'Yes.'

'So what?'

The next call George got was from Axel, from a pay-and-throw phone, using his English accent.

'Is that George?'

'Yes.'

'It seems we have a mutual friend, called naughty Natasha.'

There was silence on the other end of the line. Axel carried on.

'I believe you're attempting to steal our goods, George.'

'I don't know what you're talking about.'

'Oh, indeed you do, George. You see, I have pictures of you both together. I'll send a sample.'

Axel texted through a picture of George and me kissing, with his hand up my skirt. Another stunned silence. Axel went in for the kill.

'We don't take kindly to people stealing from us, George. So let's call it ten thousand and you can have the pictures and naughty Natasha.'

Axel hung up and, immediately, my phone started ringing. I didn't answer it for a moment or two, letting George stew. I tried to act concerned, but not surprised, as he told me what had just happened.

'I'm not paying them, Natasha. What if they come back for more?'

Axel had obviously convinced him.

'I told you, George, these are dangerous people. If you don't pay them, they'll put what they have all over the internet.'

'But ... but ...'

'Strange as it may seem to you, George, they have a code of honour. If you pay them they won't come back.'

'Are you sure?'

'I'm positive.'

George paid up. Axel met him in disguise and handed over the 'evidence'.

George rang me again when the exchange was completed.

'It's done, Natasha, I gave them the money.'

'Thank you, George.'

'But we can never meet again ... I'm sorry.'

'I'm sorry too, George.'

Axel considered the £10,000 to be his money, not mine. But at least it freed me from his threats of blackmail. He was still on the run and didn't want to risk being at my house all the time, so he drifted away and I didn't know where he went to. But we were still married and, from time to time, he'd come back. One night Nicky had the children while I went for a drink with some friends. When I came home, Axel was sitting in the house waiting for me. He stood up and kicked me straight in the stomach. I fell backwards and hit my head against the wall. He put his hand over my mouth to muffle my screams while he continued to punch me all over my body. I could feel blood trickling down my face before I passed out.

When I came to, I was tied to a chair. Axel put a bin bag over my head and taped it up around my neck. Very soon the air in the bag ran out and I was suffocating. I was struggling like mad with only moments to live when Nicky came though the door with the children. Daniella screamed and ran to me and ripped the bag off my face, while Nicky rang the police. Axel took off out the door. If I didn't know already, I knew now that this man was going to kill me, sooner rather than later.

I filed for divorce and the papers were served to the house where Axel used to live.

I'd run out of money and a new escort agency opened up in St Fagans – they didn't know about me and they took me on. One of the clients was a man called Gilbert who was even richer than George, and he took a liking to me. He was younger than George and better looking and he became a regular. We went out for meals and to shows and things, just like a regular couple. I cut down on clients so I could spend more time with him because he was a decent, kind man and unlike the usual escort agency punters. He'd split up from his partner, with whom he had two children, and he was looking for something to replace the hole in his life.

Eventually, our relationship blossomed into something bigger than client and escort: he met the children and we went bowling and to the cinema and did the usual kinds of things normal people do. But Gilbert's business was taking him away to Llanelli, almost a hundred miles away, and he wanted me to move there with him and start a fresh life.

It was my opportunity to finally get away from Axel, but I was reluctant. What if something went wrong and I was stuck in a strange place? Things had disintegrated before, many times. In the end, Gilbert signed a contract with me promising to pay me £5,000 if anything went awry between us; that way, I'd have enough money to move back to Cardiff.

Gilbert bought a house in Llanelli for £250,000, which was a lot of money, and we were ready to go there in June 2006. The removal van was outside and all our belongings were being loaded up when Axel turned up. And he was angry.

'What d'you think you're doing, Tara?'

'Leaving. You got the divorce papers, didn't you?'

'I told you, there's only one way you're leaving me.'

'Is that so?'

I'd had a premonition Axel might turn up, like the bad penny he was, so I'd placed Daniella on the lookout. She'd already called the police and we could hear their sirens approaching in the distance. Axel clenched his fist and put it right up into my face. I didn't flinch. He was gone by the time the police arrived and they gave us an escort off the Splott estate.

A new chapter was beginning for my family, or so I hoped. We were off to a little place in West Wales I'd never heard of before. A new life and a new start, as the motorway faded behind us – myself and my two children – with a man I barely knew.

But anything had to be better than what I was leaving behind.

Chapter 18

Sexual Abuse

My new home was in the Swiss Valley area, a suburb in the Llanelli rural districts, where some of the people spoke in the native Welsh language. Llanelli looked like a coal-mining town to me and my heart sank as we drove through it – empty roads and old houses, everything sparse and bare. I wondered how a house could cost a quarter of a million pounds there. But when we reached Swiss Valley, it was like a different world. The place was beautiful, with large houses and a modern shopping centre and a good local comprehensive school. Gilbert's house was newly built, with en-suite bathrooms for each of the four bedrooms and astro-turf covering the back garden. It was a community for professional people – doctors and lawyers and accountants.

As soon as we settled in, neighbours came bearing gifts, like the Magi to the stable in Bethlehem. But, instead of gold, frankincense and myrrh, they bore baskets of fruit, scented candles and potted plants. I could tell they were all very middle-class women who'd led relatively sheltered lives: graduates from Oxbridge with little or no real-life experience. I was surrounded by a group of them and they wanted to know all about me.

'I suppose you could say I'm a desperate housewife.'

I was referring to the American comedy-drama series, which was all the rage at the time.

'And which character are you, Tara?'

'I'm Gabrielle ... you know, the one who's shagging the gardener.'

They were still smiling, but I could see their faces starting to crack with the effort. Gilbert took me to one side.

'We don't speak like that around here, Tara.'

'Don't we?'

The thing about Gilbert was, I could have sex with him when he was paying me as a client, but I couldn't stand him physically as a partner. I did try, I really did, but I wasn't used to nice, I wasn't used to normal. I wasn't used to having his tea on the table at six o'clock when he came in from work. Maybe if he hadn't been a client first and a would-be lover later, I'd have treated him with more deference. But we had nothing in common and there was no emotional connection. I think he was another one who thought he should save me from myself and help turn me into a bourgeois Betty. But I was a nightmare and perhaps that's what attracted these men to me. Perhaps they liked that element of wildness in their safe and predictable lives?

After the initial greeting ritual, it became very obvious that I didn't fit in with the neighbours, either – drinking in the garden and playing loud music. Gilbert said I should be more discreet and I told him to loosen up a little. I made every excuse not to sleep with him. I'd get drunk, I say I was on my period for weeks on end, I'd sleep in Daniella's room – anything. I even crushed up temazepam and put it in his tea to make him drowsy.

Everything about him started to annoy me, even the way he breathed. I just didn't know how to adapt to his version of 'normal'. I'm not saying that was Gilbert's fault – no, it was mine. I was a fish out of water, a square peg, a cuckoo, a misfit, a false note.

After about a month of living with Gilbert in Llanelli, I received a message from Axel. He wanted to know how I was doing in my new life. The message had a threatening, sarcastic ring to it but, to me, it was like a psychic epistle that had seen into my soul, a shaft of light piercing the miasma of mediocrity, a siren voice summoning me home. I told him I was really unhappy.

'Do you want to come back to Cardiff, Tara?'

'There's nowhere to come back to.'

'I could get you a caravan ... temporary, like, until you can get sorted?'

But it would cost money and he had none. I had the contract with Gilbert for £5,000 and that would be enough.

It will probably seem as if I was completely insane, wanting to leave a life of stability and security to go back to the chaos of before. And how could I trust Axel, of all people, the man who said he'd kill me before he'd let me leave him? But I was a thirty-four-year-old who'd never really grown up. I had no real self-esteem and no loving support network. I was a woman who didn't know how to change, who felt homesick for the haphazardness of street life. The routine and rectitude of life with Gilbert was totally alien to me and I wanted to go back to what I knew – to the comforting familiarity of calamity.

Axel messaged me again, asking me to come to Cardiff for a drink, and to bring the children because he was missing them. I told Gilbert I was miserable and things weren't working out the way I had believed they would. I'm sure he already knew, as I was constantly avoiding having sex with him. He asked me if there was someone else. There wasn't – I didn't want to go back living with Axel, but he was helping me escape from this purgatory, so it was the easiest way to convince Gilbert I wanted to go, otherwise he would probably have tried to convince me to stay. So I lied.

'Yes. It's Axel.'

'How can you go back to that crazy man, Tara?'

'I don't know, Gilbert. I don't know!'

'Maybe you're just as crazy as he is.'

'Maybe I am, I can't explain it.'

'Go, then.'

'I need the five thousand we agreed on.'

Gilbert went to stay with his family in Swansea while I sorted myself out. Axel came to visit and stole everything in the house that wasn't bolted down, and I handed over the £5,000 to him, too.

Getting into the car, Axel told me to buy some chicken fillets, as he'd be back in Llanelli in a few hours to cook a curry for me and the children.

'Where are you going?'

'To Cardiff, to get you the caravan.'

Christopher asked if he could go with him and Axel agreed. I went shopping and waited patiently for them to come back. Hours went by and evening came and there was still no sign of Axel or my son. His phone was switched off and I couldn't contact him. I was starting to get really worried. Then I got a call from someone I knew in Splott.

'Where are you, Tara? Christopher's been waiting ages for you.'

'Where's Axel?'

'I don't know. He dropped Christopher off and he hasn't come back.'

Me, the great hustler, had just been hustled. Karma!

When I collected Christopher, I asked him if Axel had said anything to him.

'Yes, Mum, he said, "Tell your mother that's what she gets for trying to leave me."'

I called Gilbert in Swansea and told him I'd had a change of heart and could we give it another go. He said no. So now I was left with nothing – no money and nowhere to live. Not only had I destroyed my own life again, I'd destroyed my children's lives, too. There was no excuse for that kind of selfishness. I was a disaster as a mother – as a human being. All our belongings were in boxes, what little belonged to us, and what Axel hadn't stolen.

I was in a very dark place, and I thought Daniella and Christopher would be better off without me. If I killed myself, Gilbert would let them stay with him and he'd take care of them and bring them up properly.

I went to the supermarket and put a litre of vodka and three packets of paracetamol into my basket. I was crying uncontrollably as I stood in the queue for the checkout. I stumbled out of the shop in a daze and sat in my car with my head on the steering wheel. Then I heard a knock on the window. I looked up, with tears streaming down my face. A woman was standing outside the car, mouthing the words, 'Are you all right?'

I wound the window down.

'I saw you in the shop, *annwyl*. What's wrong?'

'I can't be here any more. I can't do it.'

She came round and sat in the passenger seat. We spoke for a long time and I told her how everything I touched turned to dust and I'd left a trail of disaster after me as I stumbled my way blindly through my completely dysfunctional life. My children needed to be free of me so they could lead proper lives, not this roller-coaster of chaos that I was taking them on. She asked me to wait, sleep on it, that things might seem better in the morning. I doubted it – I'd heard all the clichés before.

'Why don't you came back with me, *annwyl*?'

'Where?'

'To my house.'

'The children ...'

'We can collect them.'

Which is what we did.

Her name was Drinda and she was getting divorced. I fell into a deep sleep at her house and, in the morning, we spoke again. It was as if she'd been sent by God to save me.

I owe her my life.

We stayed with her for three weeks and she helped me find a place to live. There weren't many available houses to rent in Llanelli, but Drinda found one in the local paper – we couldn't stay with her as her place was being sold because of the divorce.

The little house in Pembrey Road was horrible, on a main thoroughfare, with no garden. Inside it had threadbare curtains and peeling wallpaper. The fridge had mildew and the carpet was alive with little insects of some kind that I thought were fleas. The two bedrooms were so tiny we couldn't even get a wardrobe into them, but at least it was a roof over our heads.

You're probably wondering why I didn't go back to Cardiff, if I hated Llanelli so much. Well, first of all, the children were in a good school and they didn't want to go back to Splott. In any event, I'd given up my council house there to go with Gilbert and there was no possibility of the council rehousing me after that. Pride and shame were other factors – I'd messed my life up again and I didn't want people to know. I had to beg for a little money from Gilbert so we'd have something to eat until I could decide how we were going to survive. Drinda also helped us out with supplies of essentials.

Christopher was OK with it all – he was thirteen now and as long as he had a football and a full stomach, he was happy. Daniella was a different matter. She was almost fifteen and appearances were important to her. She'd made friends in Swiss Valley and she hated having to move from Gilbert's big house. She blamed me, and rightly so.

Time passed, but I still couldn't get over what had happened to us – how I'd totally messed up our lives. On top of that, I got an anonymous text message which said: 'Enjoy life while you can' and listed my new address. I knew it was from Axel and it was telling me he was going to come and kill me. A few months earlier, when I was suicidal, I wouldn't have cared, I'd have welcomed it. But now I wanted to live again. I was frightened, as I knew he could get to me if he wanted. I couldn't eat and I weighed less than 100lbs. I started self-harming like I did when I was young on Alderney, and I thought I was having a nervous breakdown.

I needed help.

I'd heard about Women's Aid, a charity that helps victims of domestic violence, from a girl in Swansea market who used to do my nails. So I went along there and told them I needed protection for myself and my children. They were wonderful, and I have nothing but respect and admiration for them to this day. The two ladies who helped me were Bernice and Diane – Bernice made me realise that it's never OK to hit a woman. She played a huge part in my life at that crucial time and changed my views on many things. I told her and Diane about my life and they told me about domestic violence and how it never got better with men like Axel, that it just got worse. They advised me to talk to the police and they arranged for a female detective to meet me at their offices. I told her about Axel, about the times he'd been to jail, even for attempted murder, and now he was on the run with a warrant out for his arrest. She said she'd do some checking.

Sure enough, several days later she came to see me.

'I think, Tara, we'd be better to leave this man where he is. We don't want to open up a can of worms.'

'Can you at least get some officers to warn him away from me?'

'That might be difficult, as we don't know where he is.'

I knew, if I went to Cardiff, I'd be able to locate Axel within a matter of days, but they didn't seem to want to. I was at my wits' end. I could see myself being brutally murdered by this man and no one would listen to me. My relationship with my daughter was suffering as well. She still blamed me for our reduced circumstances and wouldn't speak to me unless she absolutely had to. One evening we had a blazing row and she threw a CD against the wall and broke it. I was angry.

'Don't do that, Daniella!'

'Why? It's just that paedo's.'

I didn't know what she was talking about. Paedo? What paedo? The CD was one of Axel's, that had come with us from Cardiff.

'What do you mean, Daniella?'

Something had come out of her that she hadn't meant to come out. She just stared at me for a moment, then she ran over and clung to my dress, as if she'd reverted to being eight years old. I held her close to me.

'I need to know what happened, Daniella.'

'Nothing, Mum, nothing happened.'

'I won't be angry, I promise.'

I knew she felt the way I did, all those years ago, when I was the black lamb.

'I made it up. I dreamt it. I'm sorry, Mum.'

I didn't want to push her, damage her, but I had to find out if Axel had laid a hand on her. My heart was breaking – something must have happened for her to say what she did. Then again, I tried to tell myself I would have known. I always wondered if my mother knew what Bruno did to me and I told myself I'd know if I was living with a paedophile because I wasn't my mother – or was I?

When Daniella went to sleep that night, I asked Christopher if he'd ever seen or heard anything. He hadn't.

It played on my mind so much it was driving me insane. In the end, I had to report it to the police. Specially trained CID officers came and interviewed Daniella without my knowledge. They took her from school to a location which was specially set up for it, with cameras and recording devices. I don't know why they didn't inform me beforehand; perhaps they didn't want to jeopardise the investigation. Or perhaps they thought she might not have told the truth if I was there.

Daniella did tell the truth: Axel had sexually assaulted her on a number of occasions, beginning when she was only eleven. Once he'd climbed into the bath with her, another time he'd put his hand down her pants while she was sleeping which woke her up, and he'd also masturbated in front of her.

It was the end for me, it really was. It confirmed that I was a bad mother, that I couldn't even protect my children. I was on the verge of crumbling completely, but the anger inside me kept me focused. He could do what he liked to me, but how dare he do that to my daughter!

I wanted to make Axel pay, but I knew he was a very clever and charming man when he decided to be. People believed him and were taken in by him. CID were very helpful, but they needed more than just Daniella's word. It wouldn't be easy: I'd have to be more clever than he was, I'd have to be one step ahead of him. It was also very dangerous because, if he found out what I was doing, he'd almost certainly go through with his promise to kill me.

I bought another phone and texted him, pretending to be Daniella – I was trying to get him to admit what he'd done to her. One text led to another as he began to reply, and I had to use more phones. This might seem strange, but these phones only saved about thirty messages at a time and I was worried in case anything got deleted or destroyed. I had to build up evidence, so the more texts I had the better. I'd make excuses like I lost my phone or it broke, just to keep him from suspecting anything. As well as admitting what he'd done, he was asking her to run away with him and be his girlfriend, even though she was under age. He was explicit about what he wanted to do to her, and a pattern of grooming emerged.

It was difficult to keep myself from driving over to Cardiff, finding him and stabbing him to death, but I kept my composure. When I had enough evidence, I arranged, as Tara, for Axel to take Daniella and Christopher for the weekend, saying they were missing him and wanted to spend some time with him. It was extremely difficult for me to do that, but I knew it was never going to happen … that's what I kept telling myself so I could stay cool enough.

I then went back to CID and gave them the three phones. I told them Axel would be at my house that weekend and they could catch him.

Everything was going to plan: as soon as Axel arrived, I was to tip off the police and he'd be arrested. I sent Christopher swimming so he'd be out of the way in case anything went wrong, but Daniella wanted to stay with me. We sat in the front bedroom, waiting and watching. Time ticked by, but there was no sign of Axel. My mouth was dry and my heart was beating like a metronome on speed. Then my phone pinged with a text – it was from Axel: 'I'm outside.'

I couldn't see him anywhere on the street out front, but the house we lived in backed onto narrow lanes and he'd driven down there so as not to be spotted by police. I ran to stop him coming in the back door, which was unlocked, dialling 999 at the same time. I was too late: Axel had already opened the door and was standing in the kitchen.

I whispered into the phone: 'He's here.'

I was standing there, looking at the man who had abused my daughter and I wanted to kill him, but I knew I had to keep it together until the police arrived, so as not to spook him. One of the first things I noticed was that he'd had the tattoo of my name covered over on his face – now it was a tribal design. It was something to talk about, to keep him occupied until the police arrived, but he started getting impatient. He just wanted to take the children and he became agitated when I said Christopher had gone swimming and wouldn't be going with him, just Daniella.

Suddenly, I could see blue light coming down the lane, but no sirens, and then, after what seemed a lifetime, four CID officers were behind Axel, looking directly at me. I pointed and nodded, to indicate it was him.

They arrested him and charged him with two sexual assaults and threats to kill. He was completely shocked but didn't try to resist arrest. I ran towards him, hoping to sink my nails into him, but the police grabbed me and kept me at bay. Later, when they searched his car, they found a shotgun in the boot.

I knew I had to move. Even though Axel was in custody and wouldn't get bail because he'd absconded the last time, he had many Hells Angel friends and I remembered the threats and harassment I was subjected to the last time he was on a charge and due in court. I was afraid he'd come and find us – I kept seeing him in the town centre, even though it wouldn't be him, just men who looked like him. I had nightmares about him being dead with his eyes open in a coffin, which gave me panic attacks.

In the end, I went back to Women's Aid and explained the situation – it wasn't just me who was at risk this time, it was Daniella as well. If Axel knew where I lived, his friends would know, too. Women's Aid fought my case with the council. They wrote letters of support and came to meetings with me and gave me the encouragement I needed when I felt like giving up.

The new house was well out of the way, in a cul-de-sac. You would drive straight past it if you didn't know it was there. It was lovely, with three bedrooms, an open-plan living room leading into the dining room, a huge kitchen and two big gardens, front and back. Nicky came and helped me move in. The area was very quiet, with lots of elderly residents. Everyone looked out for each other – you could leave your door open and your car unlocked, that's how safe it was. It's the house where I am still living today.

Despite the secureness of the area, Women's Aid still made sure there was a spyhole and hefty security chain on the door, and bolts on the windows. There was a panic alarm straight to the police station and we had to carry personal alarms with us at all times.

Axel was on remand for five months and I knew he was pleading not guilty, so there would be a trial and Daniella would have to give evidence and be cross-examined by hostile defence barristers. I was worried, worried what Axel would say about her and what he'd say about me. Would we be splashed all over the tabloids? The trial date was set for 2 April 2007 and I was trying to be strong, for Daniella's sake. She had to be strong, too. I was back in the gym and I'd stopped drinking, as I knew I had to be focused and in complete control of myself.

Then, the day before the trial, I had a call from Witness Protection.

'Some good news, Tara – Axel has changed his plea to guilty.'

It was a huge relief, but Daniella still wanted to go to court and I took her with me.

I hadn't seen Axel for a long time and he looked slimmer when they brought him up into the court. He also had a black eye, as if he'd been fighting in prison. He looked around and saw us – his face was expressionless. In his summing up, the judge said he'd preyed on a vulnerable single mother and his actions had almost destroyed a family. He commented that the victim of such a crime never really gets over it and the trauma stays with them for life. Axel was sentenced to three years in prison, put on the sex offenders register and prohibited from working with children under the age of eighteen. I had to try to restrain myself in the court and I did it by clasping Daniella's hand tightly.

As Axel was being led away, he turned and winked at us.

Chapter 19

Attempted Suicides

When we left Cardiff Crown Court and drove home, you would think we should have been triumphant and jubilant, but it wasn't like that. There was total silence in the car. Something had been broken between me and Daniella; this thing that had happened was like a wall between us. Daniella was damaged and I could sense she hated me for all the times I had gone back to Axel or taken him into our home again. It was something I couldn't explain to her and, even if I could, she wouldn't have understood. Axel and I were like kindred spirits, despite his violence. We shared highs as well as lows and we went through so much together. He understood me, even if I didn't understand him. We were partners in crime and, even now, even after what he'd done to Daniella, I still had feelings for him and that filled me with shame and guilt. I loved and hated him at the same time, if that's possible. He was my love/hate man – my hate/love man.

Trying to live a normal life after the court case was extremely difficult; but then, my life had never been what you could call 'easy'. Daniella was almost sixteen and I got her a beautiful dress and hired a limousine for her prom night. I used some of the £2,300 criminal injuries compensation – not a lot for a ruined life. But no matter what I did or bought for her, it didn't take the pain away and she began to rebel against me. She was just not in a good place and neither was I. Money was also getting too tight to mention and I knew I'd have to snap out of my self-pity and do something about it very soon. I wanted to go back to escorting, but there wasn't the same demand for such services in remote West Wales as there was in the cities.

One day, after I'd gone for a walk and was sitting on a bench in People's Park, lost in my own thoughts, this man came and sat beside me. I was so deep in my meditation that I didn't even notice him until he spoke.

'*Ceiniog iddyn nhw.*'

'What?'

'Do you speak *Cymraeg*?'

'I speak English.'

'There's nothing wrong with that.'

He offered me a cigarette and I took it, I don't know why. I was sorry as soon as I did.

'You seem to have a lot on your mind, if you don't mind me saying so.'

I wanted him to go away. He was getting on my nerves. Then I noticed what he actually looked like – in his late fifties, with greyish hair and a short white beard. He was wearing corduroy trousers, with a brightly coloured waistcoat and a silk handkerchief cascading from the top pocket of a jacket that was striped like a deckchair. 'How very odd looking,' I thought. He was quite chatty and said his name was Cadwaladyr and that he was a businessman, thinking about setting up some kind of enterprise, but wasn't sure exactly what.

I gathered that he had money and didn't know what to do with it. The hustler in me sat up and took notice.

He gave me a little leer.

'And what do you do ...?'

'Germaline.'

'What an extraordinary name ... Germaline.'

It wasn't. It was the name of an ointment you put on haemorroids, but it was the first thing that came into my head.

'I'm an escort.'

'An escort, eh? And what does that entail?'

'Sleeping with men for money.'

Cadwaladyr almost spat his cigarette across the park.

After I explained the basics of the escort business and how there was so much money to be made, he was hooked. It was just the enterprise he was looking for – he'd set up an agency and, with his business acumen and my experience, it would be a goldmine. Of course, I knew it wouldn't be, because there wasn't the volume of clientele. But I didn't disillusion him.

'What would the terms of this arrangement be?'

'Equal partners in everything, Germaline.'

'Everything?'

'Everything.'

He took me back to his house in Carmarthen, about a half-hour's drive away. It was a beautiful rustic area and the house itself looked idyllic from the outside. It was in a quaint, picturesque cottage, with ivy growing up the walls, set in its own land, amongst little farms and winding country lanes. Inside was a different story. Cadwaladyr kept about a dozen dogs and it looked as if they slept and sat at the table with him. The whole place had a hound-stink about it, with bits of dog food and detritus everywhere. There was no floor covering and dishes were piled up in the huge, old-fashioned sink, with empty cider bottles strewn far and wide.

When I got home, I sat there trying to plan how I could hustle this man. I rang him and invited him for lunch the following day to talk business. I made a beautiful lasagne, with Welsh salad and new potatoes.

During the meal, I mentioned that I might not be able to go into business with him.

'Why not, Germaline?'

I told him I owed a lot of money to some very violent people and I might have to move away to avoid getting hurt by them. He was genuinely concerned.

'How much do you owe?'

'Ten thousand pounds.'

He didn't bat an eyelid, just sat there chewing a mouthful of food, mulling it over in his mind.

'What if I pay off your debt?'

'I couldn't ask you to do that, Cadwaladyr.'

'Think of it as a loan, to be paid back out of your half of the profits.'

Music to my ears.

'Well ... if you put it like that.'

The following morning, he took me down to his bank. By then I was getting a bit worried in case he had connections with the local police or judiciary. He seemed like the type of eccentric who drank cerise gin cocktails with the magistrate at rugby matches.

'Which account would you like it transferred to, Germaline?'

'I'd prefer cash, Cadwaladyr.'

Then I asked him to give me a letter saying the transaction was made of his own free will and he wasn't coerced in any way. The bank manager looked bemused when he signed as a witness. The deal was done.

I used a lot of the money to decorate and furnish the house: I bought a cooker and a fridge freezer, a washing machine and microwave and beds and sofas and a big television.

After I got the cash, I had no further use for Cadwaladyr, but he kept ringing me to know when we'd be getting our first clients.

When the punters didn't materialise, as I knew they wouldn't, he came round to my house with a present. I opened the small package to find a skimpy bra and panties set.

Cadwaladyr was rubbing himself up against me.

'There are other ways to work off the debt, Germaline.'

I pushed him away and told him I had very bad diarrhoea, but I knew he'd be back again. And again. And again. I had to think of a way to get rid of him for good.

I had some builders in doing minor renovations to the house and they were a jolly bunch, game for a laugh and up for anything. I asked them if they'd do me a favour and there would be a good drink in it for them. The next time Cadwaladyr called, I was ready.

'Yes, Cadwaladyr, I have four clients at my house right now.'

'Very good, Germaline, do you need anything from me?'

'I need you to come over.'

'Really?'

Fifteen minutes later, Cadwaladyr turned up in his orange 1970s Mini Clubman Estate, which looked like it had spawned the Trotters' three-wheeler in *Only Fools and Horses*. By the time he came through the door, the four builders were standing in my living room in their boxer shorts.

'I don't understand why you need me here, Germaline.'

'Well, I can't take care of them all together. They're very big boys.'

'I don't understand.'

'You take two and I'll take two.'

Cadwaladyr's complexion turned a shade of pale green I'd never seen before, as two of the burly builders approached him, grinning lewdly.

'If we perform well, they've promised to tell all their friends.'

'I think you may have misunderstood our arrangement, Germaline.'

'No, I don't think so. Equal partners in everything ... isn't that what you said?'

'Yes, but ...'

By now the builders were fondling his testicles and nibbling at his ear.

'Come on, Cadwaladyr, let's get down to business and give these men a good time.'

'I'm sorry, I think I left something on the cooker.'

I've never seen a man of his age move so fast, with the builders shouting after him: 'Oi, come back here!'

Once I was rid of Cadwaladyr, I realised there must be other men like him lurking in this part of West Wales. I began looking in the lonely hearts columns of the local newspapers. I could always tell the ones who were married – their ads would say the same kind of thing: 'Looking for *discreet* fun' or '*No-strings* adult fun.' Once I got one in my sights, I did my homework on him and I only bothered with the men who had money. I'd go out with them and give them the impression I was up for all kinds of sexual adventures to get them to part with their cash, then I'd think up some excuse to get rid of them. I wasn't worried about violence – I'd dealt with tougher men than these rurals and I was fit and able to take care of myself. They wouldn't go to the police and risk a scandal that might get back to their wives, so they usually realised in the end that they'd been hustled and just paid the price for their illicit lust.

And so life went on and I kept numbing the pain in my heart by taking it out on every man I came into contact with. I'd been hurt, but now I was hurting back, and the only way I knew to do that was to take their money away from them, which they seemed to care more about than their wives and children.

Around this time, I met a woman called Laura in the doctors' surgery in Llanelli. My accent was different to the locals' and she asked me where I was from. I was defensive, in case she was fishing for information – I was still wild then, and didn't take kindly to strangers asking me questions out of the blue.

'Why do you want to know?'

'Sounds Cardiff to me.'

'Is that so?'

She chatted on about Cardiff and it turned out we had mutual acquaintances there and that established common ground. She gave me her number in case I ever wanted company, but I didn't call her for a while as I had other things on my mind.

Eventually we got together for a drink and we became friends – tenuous friends, rather than great friends, like I was with Nicky. Laura was a single parent, but she was always dressed well, hair and nails immaculate, and her three children had the best of everything. She drove an expensive car and lived in a lovely home. Her lifestyle was elaborate, she dined out a lot and took nice holidays and never seemed to want for anything – and neither did anyone around her. Laura was nocturnal, you'd rarely see her during daylight hours and she'd only really come alive at night. I could tell she was a handful, like myself – a tough woman. Unlike me, she was also a drug dealer.

When we first got to know each other, she was on a charge for beating up a woman on the street and I went along to the magistrates' court with her, for moral support. I always tried to be there for my friends, if at all possible. She was fined and given an eighteen-month suspended sentence.

I didn't like some of Laura's friends and acquaintances: they were users in more than one sense of the word and generally sly, devious and over-friendly. They were on heroin and were often not with it, slurring their words. They smoked heroin in front of me, which I didn't like so I would leave. I suppose I was judging them in a way, which I shouldn't have, but I never liked heroin and I didn't like the people at the top of the supply chain. I thought they were using Laura and I told her so. But she didn't listen to me and carried on down the path to her destruction, which wouldn't come for another eleven years. But when it did, it was disastrous for her.

Christmas 2007 was coming and, when it arrived, I took Daniella and Christopher away to Butlins in Minehead and spent lots of money on them. I probably overdid it with the physical things, to compensate for my deficiency at the emotional level.

When we got back, I was broke again and I'd run out of marks to hustle. I'd never stopped drinking completely and the wine consumption was creeping up – a bottle a night became two bottles and, when that didn't have the desired affect, I went back to the vodka. In reality, I was still a broken mess. I was in a spiral of despair and loneliness. I'd sit there at night, crying and looking at photos of my wedding to Axel, then reading the reports of what he'd done to Daniella in the *South Wales Echo* and *Take a Break* magazine, until one night I couldn't endure it any more. The children were in the living room and I walked into the kitchen and slashed both my wrists with a knife. Blood spurted everywhere – up the walls and onto the ceiling.

I passed out.

When I came to, I was in the back of a speeding ambulance, sirens blaring, on the way to Prince Philip hospital. They stopped the bleeding and stitched me up and, next morning, a psychiatrist came to evaluate me. They sent someone to take away all the knives from my kitchen, which was rather ridiculous, because I could just buy more. If the children had been younger, they might have tried to take them from me but, as Christopher was fourteen and Daniella was going on sixteen, they didn't deem that to be necessary. I had no further support from the psychiatric team.

It wasn't long after that Daniella followed my example and took an overdose of beta blockers, which I'd been given to help me through the court case. She thought they would stop her heart from beating. Christopher discovered the empty tablet strips in the bathroom and alerted me. We found Daniella slumped against a wall in the garden, almost unconscious. She was rushed to the poisons unit at Singleton hospital in Swansea and kept there for five days. She was put on an antidepressant called citalopram and referred to a counsellor, who discovered that she'd been suffering from nightmares about Axel coming back to take revenge on her for putting him in prison.

Through all this with Daniella and me, Christopher was as strong as a fourteen-year-old boy could be expected to be, under the circumstances. I am desperately sorry for what he had to go through then and I'm extremely proud of him now. He continued to do well at school, which is a miracle in itself. Football was his saviour – his escape from the grotesque world around him. He was always there for me and Daniella and I'll never forget that. When there was nothing else, there was always Christopher. Sometimes I didn't fully appreciate that, but not now – not ever again. He is one of the very few fabulous men I know.

Even though I was mentally disintegrating, I knew I still needed to make money to ensure the children had food on the table and clothes on their backs and a roof over their heads.

As I said before, I'm certain I could have found a job stacking shelves in a supermarket or cleaning somebody's toilet for less than a living wage, while the supermarket owners and the rich people who were too delicate to clean their own toilets exploited me and my time and took long holidays in the Bahamas. But that wasn't me.

I wanted to go back to escorting, legitimately, not scamming the clients as I did with Axel. But there was nothing in Llanelli, so I called Wylie at the Bayswater Agency. I put on an Australian accent and said my name was Alice and I'd just moved to West Wales. He told me to come for interview, just like before.

My appearance had changed a lot since the last time I worked for Wylie. I was much thinner and my hair was dyed black. My address was also different and so was my car. I hoped he wouldn't recognise me. When I got to his farm in the valleys, guess who was waiting to test the merchandise … Charlie.

'Haven't we met before?'

'I don't think so, Bruce.'

'Charlie.'

'Come again?'

'Charlie, not Bruce.'

He lasted less than a minute and I'd earned £180.

Wylie took me on and I was straight with the agency and the clients. I paid my commission and behaved myself – no more body swerving with the cash without performing.

All the work was in the cities, but Daniella and Christopher were old enough to be left on their own. I always provided them with telephone numbers for the police and for friends and neighbours, and there was always somewhere they could go in an emergency.

Wylie had plenty of clients, as usual, and I was offered two jobs on my first night. The first was a man in Carmarthen who wanted me to dress up as Catwoman and hit him with my tail; then I had to go straight to a couple in a hotel in Newport who wanted me to role-play as the guy's secretary. I did the Catwoman job and changed into a secretary outfit on the hard shoulder of the M4, pulling my hair back and putting on a striped shirt, pencil skirt and glasses. The couple wanted to record the session and I was all right with that – I never cared if people saw me on sex sites or social media, as I wasn't ashamed of what I did for a living. It was better than being a slave.

There was a lot of driving involved that night and I didn't get home until after 2 a.m., but I'd earned £500 for two hours actual work, if you didn't count the travelling.

When I got back, Christopher was on his own – no Daniella. I woke my son up.

'Where's Daniella, Christopher?'

'I don't know, Mum. Isn't she in bed?'

I panicked and started ringing everyone I knew – I didn't care what time it was. I finally found her in Fairwater, the place we moved to when we left Coleford Drive in Cardiff. She'd taken a train there to my old friend, Janet. She didn't want to talk to me and didn't want me to come near her. Janet assured me she'd be all right, and I decided a separation might do both of us good.

We wouldn't speak again for a year.

Daniella knew my door was always open. Was it the déjà vu of me and my mother? I didn't want it to be, so

I wrote her a letter every week, telling her I loved her and she was welcome to come back at any time.

I kept working for Wylie's agency but, after Daniella left, something changed inside me and it wasn't the same as before. I'd lost my enthusiasm for the work. I did one or two more jobs, then I called Wylie and told him I was finished. But what else was I going to do? I didn't know anything different. I thought maybe if I went back into the massage parlours that might work. There was one in Swansea called Bunnies, which was much nearer than Cardiff. I suppose I did it because it was the only job where I felt I had some worth. I fitted in. People liked me. It wasn't rule-heavy and the girls were good company, the money was decent and I felt safe.

They took me on and, on my first shift, I met and made friends with a girl called Saskia. She was a nurse from Bristol who did this to support her family back in Jamaica.

I wasn't there long when, one night, this girl from Liverpool who'd been drinking attacked Saskia with a pair of scissors. I got between them and gave the drunk girl a backhander that landed her on the floor. I took the scissors and gave them to the receptionist. The police weren't called and the incident blew over – or so I thought.

I got a phone call from Bunnies.

'We have to let you go, Tara.'

'Why?'

'Because you assaulted one of the girls.'

'She was attacking Saskia with scissors!'

'Nevertheless …'

I hung up. It wouldn't have mattered what I said. It was because the girls involved in the scissors incident were both black and the parlour had a shortage of black girls. They had to make an example of someone and I was the obvious choice. Besides, I wasn't 'fresh meat' any more.

Around this time, I started feeling unwell. My doctor sent me for blood tests. The results showed that I'd entered the peri-menopause, which is the transition period before actually reaching the menopause. It usually occurs in women between the ages of forty and fifty.

I was thirty-seven.

I was very young to be having the symptoms of mad mood swings and stomach pains, raging hormones, hot flushes, night sweats, and irrational thinking and behaviour. I still felt guilty for having the two abortions, and perhaps this was payback for all the wrong things I'd done in my life. They put me on hormone replacement therapy and I had to be seen once a month to have my blood pressure checked.

It was an awful time, which I wouldn't wish on any woman.

Chapter 20

Lesbian Love

I was still drinking heavily when I met a woman called Dawn Sandells at a club in Llanelli. She was a young jazz singer and really different to any woman I'd met before. She smoked cigars and dressed quirkily and spoke with a husky voice. Even though she was eight years younger than me, she was more mature and grounded than I was. I had respect for her, which I didn't have for many people, because she had integrity and hated injustice. She was very straight and never did anything illegal, but she was open-minded and understood what I did and why I did it and she never preached or pontificated. Once she got an audition for *The Voice*, the television talent contest, but she didn't believe in the ethics of the show, so she refused to participate. She still performs in clubs and pubs around the UK and has a few CDs out as well.

We became good friends, but the relationship was chaotic because I was drinking and being a nightmare and she wasn't in the same place as me. She was studying as well as making music and I was affecting her work, turning up at all hours when she needed to be concentrating. I remember once, it was her birthday and

I showed up with a pair of suede boots for her. I threw them at her and explained how I paid for them.

'That one was a wank, and that one was a blow-job.'

She just couldn't handle being with me; I was too much for her. She was trying to make something of herself and I was a disruptive force in her life. But we had some good times and I'd go and watch her play and was really proud of her – she had such a lovely way about her and she was there for me emotionally. We weren't lovers or anything like that, but I wanted more of her time than she could give me.

In November 2008 she organised a huge Thanksgiving dinner for some American musician friends she knew and I went down there drunk and ruined everything by trying to do a strip on top of the table and then falling face-first into the homemade pecan pie. Dawn tried to stop me from driving home, but I wouldn't listen to her.

Next day, I texted and apologised, but she didn't reply and I knew I'd gone too far. I went to see her and she was angry. She told me we couldn't be friends any more. It was too chaotic. It had to end. I'll never forget the words she said to me.

'You're wasting your life, Tara. You're beautiful and clever and you're wasting your life.'

It just confirmed what everyone who came into contact with me had already said:

'Tara is a write-off.'

'She'll never make anything of her life.'

I always hated being told the truth by people. I despised them for telling me what I didn't want to hear, but it was different coming from her. Dawn's words pierced my heart like no one else's had ever done before. It was a wake-up call and I decided to take notice.

I told myself it was time to change.

I gave up the brothel, got a job at a local health club and enrolled in Swansea University. I blagged my way through the interview and was given a grant and accepted onto a Humanities BA (Hons) degree course. My life was far from together, but I liked being able to tell people I was going to be studying at university. It gave me a sense of being somebody – as if I was embarking on a new journey, just as I did when I got on that little yellow G-Joey Trislander at Alderney Airport, over twenty years earlier.

And then I found out that Daniella had married Janet's son, Peter, without telling me.

The boy was in jail for thieving and the ceremony was carried out in Parc Prison, Bridgend. I was devastated – just when I'd resolved to put my own life in order, she was destroying hers. As time went on, I heard she'd been back over to Llanelli to visit friends, but hadn't come to see me. All I could do was keep writing to her and hope that she'd write back one day. Was that the way my mother felt about me?

Life was a bit of a blur: I was at university, not having a clue what I was doing, and working in the health club gym in the evenings, doing induction courses for people who'd just signed up – assessing them and showing them how to use the equipment, as well as advising on nutrition. I'd decided I was finished with the escorting and brothels for good and I'd even stopped drinking heavily.

One evening, this amazing-looking Japanese woman came into the club. Her name was Kazumi and she had short, jet-black hair, olive skin and the most amazing green eyes. She was a sensei, which means instructor, in jiu-jitsu, and she worked as a bouncer in Swansea town centre. She was forty-three years old and she asked if anyone wanted a shiatsu. I was curious.

'What's that?'

'Japanese finger massage.'

'Sounds intriguing.'

Everybody laughed. I stood up and walked over to her.

'I'm game if you are.'

She explained, as she pressed into my neck, back, arms and legs, that shiatsu translated as 'finger pressure' and it aimed to restore alignment along the body's energetic lines. We exchanged phone numbers afterwards.

It was late summer 2009 and one morning, out of the blue, I had a call from Kazumi. It was 7 a.m.

'I'm walking my dogs on the beach. Would you like to join me?'

I did and, later that day, she invited me to a boxing match in Newport. I can't remember who was on the bill, but it was a promotion for Ricky Hatton, the former light-welterweight world champion. Kazumi wanted the celebrity boxer to sign a book for her, but she couldn't get close to him because he was surrounded by security. I took it from her and flounced through the throng for the signature. Afterwards, we had some drinks together and she asked if I wanted to come round to her house to see her trophies. I agreed. The trophies were upstairs in her bedroom and she brushed my hand and looked at me in a way I'd seen once before – from Shayla on the beach in Turkey that night.

We kissed and it was both sensitive and passionate, and I was consumed by the philtre at its essence. It felt so good to be with her.

It felt right.

We became lovers that night.

Kazumi and I spent evenings together working out in the gym, or watching movies, or conversing over a drink, or making love. She met Christopher and he liked her, although he just saw her as his mother's female friend and not my lover.

In the beginning, it was wonderful – magical. We got on really well, we had fun together and forgot about the brute swagger of the world around us. But Kazumi could be jealous and hated anyone chatting to me, especially men. She hated men and the fact that I'd been with so many of them made her feel insecure. One night we were having a drink in a club when the barman tried to chat me up. Kazumi threatened to knock him out, so we had to leave.

We wanted our relationship to be out in the open, and the first person I had to tell was Christopher. I'd come clean to my children about some of the work I'd done previously in the sex industry and they accepted that I always tried to do what was best for them. If they could accept that, I was sure they could accept Kazumi. He was playing on his Xbox.

'I've met someone, Christopher.'

He didn't even hear me, so I stood in front of him.

'I've met someone I want to be with.'

'Not another Axel, I hope?'

'It's a woman … Kazumi.'

'God, Mum, what're my friends gonna say?'

He wasn't happy at first, but Kazumi was good to him. She bought him lots of presents and took him to the boxing gym so, as she and I began to see each other openly, he gradually got used to it.

One night we were both at my house relaxing when a text came through on my mobile. I didn't recognise the number. It read: 'Leave me alone. Stop writing to me.' It took me a moment or two to think who it might be from, then I realised – it could only be Daniella. I called the number immediately. Her voice was fragile on the other end.

'Why are you writing to me, Mum?'

'Because I want you to know I'm sorry for everything and I love you.'

She told me she was back in touch with her father and it shocked me – Michael hadn't bothered with her properly since she was a baby. But I didn't want to upset her and was prepared to go along with anything that made her happy.

'As long as you're happy, Daniella.'

Silence on the line.

'Are you happy, Daniella?'

She started to cry, then whispered that she'd been taking speed and felt bad about it. I was shaken: I knew Daniella would never take drugs of her own accord. My surprise gave way to anger.

'Is Janet there?'

'Please, Mum, don't go mad.'

'I'm coming to get you.'

'No, no ... please don't.'

Daniella knew if I came to Cardiff, there would be a major fight with Janet.

I'd been drinking wine with Kazumi, so I got Michael's number from Daniella and told him to go and get her. He was surprised to hear from me after all this time, but he agreed to do as I asked. Then I rang Cardiff police and told them my daughter was being held against her will and I was worried for her safety – just in case Michael ran into trouble from Janet or her family. Her original text to me was a cry for help, but she couldn't say too much because Janet was watching her. Daniella said she didn't want to stay with her father – he'd had another two children with his new partner and he was really a stranger to her. I told him to bring her home to me.

I was so happy to have Daniella back, but I knew I had to tread carefully with her, as she was still very vulnerable. I told her how much I missed her and loved her and I'd never, ever turn my back on her. The next step was to get rid of her husband, which wasn't going to be easy. Daniella was in two minds about it: they'd been close childhood friends and she believed he loved her. I felt I had to be firm, rather than faint hearted and I told her I didn't want to be involved with Janet's family – they were trouble and I didn't need that in my life just then. I couldn't have Peter coming over to Llanelli when he got out of prison, looking for her – he was too dangerous. The whole family were dangerous and I didn't want Christopher exposed to that, so she'd have to make up her mind what she wanted to do.

When it was time to introduce Daniella to Kazumi, we all went out for a meal together. I was worried how my daughter would take the relationship, but I think she was relieved that I was with a woman and not another man. Kazumi was good with her, gentle with her. We both assured Daniella that we'd get her a divorce from Peter before he got out of prison, if that was what she wanted. She agreed it was the best thing to do. Kazumi came with me to Cardiff to collect Daniella's belongings from Janet. We expected trouble, but there wasn't any.

Janet knew it was over, and so was our friendship.

I had my daughter back home, I had my son, I was in a steady relationship, I'd stopped drinking, and I was taking a degree at university. Life was coming together for me. At last!

Kazumi was really something else – I thought sex on the beach with Shayla was the ultimate and it was, for one night. But sex with Kazumi was more long-term. We were very sensual together and we didn't need drink or drugs to enhance the stimulation.

I was nervous at first, even questioning myself – looking at her arched back and listening to her gasps of pleasure. Kazumi's body was perfect and I would kiss it all over. She'd lean on me and grind against my hip, which turned me on immensely and all I wanted was her inside me. Kazumi was the only person who ever brought me to orgasm. She would slip her fingers into my vagina while kissing me and it was done softly and sensuously – not harshly or roughly, as I'd experienced with men. When I was moist, she'd put her head between my legs and her tongue was like a velvet butterfly brushing my clitoris until I reached orgasm. I would then assume the 69 position and do the same for her.

We were not just having sex – we were making love.

Afterwards, we'd sleep for a while and then start again and it would go on like that all night long. When Kazumi came to orgasm, her knees would tremble and she'd grip my hand as I gripped her thighs. We experimented and role-played and used pillows to arch each others' backs. She would pinch my nipples, which I normally didn't like, except the way she did it, and I would bite her lip. We'd scissor a lot, which was lying on our sides, grinding and rubbing pelvises until orgasm, or spit-swop, which turned both of us on. I loved her breasts – they were big and firm, and her dominant personality excited me, as I gave in to the voluptuous dolce vita.

She'd hug me in bed and I felt so safe with her. We'd whisper things to each other that nobody else needed to know; I felt I didn't have a care in the world when I was with her. We never used vibrators, as Kazumi hated anything to do with the penis and she just wouldn't have it. That didn't bother me – we didn't need a vibrator to get us where we wanted to go. She liked me to wear an oversized shirt with no underwear and I liked everything she did. When our emotions were in tune, as they usually were, it was truly intoxicating.

You don't have to be a lesbian to appreciate what I call the divineness of duality, and I would recommend it to any woman.

That year, 2009, was turning out to be a half-decent year. I was managing at university and Daniella's divorce was going through unhindered. We were living in a nice area and I was in a beautiful relationship. I began to think how lucky I was and wonder how I could help people less fortunate than myself. I'd tried to do what I could for Jade and October and other girls in the past, and it seemed like a worthwhile vocation to me.

Christopher's sixteenth birthday arrived and he had a limousine just like Daniella had for her prom. I organised a disco for him at Bar Luna on Market Street and all his friends came back to our house afterwards. One of them was an Asian boy called Maali – his father had been shot in some war and his mother had mental health problems. I don't know if he just had a little too much to drink or what but, later in the evening, Maali got upset. I asked him what was wrong and he told me his uncle beat him for not being a good Muslim. Maali stayed the night and, next morning, I called his uncle.

'Manzur?'

'Yes.'

'You need to stop beating your nephew.'

'Who is this?'

'The person who will report you if you don't stop.'

Maali stayed with us for a week and he's a family friend to this day.

Benny was another of Christopher's friends. His stepfather was violent and had headbutted the boy. When I found out about it, I couldn't let it go, but I didn't want to get directly involved because of Christopher. I tracked down Benny's biological father and pretended to be the television host Yvette Fielding over the phone. I said I'd been doing youth work with a team in Llanelli and the attack had come to my attention. Benny's father had words with the stepdad and it didn't happen again.

You can say I'm just an interferer, sticking my nose where it's not wanted, but I hate bullies and I've always tried to stand up for the oppressed, having been one myself. I've always had a social conscience, even if I didn't have any scruples about hustling predatory men. I think it was probably at this point in my life that I seriously started to become the altruistic woman I've evolved into today.

And it wasn't just Christopher's friends. Daniella knew a girl called Pippi whose early life was similar to my own. She'd been serially raped by her uncle, who was serving sixteen years in prison for abusing her. One night, all the girls were going out, except for Pippi. When I asked why, she said all her clothes were in the wash. I knew that wasn't the truth, so I took her into town and bought her a beautiful emerald-green dress. Pippi spent a lot of time at our home after that and we'd chat about whatever was troubling her and I'd let her know I'd always be there for her, which I have been. I always tried to make her feel special and it's been wonderful to watch her grow into a remarkable young woman who's happily married now, with beautiful children.

But, as always, things were too good to be genuine.

Life with Kazumi was great for a few months but, as the year went on, I noticed she was becoming increasingly possessive. She wanted to know who was calling me and who I was calling. I could only go to the gym with her and not on my own. She didn't like any of the clothes I wore and if I smiled at a man on the street or in a bar she'd fly into a rage. She even started turning up at university to see who I was associating with. I was walking on eggshells all the time and the cracks were beginning to show. Once I was out shopping when she phoned me.

'Where are you?'

'At the supermarket.'

She hung up straight away. I knew she was in a mood, so I left the shop and drove home too fast. I kerbed the car and went into a lamppost and banged my head. As I pulled up, I saw Kazumi's Jeep outside my house. I went in but couldn't see her anywhere. When I went upstairs, she was sitting on the bed, facing the door, as if she'd been waiting for me. She could see the state I was in, but said nothing.

'I crashed the car trying to get here, Kazumi.'

She stood up and left without a word.

This couldn't go on: I had to concentrate on my university course and I had Daniella to look after, who was prone to depression and was staying in her room a lot. I didn't know how much more of these head games I could take. It was deteriorating into a relationship of breaking up and making up, as if we were a couple of petulant teenagers.

Christmas was coming and it's always the most magical time of the year for me. I loved to make a fuss for the children and that year I decided to cook a traditional dinner for Christmas Day – turkey and all the trimmings, as they say in the suburbs. I laid the table and was really excited and looking forward to 2010, a new and promising decade. I wore a black lace dress, even though I was conscious of how Kazumi reacted to my clothes, but it was only going to be the four of us and we weren't planning to go out anywhere afterwards. I wanted to look nice for her and maybe change the emotional direction we were heading in.

Kazumi arrived at midday with presents; her expression changed as soon as she saw my dress. I knew Christmas Day was already ruined. She sat at the table in silence during the meal, which created an atmosphere you could cut with a cruel word. Daniella and Christopher offered to do the dishes, just to get out of the room and away from us.

Then Christopher came back and said he thought we might have a mouse in one of the cupboards. I went and had a look, but I couldn't see anything.

Kazumi came up behind me.

'Let me see.'

I had a lot of things stored in that cupboard and she began to empty them all out. That's when she found a condom – not a used condom, one still sealed in its packet and out of date. She held it up like an exhibit in a murder trial. I tried to explain.

'It probably fell out of one of my working bags ... I kept them in there.'

Kazumi knew everything about my past, how I'd worked in pole-dancing clubs and massage parlours and brothels and for escort agencies. I'd been honest and kept nothing back when we began our relationship.

She threw the condom at me and stormed out of the house. I went after her and watched her drive away through the winter snow, the magic and mystical element of the day dissolving into the tears that ran down my face.

I was up early on Boxing Day, sending her a million texts. She didn't reply to any of them.

Christopher came in to console me.

'It could have been anything, Mum. She wanted an argument and she would've found some way to start it.'

He was right. I'd done nothing wrong and, as far as I was concerned, Kazumi and I were over. I'd have to face 2010 on my own.

Two days later I had a text from Kazumi, asking if I wanted to make up – again. I said no. She sent another message, asking for her Christmas presents back. Normally, I'd have bagged them up and dumped them in her front garden, but I decided it would be unfair to take away what she'd given to Daniella and Christopher. My Christmas was ruined, but I wasn't going to let her ruin my children's as well.

I sent her a message:

'You can't have the presents back, Kazumi. I'm keeping them in exchange for all the free sex you've had from me. I could have charged you, as you clearly consider me to be a whore.'

She didn't reply and I never saw Kazumi again. I heard later that she married a girl called Jacinta and I truly wish them both health and happiness together.

Chapter 21

Kicking the Valium

I was halfway through my university course and my grades were holding up, even though I was fairly clueless to begin with. But I was determined to succeed – I'd failed at everything else, but not this. University was a new route for me, one of the many in my life. I'd always been restless, looking for something else, something over the rainbow, and never finding it. I'd stopped doing any kind of sex work and life was much more sedate and simple. My children were growing up and doing their own thing and I was on my own a lot of the time.

This actually proved to be a problem. I was lonely. All I ever wanted was to be loved and, due to reasons of convention, I always thought it would be a man who would fulfil me and make me whole. Now, the peace and soft-pedal were killing me, because I had too much time on my hands for soul-searching and regret.

I began to think about my parents and how I'd always missed having a role model in my life – someone to guide me and not let me grow wild and feral, which I did.

In 2011, someone from Ireland wrote to tell me my father had died of prostate cancer. Inside the white envelope was a smaller, brown envelope and inside that was a wallet with a silver crucifix and a lock of my baby hair, along with a dusty old piece of paper with the year '1974' written on it.

Even though the reality of my father had turned out to be a big disappointment, I cried myself to sleep that night, with the crucifix and little lock of hair under my pillow.

When I finally realised that nobody was going to present me with the emotional stability I'd been looking for all my life, I decided to find it for myself. The first place I looked to was a spiritualist church, where they said they could communicate with the dead. I lit a candle for my father and asked him why he wasn't a better man. He didn't answer. The lack of response didn't put me off and I kept going there, hoping some day I'd be given a sign. I lit candles with everyone else and listened to the sermons and tried to see the angels they said were all around me, protecting me. 'Where were the angels when I was a little girl?' I asked – but got no answer. I felt there was something missing from that church, something other than the mediums who began the services with opening prayers and hymns and told me I had a spirit to guide me and show me signs. If I did, I wasn't able to see it and, in the end, I became disillusioned and left to find myself somewhere else.

That's when I came into contact with Rahil, a Muslim man I heard debating outside the Madina mosque in Cardiff, when I was passing by with my friend Laura. I'd gone over to Cardiff to buy something for Daniella, and I stopped to listen. Rahil was huge in stature and confidence, with a long beard, and it seemed he might have answers to the many questions inside my soul.

Laura wanted to move on and was tugging at my arm.

'I want to listen, Laura.'

'It's just rubbish, Tara.'

Then Rahil's eyes met mine and he stopped speaking to the little group of men and boys surrounding him. The expression on his face was half inquisitive and half hostile. He handed me a card, just as Laura finally managed to drag me away.

I looked at the number on that card for a week before calling him. We spoke for a while on the phone and he said he'd be at the Islamic Centre in Llanelli in a few days' time, and I agreed to meet him for a coffee.

When we met, we really had nothing in common except training in gyms. But he intrigued me: he told me about Islam and how women were respected and valued in his religion, contrary to popular Christian belief. He even quoted from the Quran: 'Respect the women and treat them well, because women are the twin halves of men.' I thought this might be it – what I was searching for. We started dating and he didn't try to have sex with me, which was a welcome change from most other men.

I began reading the Quran and I liked the way Muslim women were taught to have respect for their virtue. Their ethos and character development were mostly a process of dealing with emotions – how to engender positive emotions and suppress negative emotions. It all seemed right for me, so Rahil and I secretly arranged to be married in the Swansea mosque. He paid me £4,000 as a dowry, which was the tradition.

On the day of the wedding, I wore a full-length black and silver *lehenga* with studded sandals and a black hijab.

Christopher was in the house with his girlfriend when I came downstairs. He looked at me as if I'd completely lost my mind.

'What are you doing, Mum?'

'I'm getting married.'

Rahil and I were married in front of two witnesses that he'd arranged. We recited the marriage vows in Arabic.

'I have given myself to you.'

'I have accepted you.'

Then, after a short sermon, we signed a contract called a *nikah* for the imam and were given a marriage certificate to prove that we were legally married in the eyes of the law – I didn't realise that was Sharia law, not British law. Afterwards, we went for a meal to a halal restaurant and, that night, we had sex for the first time.

For me, it was mechanical and robotic after Kazumi. He was rough and didn't seem to be interested in pleasing me, just himself. He could have been any one of the clients I'd had sex with for money and it meant nothing to me. Of course, it was bound to be different after Kazumi – I don't think any man could have replaced her sexually. The only reason I was with Rahil was because I was lost and I thought Islam might provide me with the signs my spirit guide hadn't.

Things worked fine for a short while and Rahil even bought me a new family car – a dark blue Fiat Galaxy. But we didn't live together all the time – Rahil had a house in Cardiff and I never went there, simply because I had no desire to. And, eventually, it was the same old story: he was charming when I met him but, after we were married, he began to control me. You'd think I'd have learned by now, wouldn't you? He'd grab my arm and pull me to him if I strayed too far when we were walking. He constantly corrected what I said and got angry if I swore, which I was wont to do at times. I wasn't allowed to wear any make-up or reveal any part of my flesh, especially when other men were present – a complete contrariety for an ex-pole dancer, brothel girl and escort. High heels were a taboo because he said the clip-clopping sound they made attracted lechers. I had to sit at the table with him while he ate, and he'd be up very early in the mornings chanting prayers in a long white *thoub*. It was really beginning to get on my nerves. Everything was so serious all the time, I couldn't have a laugh or let go, even for a single second.

When he wanted to marry off Daniella to one of his cousins back home in Syria, that was the final straw.

I began to have trouble breathing – I'd given up drinking and smoking, so I wondered what could be causing the problem. The only thing I was still taking was the Valium and, when I thought about it, I realised how dependant I was on the drug. I decided to try to give up taking the tablet that had been such a regular part of my life for so long and see what would happen. Rahil had been in Cardiff and he came to my house later in the evening. I was in some distress and I thought I could share my attempt at rehabilitation with him – he was my husband after all. I thought he'd understand and be able to offer me help and encouragement. I was mistaken.

'You won't do it. You're just a junkie!'

'I can't believe you said that, Rahil.'

'It's what you are.'

'Get out of my house!'

He swore at me before leaving – apparently, expletives were all right for him to use, but not for me.

I wanted him out of my life but I was told by the imams that he had to divorce me, I couldn't divorce him. I know

now that wasn't true – I didn't know about *khul'* then, which is how a wife can divorce her husband in Islam. Of course, I wasn't legally married according to British law, only according to Sharia law, so I didn't need a legal divorce, as I wasn't married. How stupid can you be?

I tried everything to get Rahil to divorce me, but he just wouldn't do it. In fact, he enjoyed having that power over me. One day, I'd had enough and I hurled so much abuse at him and cursed him so much that, in the end, he screamed back at me:

'I divorce you! I divorce you! I divorce you!'

And I was free again, even if it was only psychologically – a weight lifted off my shoulders. He walked out with his rucksack on his back and I never saw him again. Husband number five, who really wasn't husband number five, at least not in the statutory sense.

And then Daniella got pregnant. It was in January 2012 and she was twenty – I'd just turned forty. I wasn't sure how to take the news and Christopher believed she'd be wasting her life with a baby at such a young age. I said I had Daniella when I was nineteen and I didn't consider my life to be wasted – at least not as far as my children were concerned. Quite the opposite, in fact, as there were times in my life when I would have just given up completely if it hadn't been for my children. So, no, she wouldn't be wasting her life. I asked if it was what she wanted and she said it was. I knew she'd be a good mother – it may even have been what she needed to get over the trauma of Axel.

Her pregnancy wasn't easy and she was sick all the time but, eventually, on 8 September 2012, she gave birth to a beautiful baby girl: Amilah. Daniella was twenty-one a week later. She and my granddaughter moved out of the family house, and into a home of their own. That just left me and Christopher, who was now approaching twenty, and the Valium.

I'd been addicted to Valium for almost twenty years. I didn't realise I was addicted, just that I had to take the little blue tablets every day, sometimes as much as 80mg, to make me feel normal. I couldn't go out without a Valium in my bag and I'd get extra on the black market rather than risk running out, as the fear of being without the drug was terrifying. It was my life, it had very subtly become a part of me, establishing itself as a necessity as stealthily as a secret agent. My children had never known me not to be on Valium – how shocking is that? They'd go and fetch them for me from my bag, just as if I was asking them to get me an aspirin. But it was just a normal part of the daily routine for me, like having a cup of tea in the morning.

I googled the side effects of going cold turkey and I was worried because it said you should see your doctor first and wean yourself off gradually. I knew I couldn't do that – either my relationship with Valium was over and I stopped abruptly and completely, or I'd be taking it for the rest of my life. There was never any middle ground with me, it was always all or nothing. People I spoke to questioned my sanity and told me coming off Valium was worse than coming off alcohol, or even heroin, and I should certainly see a doctor. There was a twelve-step programme available, but that wasn't for me: it was do or die. Anyone who knows me knows I'm a strong-willed woman and, even though I realised I was facing a huge battle, I was determined to do it my way. Now that I didn't have to worry about Rahil, I could concentrate on getting clean.

After a few days without a tablet the effects began to kick in – I started to have sweats and cramps in my hands, and then feeling chilled to the bone. I developed tremors in my chest and nausea and began aching all over. I realised I could have a cardiac arrest or a fit or a seizure, that what I was doing was serious. So I prayed. I prayed and prayed, to whatever god would listen – to the mother of God, the son of God … the Lamb of God.

It took two months of cramps and headaches and cravings and distorted images and longings and cryings and fear and loathing and finally I was free of the come-down. It took a full year for me to be fully clear of the contamination. It was an uplifting moment when I woke and realised that the addiction was gone and had taken its side effects with it.

I didn't need that crutch any longer.

In March 2013 I was coming up to finishing my degree in Humanities and hoping to graduate in June. There was still something missing in my life and I couldn't put my finger on what it was. Then, one spring morning, I was in the supermarket queue behind a man in his sixties with long grey hair, wearing a cowboy hat. He was short 50p for what he wanted to buy and the cashier was being difficult, so I paid it for him. Outside in the car park he came up to me.

'Thank you. You will be blessed for helping me.'

'It's OK.'

I walked off towards my car, but he followed.

'My name is Kwatoko.'

'Unusual.'

'It's Native American. It means bird with big beak ... because of my nose.'

That made me smile. And he did have an aquiline nose that was a little larger than the norm.

'Can I give you something in return for your generosity?'

'There's no need, it was only fifty pence.'

He wouldn't take no for an answer and went over to an old red pick-up truck. He came back with a kind of handmade willow hoop. It had a woven net or web, with beads and feathers hanging from it.

'What is it?'

'A dreamcatcher.'

'What's it for?'

He told me it was from the Ojibwe tribe in North America and it was used to protect people – you hung it over your bed and the web caught evil dreams or any harm that might be in the air.

I was intrigued: maybe what I was searching for could be found in this culture. I wanted to know more. Kwatoko was his Native American name, but he also called himself Joseph, which was his white-man name. We talked in the car park for a time I lost track of, and Joseph showed me ghostly pictures of old houses and swirling shadows and it really caught my imagination. Could this fill the void in my life?

I had to get on, but I asked if he'd visit me at my house to speak more about his beliefs. He agreed.

A few days later, he came with more dreamcatchers and pictures of himself dressed in traditional Native American clothes: head feathers and beads and a painted face. He chanted and stamped his feet while performing a healing on myself and Daniella. He placed his hands on our heads and necks and asked us to chant with him. We didn't really know what it meant and I could see it was all mumbo-jumbo to Daniella, because she was rolling her eyes at me. But I wanted it to work and Joseph and I became friends. He inducted me into Wakan Tanka, which is the sacredness that resides in everything – every creature and every object. Among many other things, I also learned that life simultaneously exists in two parallel dimensions – the physical and the emotional – mass and energy, which fitted in with the way my life had played itself out up to now.

I enjoyed Joseph's company – we had a spiritual connection and he never wanted anything sexual from me. He instructed me and gave me books to read, which broadened my imagination and my ability to understand the universe around me. I even had a dreamcatcher tattooed on my back.

After I'd known him for about a month or so, Joseph told me about a place called Tipi Valley in Llandeilo, a remote part of Wales on the edge of the Brecon Beacons National Park. He asked me if I'd like to go up there.

'I'd love to, Joseph.'

We set off in his rattling red pick-up and travelled for a long time through remote, winding lanes. Then he stopped the truck and said we'd have to walk the rest of the way, as it was inaccessible to motor vehicles. We seemed to walk for miles, over hills and dales, and my feet were killing me. Then, in the distance, I could see smoke from fires and, as we came closer, I could see people – men, women and children – and dogs and horses and other animals.

When we finally arrived, it was as if I'd stepped out of a time machine into a different dimension. The people were living with nature – were part of nature. All the dwellings were low-impact, like tipis and yurts and mud huts and round houses.

It was a village rather than a commune, totally dependant on the earth and what it produced. There were people gathering firewood and children running around half naked, bathing in the river; the women walked around braless or bare-breasted. Everyone was self-sufficient and looking after themselves, the food was all home-produced; mothers gave birth there, the children were educated there ... all like it was hundreds of years ago. If need be, you could go to the toilet in what they called a 'shit-pit' and wipe your bum with a dock leaf. It was bizarre and surreal to someone like me – it was as if I'd dropped acid and was hallucinating.

There was a sweatlodge, with chanting and drumming and people playing music and smoking weed. Also a big communal tipi called the 'big lodge' where guests went, and that's where Joseph took me. It was very basic, with a floor made of rushes and an open fire with cooking pots and other people with mats and sleeping bags and sheepskins. We weren't staying the night, so we hadn't brought anything like that.

Joseph and I stayed in the big lodge with people dancing, singing, playing guitars and smoking marijuana. It felt so natural and peaceful and I really enjoyed being there. In the end I got stoned and danced with the others and became as one with them. I loved every minute of it and didn't want to go home – I felt I belonged there. We stayed well into the night and I was sad to leave when we had to say goodbye.

But I was already planning to come back with Daniella and Christopher and Amilah to live there as part of the community, away from all the crap in Cardiff and Llanelli.

Christopher was playing his Xbox when I got in. Normally, he wouldn't even notice me, but he turned round, sniffing the air, as if someone had trodden in dog excrement.

'Mum, you stink. Where have you been?'

'Stink of what?'

'Smoke and mud … and you have twigs in your hair.'

'I've been to Tipi Valley and I'm going to take you and Daniella back there to live.'

'You must be high on something.'

'No, we can dance and live free … hunt for food … become hippies.'

Christopher stopped playing and looked at me as if I'd fallen over and banged my head on something really hard.

'Good luck with that, Mum. But I'm not going, and I doubt if Daniella will.'

'Well, I'll go on my own then. You can have the house.'

He just shook his head and went back to his Xbox.

But he was right, I never returned to Tipi Valley. The real world encroached again and its commitments and distractions clouded my mind and diluted my determination. Joseph and I drifted apart and I went back to the spiritualist churches.

I started visiting clairvoyants, hoping they could find me a fairy-tale ending to my story. I wanted them to tell me I'd live happily ever after with someone who truly loved me. Sometimes they told me things I already knew and other times they frightened me. Every time they charged me a lot of money that I could scarcely afford. In the end, I stopped going to them. I knew there had to be something else, but I just didn't know what.

Then, one day in 2013, a message popped up on my Facebook page – it was from a man called Thomas who I'd known when Christopher was just a baby. Michael was on remand for threatening me with the knife at that time and Thomas and I were just a little more than good friends. When Michael got out of prison, he came to my house and kicked the door in. Thomas had been with me at the time and he'd jumped out through the window and broken his leg. I hadn't seen or heard from him since.

Back then, Thomas was a hippie type – lean, with huge brown eyes and a long mop of hair. Unlike Michael, he was quiet and didn't like trouble and he was big into the rave culture of the early 1990s. I'd put something on Facebook about Tipi Valley and the hippies there, which had caught his attention, and now he wanted to meet.

I have to admit, I was excited. It was like hearing from a childhood sweetheart after twenty years, and I wondered how we'd be after all that time.

We met for coffee in Swansea town centre and I was amazed at how well we got on. We seemed to have a great deal in common and we were very in tune with each other. It was probably the residue effect of my experience at Tipi Valley and because I didn't go back there to fulfil my hippie dream – Thomas was the next best thing.

Now, I bet you're saying: 'Here we go again' – and you're right. There I went again. After only a month together, we decided to get married.

Everyone was against our marriage, but the more they kept telling me not to do it, the more determined I grew. I suppose it was that old recalcitrant streak in me: I wasn't having people tell me what to do – even if they were right and I was wrong.

Christopher refused to even attend the ceremony.

We couldn't afford a big wedding, like I'd had before, but that didn't matter to me this time. It was a nice service at the registry office with just a few friends. I wore a pink-and-white floral mini-dress with red high heels and bands of flowers around my head and wrists. We went to a restaurant afterwards for a meal and champagne, and I was happy.

Husband number six.

Several weeks in and everything was fine. We got on well, he was a great cook and the sex was good – nothing freaky.

But you know what I'm going to say next, don't you?

As time went by, Thomas became very moody. He hated me being on the phone, he'd follow me around the house, from room to room, and I felt like I couldn't breathe. He came to the gym with me, even though he wasn't a gym person. If I went in one room, he'd come in after me. He also liked a drink and I was trying to stay off alcohol. I didn't mind him having a few cans of beer watching a football match, but I caught him drinking neat vodka from the bottle and I knew he had a problem.

Thomas had been laid off and wasn't working or bringing in a wage, which made matters worse. He hated me having friends and wanted to be my shadow – all the time. I didn't know how long I could put up with it. We'd only been married a few weeks and it was disintegrating already. Everybody was right. The final straw came when he twisted a piece of metal wire into the shape of my name and heated it over the gas cooker until it was glowing red. Then he branded himself on the chest with it. I couldn't understand that level of possessiveness.

One day I came home from Daniella's and he had his bags packed, ready to leave. I was surprised, but not sorry.

'What's happening, Thomas?'

'It's not working, Tara. I'm leaving.'

I think he expected me to try to persuade him to stay. I didn't.

'OK, I can drop you at the station.'

I drove him to the railway station and we didn't speak a single word to each other on the way. It was his game, but I wasn't playing.

We pulled up and he took his bags out of the car.

'Have you nothing to say, Tara?'

'Yes: goodbye.'

Then I drove off.

Thomas came straight back. He said it was to get the rest of his stuff, but he stayed over. I slept in the spare room and, during the night, he came in and we argued until about 4 a.m., until I couldn't take any more. I made tea and put a sleeping pill into his, which knocked him out within minutes. Next day we put all his stuff into the boot of my car and I decided to drive him to Swansea station, rather than Llanelli, so he couldn't come back again. On the way, he kept going on and on in my ear – one minute he'd be saying we could work it out and we should give it another try; the next minute he'd be calling me a slag and a whore. We were driving on the A484 and, before I knew what was happening, he had opened the car door and jumped out. I did a U-turn and drove back to him. He was unhurt. I opened the boot and threw all his bags onto the road beside him. I was so angry I slammed the boot down while my head was still halfway inside and almost knocked myself out. I saw stars, and blood was trickling down onto the pink bathrobe I was wearing.

Thomas approached me, to see if I was OK.

'Leave me alone!'

I jumped into the car and drove home. I had a large cut on my head and had to see a doctor to get it stitched.

I didn't care where Thomas was going, as long as it was away from me. But I still had one problem: I was married to him and I didn't want to be. We'd only been married a month and there is a one-year requirement for divorce. I saw a solicitor and told her the marriage hadn't been consummated, as I was living with another woman for two years previously and didn't know what I was doing when I married Thomas because I'd had a nervous breakdown. We had grounds and we applied to the court. It cost me a lot of money, but the marriage was annulled and my divorce papers came through in August 2013. I sent a copy to Thomas's parents, as I didn't know where he was living.

In 2016, I heard he took his own life and that really saddened me. He was a decent man – he never abused me or hit me. I should have realised he had issues of depression and I should have been able to help him. It wasn't totally his fault we split up – after six husbands and various female lovers, it should have been obvious that it was impossible for anyone to live with me.

I didn't go to his funeral or send a card; not because I didn't care, but because his family might have thought it to be inappropriate.

Chapter 22

God's Working Girl

I graduated from Swansea University in July 2013. My children and granddaughter attended the ceremony, which went on all day. I wore a mortar board and gown and my group was the last to go up.

Waiting to go onstage in Brangwyn Hall was an amazing feeling. I was really nervous and tripped on my gown. There was a vicar in front of me.

'Please pray I don't fall off the stage.'

He smiled awkwardly, wondering who this strange woman behind him was. If he only knew! I felt really weird when they handed me my scroll: it was as if I didn't deserve it. It was very surreal. Then everyone clapped and I was back on that stage in the Belle Vue Hotel when I won third place at the Miss Alderney contest all that time ago. We had a lot of family pictures taken and we celebrated afterwards at Frankie & Benny's in Llanelli. I drank diet Coke and was very proud of myself and how far I'd come since the bad old days.

I called my aunt Christine on Alderney and told her about Daniella's baby and my graduation. She was delighted to hear good news for once. I knew my mother wouldn't speak to me so I asked Christine, if I sent her a photo of my graduation, would she deliver it to Angela?

She agreed, but I never had any response from my mother.

I just wanted her to be proud of me.

Shortly after making contact with Christine again, I decided I was finally ready to break free of the demons that had plagued me all my life. I decided I wasn't a bad person because of what happened to me when I was little – a black lamb – and I wasn't wrong for being abused. I was wronged. I went to Llanelli police station and made a report. Llanelli police liaised with the police in Cardiff and Alderney. My medical records were examined and my family, friends and neighbours on Alderney were interviewed. Reports came back about Bruno's violence and my aunt Christine told police that I was afraid of him and she often saw marks on my body. They wanted to interview Bruno, but he was long gone. Apparently, he owed money to a lot of people and he'd fled to Thailand, where he was now living. He's in the police system and there's a warrant out for his arrest, if he ever returns to the UK.

As soon as I reported the abuse, I felt at peace. The anger that had been burning me up all my life left me. What I'd gone through was no longer a dirty secret festering inside me like a sin – it was out there in the open for all to see.

Despite breaking free of the past, and graduating, I still felt there was something missing in my life. I was straight and sober, the straightest I'd ever been, but I felt lost and lonely. Not lonely for another husband or partner, but lonely for a purpose, a meaning to my life.

I needed something to fill the emptiness inside me now that the anger was gone.

In September 2013 I was at a children's indoor play area with my granddaughter when I noticed a woman staring at me. You know me by now – it got my back up so I stared back, then went over to her.

'Do I know you?'

Her name was Selina and she turned out to be the mother of one of Daniella's friends. We got talking and for some reason I told her I was going to spiritualist churches in search of a meaning for my life.

'Don't go to them, Tara, they're demonic.'

'Why would you say that?'

'They're unchristian.'

I remembered about being a Christian: it's what I was when I was a young girl at school on Alderney. I was more than a Christian, I was a Catholic. I didn't like it much then – it hadn't stopped Bruno from abusing me, and I didn't care about it now either.

'I really don't need a bible bashing, Selina.'

'This is not Catholicism, Tara. This is being born again.'

Being born again appealed to me – just the phrase itself, even though I didn't know what it meant. Selina said she could come to my house and bring some scriptures and explain evangelism to me. My instincts told me to say no, so I can't understand why I said yes.

I really wasn't in the mood when she turned up with a Bible, so I made her a lukewarm cup of coffee and gave her a stale biscuit, hoping she'd take the hint and do a body swerve. She didn't. She started talking about God and quoting the scriptures – John 8:36 'So, if the Son sets you free, you will be free indeed.' She could see I didn't know what she was talking about and I was getting more frustrated by the minute, so she finished up by asking if I'd like to say the Prayer of Salvation with her. By then I was losing the will to live and was prepared to agree to anything to get rid of her.

After we said the prayer, she went outside and started praying over my car because I'd told her Rahil bought it for me when we were together.

'What are you doing?'

'It's a sinful car.'

'What?'

'A non-believer bought it for you.'

My neighbours already believed I was insane and I could imagine them behind their curtains, ringing up the local mental health hospital to have me sectioned.

Strangely, though, when I woke the following morning, I had an overwhelming desire to go to church. I didn't know what kind of church and I thought, after the life I'd led, no church would touch me with two barge poles tied together. But I couldn't shake the yearning – it was like being pregnant and craving celery or the smell of coal. I ended up walking into a church in the town centre and starting to cry for no reason. I just didn't know what was wrong with me, what was going on.

The next day Selina rang me and asked if I wanted to go to a house group with her. I didn't know what a house group was and she explained it was just a bunch of born-agains talking, praying and drinking non-alcoholic beverages.

'No, just leave me alone.'

But she wouldn't, and I had to agree to go in the end. Selina was totally the opposite of me, wise and gentle, but she was a pit bull when it came to converting people to her particular evangelical viewpoint.

I had no idea what to expect when we arrived at this house, full of middle-class God botherers. I hoped we weren't going to start talking about our lives, or they'd throw me out before I even got started. I wondered what I was doing in this place: I had nothing in common with these people. Then again, a lot of people in the Bible turned out to be either murderers, drunks or prostitutes.

At the end, they asked me if I'd like to be baptised and, even though I'd already been baptised as a Catholic, I thought: 'Why not? It can't hurt, can it?'

They baptised me down the north docks in Llanelli on 31 October – yes, Halloween. A couple of elders waded in with me in waterproofs – I was in shorts and a T-shirt. It was pelting down hailstones and the water was freezing. They dunked me under three times, while reading Matthew 5:14–16: 'You are the light of the world. A town built on a hill cannot be hidden. Neither do people light a lamp and put it under a bowl. Instead they put it on its stand, and it gives light to everyone in the house. In the same way, let your light shine before others, that they may see your good deeds and glorify your Father in heaven.'

I nearly drowned – but I was born again.

Hallelujah!

I started going to Kings Church at the Ebenezer gospel hall in Swansea. They did a 'healing' on me to restore my mind and make it more like Christ's – not to act in the flesh, but to act in the spirit and be obedient to His word. It's like someone is broken, but they don't know they're broken and when they speak about it and let it all out, they get release and cry and they're healed.

And, in secular terms, I wasn't broken any more; nor was I an addict or a prostitute. I did Bible study, where fellow Christians got together in a cosy circle and sang songs of worship and prayer. We read passages by the four evangelists and discussed them afterwards, and I became a follower. My friend Laura mocked me and called me a bible-basher, but I took no notice of her, just as she took no notice of me when I warned her about the company she kept.

The thing is, the born-again Christians weren't content to just save me from the devil – they wanted me to go and save other people and 'bring them to the Lord'. So I did. I brought them my daughter, Daniella. Everywhere I went, I talked to people about God – taxi drivers and people in the street, perfect strangers. They'd always have a negative excuse not to listen at first.

'If there's a god, why do we have wars?'

'I don't believe in that religion rubbish.'

'I'm happy the way I am, leave me alone.'

But I'd keep on and on at them because I was on fire with evangelical zeal.

Daniella had another daughter in 2014 and I had another beautiful granddaughter – Gabriella. I chose Gabriella, which is the female version of Gabriel, the herald of good news in the Bible, the archangel who announced the impending birth of Jesus to Mary. It seemed appropriate at the time. My daughter also moved to a new house just around the corner from me, so I could see her and my grandchildren every day.

I was approached by a Christian counsellor while I was attending one church in particular. He asked me to join his house group and I agreed. Because he was an elder and a counsellor, I divulged details of my past life to him in confidence. Shortly afterwards, the whole church knew what I was before, and people were coming up to me asking awkward and impertinent questions. It made me feel like a fraud and I was deeply embarrassed. It wasn't that I was particularly ashamed of my previous life, but because what I had said had been in confidence. Had I decided to get up in the pulpit and broadcast it myself, then I'd have been fine with it, and maybe that's what I should have done. I texted the pastor, asking why a Christian elder considered it OK to betray a confidence – he didn't respond. It really affected my 'walk with God' in that church, so I left.

The next church I joined had a pastor from America visiting. He was a lot older than me and looked like Clark Kent – very suave. After a service one evening, he asked if he could take me to see a movie. I assumed it would be a film with a religious theme, so I agreed. Next evening, he collected me in his Jeep and we went to an arthouse cinema in Cardiff to see an indie film called *Nymphomaniac*, by the Danish director Lars von Trier. It was all about a young woman who'd led a libidinous life and she tells her story to an older man. How very appropriate – for him! The things I'd said in confidence had obviously travelled further than I thought. There were lots of explicit sex scenes and I felt uncomfortable and asked to leave early. He wanted to come in when he dropped me off, but I said no. I'd told him I was thinking about writing a book and he said he knew many important people in Hollywood who could help me and turn it into a film – if I went out with him.

That was the beginning of the end of orthodox evangelism for me.

I liked the concept that was being preached: of being a good person, but the protocol of the religion didn't hold me – the mechanics, the ritual and etiquette. I was more interested in the human – the loving and helping, and not judging. My relationship with God was a personal thing, unique to me.

The thing is, it's all right praying and fighting the devil on a spiritual level, if that's what you want to do, but I needed a more earthly calling. I felt the churches I visited weren't doing enough for people on a physical level. Like when I found out a young boy my son's age had died of a drug overdose – his mother and brother were already dead and his other brother was in prison. He'd had such a hard upbringing and I thought that trying to help people like that in a meaningful way must surely be better than all the altar-thumping and hymn-singing. We were supposed to be Christians, but we weren't doing enough to *help* people.

One Sunday, I got up and took the microphone in this particular church, having decided to challenge the congregation.

'I'm sick of seeing deprived people dying needlessly from all kinds of abuse. What are we doing about it?'

There was no reply, just a stony silence.

'Well, answer me ... What are we doing about it?'

Silence. Then someone shouted back.

'What are *you* doing about it?'

And that's when I knew I was just like the rest of them, doing nothing. I resolved there and then to be more than just a benchwarmer, full of good intentions but never actually doing anything. I was always a doer, not a sayer.

Finally, I knew what the longing inside me was, what I'd been searching for. It wasn't to be found inside the four worshipful walls of any church. It was out on the street. This interpretation of God was missing from the manifesto of the so-called Christians around me – my interpretation. My interpretation wasn't a god in the sky, nor a man with a white beard. No, God was more an essence to me, an entity inside me and inside everyone – every thing. God was the oneness of the universe and beyond the universe – beyond space and time, and it manifested itself at the human level in love – love for the forgotten, the forlorn, the drugged, the destitute, the no-hopers and the neglected. That was my god. It was a difficult concept for me to grasp but, once I did, I knew it had changed me for ever.

If I hadn't gone through what I went through in my life, how could I ever have understood what other people were going through and have empathy with them? Life is for loving, once you know what the word 'love' really means. I know that now and I've been able to forgive everyone who hurt me in the past. I only hope people I've hurt will forgive me also. It's one thing to talk about spreading love and it's quite another thing to do it. I don't want to preach to anyone here – I'm not a preacher and I'm not trying to convert anyone to anything. I'm just telling my story and speaking for myself when I talk about how I found the true meaning of love.

I was driving home in the rain one night, when I saw this frail old man standing at a bus stop, soaking wet. I pulled up and asked him if he wanted a lift.

'Oh, thank you very much, miss.'

He was over ninety years old and I reckoned not long for this world. When we got to where he lived he clasped my hands in his and looked straight into my eyes. He didn't say anything and neither did I, but I knew that look – it was appreciation. No, it was more than that – and it was less than that. It wasn't thanks or gratitude – I didn't need credit for picking him up. It was genuine affection. Love, if you like. Not the popularised 'love' of the movies and magazines – this was real regard, and it was unspoken. It didn't need to be said. Just felt.

After that, I started going out onto the streets, to the roughest areas in the cities of South Wales – Swansea and Llanelli and Neath and Cardiff, meeting homeless people and drug addicts and girls on the game. I'd just go and talk to them and listen to the stories of their lives. I didn't ask them to convert or come to God or find faith or anything like that. I just listened to them and let them know that at least one person in this world accepted them for what they were – human beings. And they accepted me, because I was one of them once.

You could say I first turned the corner from being a gangster's girl to being what I called 'God's working girl' in 2014. I even had the name tattooed on my arm. I looked for people who were hurting, who needed help – teenagers and tattoo-covered tough guys, people pumping iron in gyms and drinking in pubs, sick people in hospitals and old-age pensioners close to death, gays and straights and in-betweens, atheists and agnostics, criminals and cut-throats, hookers and harlots. I had no fear because my god was with me.

And my god was love.

During the winter of 2014, I had to cut through an alley to get back to my car and I almost stumbled over a woman who was sitting in the gutter. The weather was awful and freezing cold. At first I walked past, but then I went back and sat down beside her. She'd been drinking some kind of vodka mixture and I couldn't get any sense out of her because she was so drunk. I managed to get her to her feet and we staggered towards my car, swaying all over the place. It looked as if we were both plastered and people gave us a wide berth. I got her into the car but it took me a long time to find out from her where she lived.

When we eventually arrived at her house, a man who looked really ill opened the door. We helped the woman inside. There were discarded syringe needles everywhere, the place was full of damp and the ceiling was caving in. The man made me a coffee as the woman began to sober up. We talked and I discovered that he'd been rented out for sex by his father from the age of eight and on heroin for fifteen years. The woman had also been abused for most of her childhood. They couldn't believe that I had no hidden agenda and was prepared to listen to them without judging them. I offered to write to the council about their living conditions and that resulted in them being moved to a new house. The last I heard, the man got on to a methadone programme and the woman is now off the alcohol.

I've had many encounters on the streets, some funny, some fraught with danger. Overall, I have to say how harrowing it is out there in the world of the broken. I've met many characters – eccentric, crazy, lost, dejected, rejected, hopeless, hopeful, misused, abused and all variations on those conditions and others. One man I met was called Teabag Pete, who was well known on the squalid streets of Swansea. Pete died of a stroke in January 2015 and they've now opened a homeless shelter in his memory.

Shortly after Pete died, I parked my car to go shopping and I noticed this guy who was limping badly. So I walked alongside him and asked him what was wrong. He said he had a hole in his leg and was doing the best he could with it.

'What's your name, if you don't mind me asking?'

'George.'

I helped him to his car and we exchanged phone numbers. I've kept in touch with him because he was alone in the world and believed nobody cared about him. I proved to him that wasn't true and he now has a new outlook on life, which is much more positive.

Station Road in Llanelli was particularly known for drug users and dealers and alcoholics. One night I was out there in the bitter cold when I was approached by a young girl called Kelly, who I knew from previous visits was a heroin user. She'd lost both her parents and her situation was hopeless. She was with three guys who were all off their heads on junk. I took her face in my hands and told her she had to stop doing this or she'd end up dead. The guys she was with started to get a bit agitated.

'What business is it of yours?'

'I'm concerned for her welfare.'

'Are you her mother?'

'No.'

'Fuck off, then!'

They came up very close to my face and tried to intimidate me and one of them pulled out a knife, but I stood my ground, ready to use my martial arts if I had to. All of a sudden, the place was alive with sirens and flashing blue lights. It was a police raid and everybody scattered. I don't know what would've happened but for that. Kelly turned and hugged me and said she'd be in touch, before disappearing into the dusk.

I never saw Kelly again after that, but I heard she'd had her baby taken away from her because she was still on heroin. It really upset me because she was a beautiful girl who was destroyed by drugs, like a lot of other young people. I only wish I could have done more for her back then.

The thing is, I've never felt fear in the dark of the alleyways or the grime of the gutter. I've continued to go out onto the streets and conduct my little one-woman crusade against conceit and indifference. In the spring of 2015, I was taking Daniella to the doctor's and there was only one parking space, close to where a group of men were drinking strong cider. My first inclination was to drive on and find another place to park. Then I realised that would be judgemental, so I parked the car in the available space close to them. When we came out of the doctor's, one of them was jumping on my car and kicking it. I shouted at him and the group began to approach me and Daniella, with the one who was kicking the car becoming verbally abusive. I dialled 999 and the police quickly arrived on the scene. The men were local alcoholics who were known to the police and the one who was kicking my car was bundled into the back of a van. There was no real damage done, so I told the police I didn't want him to be arrested or charged. They looked at me as if I was the one they should be arresting, for wasting their time. I tried to explain my reasoning.

'Look, you can see he has problems, and I don't want to add to them.'

They let him go and Daniella and I drove off. Later on, when I thought about it, I regretted not getting his details, so I could try to help him.

The following week I had to go to the library and there was the car-kicker with the same group of men. I walked up to him.

'Do you remember me?'

Of course he didn't. He had no clue who I was.

'What's your name?'

'Dai.'

'Well, Dai, my car knows you.'

I asked him why he did it and he said he was angry at the time – angry because he'd lost his home and his family.

'Because of the booze?'

'No, the booze came after.'

I took the whole group to a café and bought them tea and sandwiches. Then I took Dai to a clothes shop and bought him new boots and a hat and coat. He couldn't understand why I was being so kind to him, after he'd been kicking my car – he thought I was police, trying to trick him in some way.

'Of course I'm not police. If I was, you'd have been arrested.'

I still see the group now and then and take them for tea and traditional welshcakes and they know where I am if they need me. We're all broken in one way or another and just need someone to listen to what we have to say.

Despite these good deeds, I was still human and I had a row with my sometime friend Laura in the summer of 2015. There was a stabbing in a Cardiff nightclub and Christopher was a witness. CID came to my house and took him away to be questioned. I was extremely worried so I called Laura, who had a criminal record, for advice. She was cool with me for some reason I never understood and wasn't prepared to help. Christopher was allowed home after the questioning and wasn't charged with anything, but I was really angry with Laura's attitude, especially as I'd gone to court with her and was there for her when she needed me. I told her never to contact me again and I deleted her from all my social media. Very un-altruistic, I know, but that was it as far as I was concerned, we were no longer friends.

I didn't see her about anywhere for nine months or so, which was unusual, then one night I dreamt I saw her face and she was crying. I could remember it plainly when I woke. 'How unusual,' I thought, because I'd never seen Laura cry in all the years I'd known her. I felt I should go and make up with her, but I was hesitant, not knowing what kind of reception I'd receive.

Before I could drum up the courage, I saw her one day, sitting in her car, crying, just like in my dream. I jumped into the passenger seat beside her.

'What's the matter, Laura?'

She was so surprised to see me and wiped her eyes immediately, pretending she wasn't weeping.

'Tara ... How're you?'

I didn't want to pry, so I put my arms around her and gave her a hug.

'It's all right, Laura ... Whatever it is, it's all right.'

'Can we be friends again, Tara?'

'Of course.'

Christmas was coming and my children were grown up and I had this brand-new fibre-optic tree complete with decorations. So I decided to give it away. I put it up on Facebook and said I wanted to help someone, preferably a struggling single parent. I had lots of replies but one in particular touched me. Darren had two young children, a girl and a boy, and he lived close to me, so I went round there with the Christmas tree. The cold inside the house was eerie – it was colder than outside. There was no carpet on the floor and no curtains on the windows, and that unique smell of destitution pervaded the place. The children were delighted with the tree and, as I left, the little boy spoke to me.

'Lady, did Santy Claus send you?'

I walked to the car with tears streaming down my face.

The following Sunday I went to the Liberty Church in Swansea and made all the good, upright Christians put their hands in their pockets for a collection. I raised £380. I went back to the house and asked the children to write letters to Santa and give them to me. They didn't ask for much – the girl wanted a doll and the boy wanted a water pistol. I bought those toys for them, and others, along with new clothes – pyjamas, underwear, shoes and coats. With the rest of the money I bought food – a turkey and other Christmas fare. Word of my efforts got around the area and people started donating other stuff: curtains, duvets, cutlery – even beds. My son Christopher gave brand-new trainers and jeans for the father, who cried when all the gifts were taken round to him. It was like a scene from Charles Dickens's *A Christmas Carol*. But, at least for one year, it would be real for that family.

Random acts of kindness can change lives.

These are just some of the instances of empathy for fellow human beings that I've been part of and continue to be part of. And I'm not telling you about them because I think I'm wonderful or angelic – I'm not, as well you know by now. They're just little things that don't cost a lot, but can mean a great deal in people's lives. I go into the massage parlours and talk to the girls – I don't preach, just listen and try to understand the hand that's been dealt to them. I talk to working girls on the street and advise them on how to stay safe and clean. I try to get addicts into rehab and alcoholics onto programmes. It can be dangerous at times, going where no one else wants to – talking to people the rest of the world has forgotten. But they see me for what I am most of the time, a person who poses no threat to them and who has no hidden agenda. Someone who just wants to understand why they're the way they are and offer some constructive advice on how to get their lives back on track.

For me, being a Christian isn't about sitting in a pew on a Sunday morning; it's about stepping out into a world that's full of pain and broken people and offering them a little kindness. You should try it sometime. Buy a bunch of flowers and hand them to a sad stranger on the street. Help a bewildered person who's struggling to understand something. Ask a depressed individual why they're crying. Sit on the side of the street and talk to a dishevelled beggar.

You'll feel much better for it.

Chapter 23

Cancer

Having Daniella and my granddaughters living close to me made life a lot easier. I was back in the gym and very fit for my age. I was also back at university, doing two courses: 'An Introduction to Counselling' and 'Counselling in Context'. My aim was to become an accredited professional, as I felt I had the right life experience to do that job, along with being empathetic, compassionate and non-judgemental. Christopher was in a solid relationship with his girlfriend and enjoying his football and his job, which had very good prospects.

Life was good.

In June 2016 I had a minor injury at the gym and couldn't train for a while. I seemed to be tired and short of breath all the time and I didn't know what was wrong with me. One day, I was showing a woman around one of the churches I used to go to and my legs suddenly went all wobbly and I ended up on the floor. When I looked down, my belly was moving, as if it was full of frogs. I know this may sound bizarre, as most people would have been very worried, but I just put it down to some kind of religious manifestation or trapped wind or something, because I really didn't know what was happening. That night, however, my stomach was quite swollen so, next morning, I went to see my doctor.

The expression on his face started to change as he examined me.

'I need to send you for an emergency scan, Tara.'

He arranged for me to be seen at Glangwili hospital in Carmarthen and that's when I began to suspect something was really wrong. I felt incredibly scared and I started to cry as I left the surgery.

Christopher came with me to the hospital, where I was seen by a specialist. He asked me how old I was.

'I'm forty-four.'

'Oh, you're too young.'

'Too young for what?'

'Nothing … nothing.'

They gave me a CT scan and an MRI scan and they told me I either had a complex cyst or cancer.

A blanket of fear came over me when I heard that word 'cancer'. Christopher was sitting opposite when I got off the bed. We were both crying. They made me a cup of tea and put me in a big rocking chair in the day room because there were no beds. I tried in vain to calm down and, after several hours, they came and said they had a bed for me.

'Why do I need a bed? I'm going home.'

All my instincts and anxieties were screaming inside me: 'I can't do this! I can't do this!'

Christopher begged me to stay and do whatever they asked.

In my heart I knew I couldn't run away from it, as I'd run away from so many situations in my life. This would have to be faced. My son came to the ward and stayed by my side and I heard him praying in a low voice.

'Please don't take my mum. I'll do anything ... please!'

I had tried to get him to find God when I was full of zeal and fervour, as I had. Maybe it came to him at that moment, or at least his own interpretation of what God truly is?

I was put on morphine, which gave me a nice feeling of intoxication I hadn't experienced in a long time. Next morning, a senior consultant came to see me with a set of questions. I think I was still on the morphine high.

'Have you been losing weight?'

'No.'

'Have you been urinating excessively?'

I smiled to myself – that could have been a useful disorder back in the brothels.

'No.'

'Have you been tired and oversleeping?'

A little, but I lied, hoping the deception might confuse the cancer and it'd go away.

'No.'

'Have you been feeling full after eating?'

I always felt full after eating – didn't everybody?

'No.'

He told me I had a mass. I thought he said I had to go to Mass.

'But I'm not a Catholic ... not any longer ...'

He gave me a worried look, as if whatever was in my stomach was now affecting my brain.

Afterwards, I had to go for another MRI scan and wait two days until they assessed the results. The waiting was the worst part.

When it was over, they told me I had stage 1A ovarian cancer. They wouldn't know how far it had spread until they operated.

'The tumour is a large one, Tara.'

By now my stomach had swollen so much I looked about six months pregnant. They booked me in for a radical hysterectomy. A radical hysterectomy is a surgical procedure where they cut down from the breastbone and across the stomach to get the tumour out without it bursting. The surgeon told me everything would have to be taken away: my uterus, ovaries, cervix, fallopian tubes, womb, lymph nodes, upper vagina and vaginal tissue. I'd be left with a scar in the shape of a cross.

How ironic – I'd lose the tools of my previous trade in exchange for the mark of Jesus. A modern-day Mary Magdalene.

While I was waiting for the operation, Daniella told me she was pregnant again. Although I was happy for her, it was actually the last thing I wanted to hear because I didn't know if I was going to survive. I told her I wouldn't be able to help the way I did with Amilah and Gabriella, and I had to think of Christopher, who was taking my illness very badly – not eating or sleeping, just crying and saying he wouldn't be able to carry on without me if I died.

The day of the operation came and they'd tested my blood pressure and given me ECGs and all sorts of other examinations and I didn't know whether I was coming or going. A vanguard doctor arrived and told me it was a big operation and I'd probably be on the table for at least seven hours.

'There could be complications.'

'I know what you're saying ... I could die.'

'Worst-case scenario.'

A calmness had come over me.

'It's all right, I'm prepared.'

He looked at me and smiled.

'You have the faith, don't you?'

'Yes, my own faith.'

'Look at my name tag.'

I looked. It said: 'Dr Jesus Rodriguez'.

'I'm with you, my child.'

We both laughed and I gave him a huge hug.

My surgery was the last one in the afternoon of 31 July 2016. They sat me up and sprayed my back with anaesthetic to make it go numb so they could give me an epidural. I remember nothing much after that until I came to in the high-dependency unit late in the evening. I was hooked up to lots of machines and had a breathing mask on me and a catheter inserted. I was on an IV of saline and morphine and I was so drained and groggy I hardly noticed Christopher sitting close by, waiting for me to come round. He was holding my hand and stroking my face.

'I love you, Mum.'

'I love you too, son.'

I fell back asleep and the next day the surgeon came to see me. He said the tumour was 10lbs in weight and it had taken two of them to lift it out of me. My belly had gone flat again, like a balloon that had been burst with a knife.

I was in hospital for five days and I have to say our NHS is the best health service in the world. For the sake of generations to come, I hope we don't allow the politicians and profit-makers to destroy it.

Christopher was very helpful when I came home. He took two weeks off work, cooked for me, went shopping, cleaned, helped me get dressed, brushed my hair and fetched and carried for me, even in the middle of the night. I don't know what I'd have done without him. I couldn't sleep on my stomach or on my side, only on my back. I couldn't walk properly, just shuffle; I couldn't sneeze or cough and I had to hold my stomach with a pillow because it felt as if it was going to spill out into my hands.

Three weeks later I went back to the hospital and they said the cancer had been growing for about two years, but they'd got it all and I wouldn't need chemotherapy. I'd have to return for check-ups every six months for five years, which I'll be doing until 2021.

I'm still not back to my normal self, or what I call my normal self, and probably never will be. My stomach is scarred and I can't use the gym like before because of how many muscles they had to cut through. I hobbled around for the first four months recovering, and I tried to make Christmas 2016 special, as usual. After all, I was alive, Daniella was due to have her baby in February 2017 and there was a lot to live for.

My daughter went into labour on 29 January 2017, which meant the baby was going to be premature, so I stayed with her in the hospital. There was so much peace in that delivery room as she gave birth to a boy the following day; he looked so beautiful as I cut the cord. Daniella called my grandson Elijah-Blu.

The original Elijah was a prophet and miracle-worker in the ninth century BC – long before the coming of Christianity. He was a man for all roads and religions; a true ecumenical; a universal man – a man of the universe. I hope my grandson turns out to be the same.

*

In June 2017 I had a phone call from the daughter of my friend Laura. I was surprised and wondered why she was ringing me instead of Laura herself.

'Hi, Tara. Mum wants to know if you'll pray for her.'

That surprised me even more. Laura never believed in anything spiritual and she used to mock me when I was an evangelist.

'What's going on, Sienna?'

'Mum's going to be remanded in the magistrates' court.'

'What for?'

'The drugs.'

I hurried down to the magistrates' court and met with Sienna and other members of Laura's family, along with their solicitor.

The solicitor asked if I was Tara, and I told her I was.

'Can we have a private word, Tara?'

She took me into a room.

'Laura's spoken highly of you and your relationship with her children. They may need you now.'

I was bewildered. A feeling of foreboding came over me.

'How serious is this?'

'Well, they're saying she's the most dangerous woman in West Wales.'

What? I was with her a couple of days previously in the splash park, eating ice creams. Most dangerous woman? OK, I knew she dabbled in drugs a bit, but surely there had to be some mistake?

We all went into the court and there was Laura, lined up with five other accused. The prosecuting solicitor called her a 'lieutenant' and said they had photographic evidence and talked about 'conspiracy'. In the end, Laura was remanded on a charge of conspiring to supply class-A drugs from 2014 to 2017.

Back at her house afterwards, the door had been rammed in and the place ransacked by regional crime police, who'd taken everything: money, computers, phones, paperwork, bank details, the lot. Drawers were pulled out and stuff scattered everywhere. It was as if the house had been burgled. I was heartbroken. What about the children? Laura's two sons were taken away by their fathers, but Sienna was twenty and had her own house – I was determined to stick by her and help as much as I could.

Over the next few days, we were able to find out that Laura had got herself involved with some big-time gangsters from Liverpool – they had two main supply people for their drugs in Llanelli, and Laura was one of them. The police operation, which had been going on for some time, was called Operation Ulysses and it had netted twenty-eight high-level drug dealers from around the country.

All Laura's 'friends' disappeared, they faded away like ghosts in the gloom – all except me.

In the meantime, once I recovered from the cancer, it was time to get back to doing a Level 6 in counselling skills at the University of Wales Trinity Saint David, which I started in September 2017. The course consisted of three modules and I had to do assignments, assessments and triad work in groups of three or four, with role-playing as client, counsellor and observer. I really enjoyed the course. I loved stretching the scope of my knowledge and going to academic levels I hadn't been to before.

I also made some really genuine friends there, three in particular who I won't name, but who are now friends for life.

While I was studying, Laura was languishing in Eastwood Park prison, waiting for her trial. I visited her there and brought her everything she needed. It really affected me having to leave her: she looked so forlorn, not the tough, confident woman who'd been my friend for so long. Sienna couldn't handle things on her own, so I searched around and found a good solicitor. He found a barrister to represent Laura in court and they tried to persuade her to plead guilty, for a lesser sentence. Laura wouldn't agree. I was angry with her – they had all the evidence – Operation Ulysses had been going for three years and all the other defendants were pleading guilty. But Laura wouldn't budge. I was constantly on the phone to the solicitor, pleading with him to convince her. In the end she agreed to plead guilty to one year of drug dealing, and we thought that might be enough to get her a deal.

The Crown Prosecution Service, on the other hand, decided they could prove three years' guilt, and Laura wouldn't back down until it was too late. She eventually pleaded guilty, but the delay had diminished any hope of a reduced sentence.

I attended the trial with Sienna at Swansea Crown Court in March 2018. We were told Laura would probably get eight years. There were five other people being sentenced that day and they all had references and testimonials. Laura had none. I wondered why I hadn't been told. During the lunch break, I ran across to the solicitor and wrote a testimonial for her with shaking hands. Whether the testimony of an ex-prostitute would do her any good or not, I didn't know. But I was respectable now and a university graduate, and I knew her better than anyone, so I was as good as anyone else, wasn't I? I then went to see Laura and managed to clasp fingers with her through the gap in the plastic barrier. Her eyes were glistening – I felt so helpless.

Laura was sentenced to twelve years. The judge said she was responsible for over thirty drug-related deaths and had shown no remorse. She was a 'truly wicked woman'. I knew better – she was a victim, just like those she sold to. Someone got her onto the drugs in the first place, then encouraged her to sell drugs to pay for her habit. That's the thin end – it escalates from there, especially if life has little else to offer in deprived areas of big cities that have been written off by the politicians and property developers. In some ways Laura was lucky – she'd get out of prison and have a chance to rebuild her life. Others got sent to the cemetery.

Sienna clung to me as her mother was taken down.

I write to Laura every day and I visited her when she was at Eastwood Park prison. Her father died in July 2018 and she was allowed to attend the funeral. I met her there and we hugged, walked together and cried. She was and is my friend and I'll be waiting for her when she gets out.

I finished the university course in May 2018 and my graduation was held on 9 July 2018, almost a year before this book will be published. I know you'll find this difficult to believe, but I'm not big on events and I do get rather shy at times – you're probably laughing and rolling your eyes – and I wanted this graduation to be low-key.

Daniella decided to ringlet my hair in bendy curlers so I'd have the Lady Gaga look and I had to sleep with them in overnight. Next morning, though, I looked more like Lady Macbeth and I was going frantic. Daniella thought it was hilarious as she tried to drag the frizz straight and, the more she laughed, the more irritated I became. Not a good start to the day.

When we got to the hall where the ceremony was taking place, some women were registering people and allocating numbers. We then had to queue to collect our mortar boards and gowns. My feet were killing me, so I jumped the rail to get ahead of the line. The woman at the kiosk would know I'd jumped the queue because the allocated numbers were going in order, so I asked the person in front of me what their number was – it was 207. My turn came.

Mrs Middle-Class looked at me.

'What's your number?'

'208.'

She looked at the corresponding names.

'And you are Asaf Bugti?'

'Asaf, As if . . . you can call me whatever you want.'

I've never seen a pen stick so hard into paper.

It was a very hot day during the heatwave of July 2018 and, wearing a black mortar board and gown over a striped trouser suit, I was sweating through my make-up as we queued again for the official photos. Christopher was stuck in traffic and running late and I wanted him in the pictures with me and Daniella. I allowed other people to go ahead of me as we waited.

Photos over, we went for the presentation and I was confident on stage, doing my catwalk impression with my left hand in my pocket. The vice-chancellor said he hoped I'd go far in life and he wished me every success for the future.

'Thank you so much.'

I waved to Daniella and Christopher and blew them a kiss, then we went out into the grounds and took some nice family photos by a tree. Afterwards, we went to a restaurant to celebrate with friends and I was in bed by 8 p.m., exhausted.

It really affected me when my friend Laura went to prison for twelve years. I said to myself: 'There but for the grace of God …' I mean, my life could have gone a different route at any stage in its erratic and chaotic trajectory. I completely understand how people get involved in serious crime, either through circumstance or wrong choices – I've been affected by both myself.

Due to my outreach work in the rough parts of city centres, I'd been able to get to know a lot about what goes down on the streets – who was involved in what and who the really bad people were. Rumours circulated and names got mentioned. I began to hear about one group in particular – violent bullies who intimidated others lower down the drug-dealing pecking order. These were men who went to people's houses with baseball bats and set others up to take the fall for them and go to prison for years. Normally, in the criminal fraternity, people keep information to themselves and don't 'grass' on others, no matter what. It's an unwritten code. But this gang didn't care about that code and broke it with impunity when it suited their own purposes. They had no scruples whatsoever and literally seemed to be able to get away with murder because everyone was so frightened of them.

Some of the people I'd been helping were involved with the gang and wanted a way out, but didn't know how to escape without putting themselves and their families in danger. There wasn't much I could do except offer them understanding and solidarity, not being directly involved myself.

One day I was having a coffee in the town centre with someone whose life was on the edge due to involvement with class-A drugs, when I noticed a man watching me from across the café. I didn't know who he was, but I assumed his surveillance was because of who I was with, rather than who I was. I believed the observer was part of the gang and was trying to intimidate the person I was counselling. I wasn't one to be frightened by that kind of thing, so I walked across to him.

'What's your problem, mister?'

He looked at me without speaking for a moment or two.

'You're Tara.'

'That's right.'

'Can we have a word outside?'

I don't know why I agreed, but we were in a busy part of the town centre, so what could happen?

Outside, he started walking towards a dark van that was parked down the street. I followed. There was another man sitting in the front of the van. The one from the café opened a sliding door on the side.

'Get in.'

'Not likely!'

He flashed a badge at me.

'We're CID.'

I didn't know if that was genuine or not, or what I was getting myself into, but I got into the van and the two men got in after me. Looking back, it was such a reckless thing to do and I might not be here now to tell the tale.

It turned out they were genuine CID, working with informants for Carmarthenshire police.

'We've done some homework on you, Tara.'

'Have you now?'

'We think you can help us.'

'Do you now?'

They recited some names to me and amongst them were the names of a couple of the gang members who were terrorising people. I told them what I knew, not because I was a grass, but because I wanted to help the poor people who weren't strong enough to help themselves – the ones whose lives these bullies had ruined and were continuing to ruin. I'd already seen one of my good friends sent to prison for twelve years because of people like these and, if I could help prevent the same thing from happening again, then I made no excuses for it.

The CID men asked to see me again. I told them I'd help in any way I could. A week later we met, this time at a petrol station in a place between Llanelli and Carmarthen. I parked my car and climbed into the back of the van again. They gave me a declaration to read, which set out the conditions for working as an undercover agent. I was confused and didn't know what to do.

'We want to make it formal, Tara.'

'I don't know ... People won't trust me ...'

'No one will know.'

'It's dangerous – my family ...'

'We'll protect you, and your family.'

'I don't know …'

'You helped us before, Tara, to put away Axel Preece.'

'He abused my daughter.'

'This gang is abusing other people's daughters.'

They were right. I'd be a hypocrite not to help get these thugs off the streets. So, the poacher turned gamekeeper.

I signed the document and they took my fingerprint and gave me a password so that, when they rang me, I'd know it was them. If I called them, I had to use the code name Bo Reed and I was given a diary to log relevant information.

It was the stuff of movies and, to be honest, it excited me in a way I hadn't been stimulated for a while. I'd also be able to reassure the people I was counselling that their troubles would soon go away and they'd be able to live in peace and not be afraid to go outside their front doors.

I continued to make regular trips to the city centres, where the forgotten people trusted me and shared information that would help me to help them. After a few months, arrests were made for money laundering and other serious crimes and the gang members were taken off the streets. For obvious reasons, I can't divulge too many details here and I'm not saying I was instrumental in this, but I hope I played a small part in making the streets safer for the abused and vulnerable. I don't regret what I did because people like that gang ruin lives – even their own.

I was an undercover agent for seven months altogether and every now and then I still get calls from the unit.

'Hey, Bo, how are you?'

'I'm good.'

'What's happening?'

'Nothing much.'

If I'm honest, I never really had much time for the police and I know there's a lot of corruption and discrimination in the force, but sometimes they do the right thing and I hope this was one of those times. As for now, Bo Reed's career as a wannabe Jane Tennison is officially over.

Mission accomplished.

Chapter 24

Anyone Can Be Me

I've known a lot of gangsters. Some I've written about and some I haven't, for legal reasons. I've known very dangerous men and some not so dangerous. I've known gun runners, drug dealers, 'celebrity' gangsters, men with connections to terrorist groups, and gangsters who now write books and make films. However, my book is about more than my association with gangsters; it's about my life: from a dysfunctional and abusive childhood to the person I am now. I wanted to show people how it's always possible to change your direction in life, no matter how difficult it might seem at the time – you just need to decide what you want to do and have the determination to get out there and do it. I hope I have achieved that over the course of my narrative.

In reading this book, many people will probably say I was a bad mother and maybe I was – that's for others to decide, not me. But to provide the full picture, I'd like to include a little testimonial to my children in this final chapter. Please bear with me and I'll try not to sound too twee. I know I've been writing about my children throughout, but it's because of them I'm where I am in my life right now, and not dead or drugged up or in prison. They're a very important part of my story and I just want to tell you who they really are in their own right, as individual people.

Daniella was the most perfect baby when she was born – big blue eyes, rosy lips and a mop of dark hair. I could see from a young age that she was quite reserved, unlike me. She remained like that right through school and she grew prettier as she grew older. She wasn't the most popular girl and only had a small circle of friends. She liked to read books, just as I did when was young – she was always reading something. I'd often have to fight her battles for her because she was a shy girl. She was very accepting of what people, including myself, said or did and sometimes I had to step in and say, 'No, Daniella, that's not right.' Through her teenage years, Daniella made a few mistakes, but who didn't? It's all part of growing up. But her heart was always right and she was kind to others.

As Daniella grew, so did her personality, and she became a little impulsive – like when she ran off to Cardiff and married Peter while he was in prison. But that was me all over and, just like me, she had to learn the hard way. As well as bad, some people might say I was overbearing and headstrong with my children, but I don't accept that. I was just trying to be protective in the only way I knew how, even through the crazy times. I'll always regret not being able to protect Daniella from Axel; maybe that's why I'm so watchful with her and my grandchildren now.

Daniella's always been über-loyal to her friends and has stuck by them no matter what anyone said about them, even though that loyalty hasn't always been reciprocated. She hates hugs and kisses and being made a fuss of. The only times she allowed me to show affection like that was when she was pregnant – then she needed me to be with her all the time. In recent years, she's come with me to buy food for the homeless and she always tells me about someone who's down-and-out or broken and asks me to help them.

Daniella is an excellent mother, far better than I ever was when I was her age. Her children come first and foremost in her life and I'm so proud of her for that. She's full-time, hands-on with them and she spends every penny she has on them. She loves being a mother and it's definitely her niche in life. Sometimes she's hard on herself and feels she might have done more, career-wise. But I always tell her that being a good mother is the hardest job in the world. Back when I was her age, I made sure my children were dressed, fed, went to school and were treated on their birthdays and at Christmas. Other than that, they had to cope with my dysfunctional lifestyle and it's a wonder Daniella turned out as stable and grounded as she is.

My daughter doesn't show emotion easily and I've only seen her cry a handful of times, mostly when she was in labour. On the other hand, she's very sensitive and sometimes I have to watch what I'm saying, as her feelings can easily be hurt. Otherwise she's usually chilled and laid-back and has an unbelievable amount of patience, especially with me. She has a humility that's rare these days and she and my grandchildren are a constant source of joy and happiness in my life.

When I was pregnant with Christopher, I didn't take care of myself as much as I did with Daniella. He wasn't planned and I wasn't prepared. Everyone wanted me to have an abortion, but I refused.

As a boy, Christopher had a big, extrovert personality and, in that respect, he was more like me than Daniella was. He was very popular in school and loved football, always telling me he'd scored hattricks. When I went to a school presentation one time, expecting him to get a trophy for 'goal of the season' or something, I couldn't understand it when he didn't. Me being me, I collared his PE teacher and demanded to know why my son hadn't got a trophy, after scoring hattricks all season. The man laughed and told me Christopher hadn't scored a single goal.

My son was a mummy's boy when he was little, always coming into my bed to be close to me. Perhaps that was a kind of insecurity because of my crazy lifestyle, I don't know. As he grew older, Christopher grew more independent and it was always difficult to get him to do something he was set against. He was very much a wheeler-dealer from an early age – washing car windscreens by the traffic lights in Cardiff and doing all sorts of other part-time jobs to make a pound or two.

Christopher was always an outdoors boy and I rarely saw him in daylight: football and his friends were his life. He was also very impulsive, like me – once he came home and said he'd taken up cage fighting, then it was mountain biking, then something else. But football always remained the constant in his life. He became a strong-minded individual and knew what he wanted. He passed all his exams and went on to college, where he got an HNC in public services and went on to become a successful sales consultant. He's now bought his first house and is moving out – I'm going to miss him so much. He's also qualified as a football coach and was mentoring the under-14s, before becoming manager of the local football team, Trallwm AFC's 1st team. He's very well known in this part of Llanelli and everyone says the same thing about him.

'Chris – he's a top man.'

Christopher has a boldness and determination about him that he gets from me. He hates losing at anything, even Snakes and Ladders, and he'll cheat rather than lose (it's true, Christopher!) He gets frustrated easily and always thinks he's right – he'll pull up Google to prove a point which always makes me laugh – I'd punch someone in the face to prove a point.

My son is very wise for his age and not easily fooled – many's the time he's given me advice about people to stay away from that's proved to be right. When I had cancer it was Christopher who ran the house and looked after me. He has my warped sense of humour and hates injustice, just like me. My son has never judged me in anything I've done and, even when I've been wrong, he's always stood by me and we have a very strong connection as mother and son. Not a day goes by without me telling Christopher I love him and he always says he loves me.

I love you, son!

I was never shown proper love and I didn't know what it was. Love and sex are not the same thing, neither are love and possessiveness. With Daniella and Christopher it was unconditional love, no matter what I did, said, or how I acted. I regret a lot of the things that happened when I was younger, but they've never judged me or said they were raised badly.

I'm so proud to be their mother.

If you've worked in the sex industry, as a dancer, stripper, masseuse or prostitute, men think you really enjoy sex. It couldn't be further from the truth, at least for me. I mean, if you work as a bricklayer, you don't want to go building walls on your day off, do you? Or if you're a farmer, you don't want to be milking cows when you're on holiday in Ribera del Duero – no, you want to go wine-tasting. Although I've been a sex worker for a lot of my life, I was never really all that good at sex and it was always just a means to an end. The only time I really felt the earth move was when I was with Kazumi. The point I'm trying to make is, we shouldn't stereotype and we should always try to see the real person behind the sometimes deceptive exterior.

I think I've always been a very spiritual person, even if I didn't know it. My previous life was probably a test of my moral fibre, if you can understand that. I hope I've passed that test and I'd like this book to be a source of inspiration to women – and men – who have lost their way in the world. I hope it's something they can find confidence and a way forward from reading. I think my story is one where faith triumphs in the end – not blind faith, but the kind of belief where hope springs eternal and wins out over seemingly insurmountable odds. I know it's a story of contrasts: of darkness that's lit by the pureness of the inner being – a light that can be dimmed, but never extinguished. I hope it will be of interest to people who've faced abuse, exploitation, violence and intimidation – and even those who haven't.

Once I thought I was no one.

Now I know I can be anyone.

And anyone can be me.

About the Authors

John F. McDonald is an award-winning writer from London; his work includes memoirs, novels, graphic novels and screenplays. Find out more at www. johnfmcdonald.co.uk

Tara O'Shaughnessey was abused as a child and later fell into a life of crime and prostitution. She is now a university graduate and counsellor, and has dedicated her life to helping 'fallen women'. Tara would like her book to be a source of inspiration to women (and men) who have lost their way in the world, something they can find hope and a way forward from reading.